CW00740715

BIRDS OF ARGENTINA & URUGUAY
A FIELD GUIDE

ARGENTINA AND URUGUAY IN SOUTH AMERICA

BIRDS OF ARGENTINA & URUGUAY A FIELD GUIDE

Fe de erratas que reemplaza a la cartografía de las páginas 4, 5 y 296.

1 Límite del lecho y subsuelo
2 Límite exterior del Río de la Plata
3 Límite lateral marítimo argentino-uruguayo

ANTARTIDA ARGENTINA

ARGENTINA AND URUGUAY
showing Argentina's National Parks

The Red-crested Cardinal, *Paroaria coronata,* was chosen for our cover because it is a symbol of the splendor of the birds of La Plata region and the pain of underserved captivity.

T. NAROSKY - D. YZURIETA

ASOCIACION ORNITOLOGICA DEL PLATA

BIRDS OF ARGENTINA & URUGUAY

A FIELD GUIDE

VAZQUEZ MAZZINI EDITORES

BUENOS AIRES

A contribution of the Asociación Ornitológica del Plata
25 de Mayo 749, 1002, Buenos Aires, Argentina, Tel. 312-8958

Published with the support of the
International Council for Bird Preservation,
Pan American Section

First published 18th. august 1987 (Spanish)
Second Edition 1988 (Spanish)
Third Edition 1989 (Spanish)
First Edition 1989 (English)
First Edition white and black 1989 (Spanish)
Fourth Edition 1993 (Spanish)
Second Edition 1993 (English)

© **VAZQUEZ MAZZINI EDITORES**, Argentina

Title in Spanish:
GUIA PARA LA IDENTIFICACION DE LAS AVES DE ARGENTINA Y URUGUAY

Queda hecho el depósito que previene la ley 11723
ISBN 950-99063-3-6
VAZQUEZ MAZZINI EDITORES
Concepción Arenal 4864
1427 - Buenos Aires - Argentina
Tel. y Fax 854-7085

SPONSORS

Ministerio de Educación y Justicia de la Nación,
Secretaría de Cultura, Argentina

Secretaría de Agricultura, Ganadería y Pesca de la Nación
Dirección Nacional de Fauna Silvestre, Argentina

Ministerio de Agricultura, Ganadería y Recursos Renovables,
Córdoba, Argentina

Museo Argentino de Ciencias Naturales B. Rivadavia,
Buenos Aires, Argentina

International Council for Bird Preservation,
Pan American Section

Fundación e Instituto Miguel Lillo,
Tucumán, Argentina

Fundación Vida Silvestre Argentina

Consejo Internacional para la Preservación de las Aves,
Sección Argentina

With the special collaboration of

Sergio Salvador
Manuel Nores
Rosendo Fraga

and a group of naturalists from the Asociación Ornitológica del Plata

Additional illustrations by

Eduardo Saibene
Juan Claver
and Gabriel Peralta

Photographs: Courtesy of Héctor Rivarola

Graphic Design: José Luis Vázquez

To the memory of Claes Christian Olrog
the master who is still with us

That there may always be a bird flying in the sky
and someone looking at it

Citation:

NAROSKY T. and D. YZURIETA, 1989. Birds of
Argentina & Uruguay. A Field Guide.
Asoc. Ornitológica del Plata. B. Aires.

CONTENTS

PROLOGUE

Although the beauty of birds has always moved man, up until only 50 years ago scientific knowledge about them was reserved to a few. Identifying the less common birds required hunting them in order to compare the sample at hand with the descriptions inserted in voluminous reference books.

However, in 1934, the first "field guide" by Roger Tory Peterson produced a true revolution in ornithology by making it accessible to the general public. From then on a small manual, easily stuffed into a coat's pocket, and a pair of binoculars was all that was needed for any mortal to recognize birds seen in a field trip and even to discern among similar species.

Identification is a "sine qua non" condition to become truly interested in animals. It is the starting point for further observations on their behavior and their relationship with the surroundings; in synthesis to have an intellectual appreciation of them.

Peterson's pionnering guide was followed by thousands of others --some copied its style, others introduced variations-- that exhibited the avifauna of continents, regions, countries, and even more limited areas.

*In Argentina, the veil that covered ornithology from the great public, was removed in 1959 by Dr. Claes Christian Olrog, with the appearance of his manual **Argentine Birds, a Field Guide**. A whole generation of nature lovers was initiated in the interpretation of our winged world with this work, unique in its kind for many years.*

*Of the few guides that followed surely the most successful one, the one most used due to its practicality --even though its illustrations were in black-and-white-- has been the A **Field Guide to the Birds of Buenos Aires Province** by Narosky and Yzurieta, which appeared in 1978 and whose basic lay-out is followed in this work. Undoubtedly, its success must have encouraged the authors to face the ambitious job of covering all of the Uruguayan and Argentine avifauna -- which with nearly 1,000 species, is among the most numerous in the world-- and it confirmed the convenience of the designed adopted, inspired on **Birds of the Department of Lima** by Maria Koepcke.*

Ideally a field guide requires--in addition to a format that allows for comfortable use--highly precise illustrations showing birds in poses that facilitate comparison, very concise texts that point out distinctive features and the most prominent aspects of their behavior, habitat preference, distribution maps, and a rigorous scientific approach, incorporating the most recent data and based on the most current taxonomic classification. The presentation of the information notably influences on the practicality of the field guide.

Obviously, no one could be better qualified to carry out this task with those requirements than our experienced and sagacious bird watchers. Whoever has accompanied Narosky and Yzurieta in a field trip has been amazed by their extraordinary perception and by their detailed and systematic annotations, which are the best basic material on which the brief and accurate texts are based on. Their photographic material has complemented the images kept in memory, to give --as a result-- Yzurieta's illustrations reflecting birds' typical poses. The numerous field trips throughout Argentina guarantees Narosky and Yzurieta's familiarity with the great majority of the country's avifauna. Together with it, Narosky's involvement with the Asociación Ornitológica del Plata and his numerous published works, ensure a greater scientific standard.

I have no doubt that this field guide will have an enormous repercussion in the appreciation of birds by the general public, not only providing a better tool for those that are already interested in birds --aside from its utility for scientific researchers-- but, particularly, bringing a multitude of people who require to be induced by a truly practical and attractive instrument, to the fascinating activity of birdwatching. And, since the survival itself of Argentina's avifauna is intimately associated with the interest awakened upon the country's population in it, this work will also mean a valuable contribution to the conservation of birds in this part of the continent.

Francisco Erize

FOREWORD TO THE ENGLISH EDITION

Here is the first English-language, pocket-sized field guide on South American birds. It covers all the species of two entire countries, with a geographic range extending from Antarctica to the jungles, and describes and illustrates almost one-third of all the birds of the continent. It has been written concisely but with quality, and uniquely offers a first-rate illustration immediately adjacent to the text describing each species. A host of other thoughtful aids to quick identification show that the authors are deeply sensitive to the needs of new birders and more experienced ones wanting to become acquainted with the magnificent diversity of Argentina's avifauna.

English-speaking birders are greatly indebted to this exceptional duo, Tito Narosky and Dario Yzurieta, and their team of collaborators, as well as to the Ornithological Association of the Plata, for producing this wonderful book. Special thanks are due for their interest in having the English-language edition available so promptly after appearance of the Spanish original in 1987.

While the importance of this English language edition cannot be overemphasized, its users shoud also be aware of the even greater significance of the Spanish original. While not the first field guide to appear in Argentina, it is the first for Uruguay. Although coverage for other neighboring countries is incomplete, it also has significant utility in Paraguay, Bolivia,and southern Brazil, where nothing similar to it exists. In Argentina it is the first field guide to cover all species in the country and provide information and colored illustrations having the quality necessary to attract uninformed readers and convert them into enthusiasts and hobbyists. Many negative factors are operating to reduce and endanger bird populations in South America. This book has the potential to counteract them by creating a sizeable, genuine constituency for birds with power to influence gobernmental and private organizations toward more prudent decisions on environmental and economic questions involving the fate of wildlife.

William Belton

ACKNOWLEDGMENTS

The idea of shaping into reality "A Field Guide to the Birds of Argentina and Uruguay" has received wide support from bird lovers alike and ornithophiles from the Rio de la Plata region. Perhaps because of that it is possible to identify in this work the influence of specialized studies from both sides of the River Plate. In addition to our own and to bibliographic criteria, consultations have been made that range from the works' great features to those small details of distribution. And the contributions have been, logically, unequal. We shall try to name those who have offered some type of collaboration. In any event, we know that there will be omissions, inevitable after five years of work and a constant and varied exchange, personal and by mail.

To all, mentioned or not, our deep gratefulness. And particularly:

to Manuel Nores, who in addition to diverse suggestions and critical oppinion is responsible for the chapter "Ornithogeograph Zones of Argentina", which without doubt gives the work greater hierarchy;

to Sergio Salvador to whom an efficient research work on the subjects of environment and distribution is owed;

to the specialized artist Eduardo Saibene (genera and family silhouettes of Passeriformes), Juan Claver (non-Passeriformes family silhouettes), and Gabriel Peralta (species requiring confirmation of occurrence and bird topography) who contributed with their valuable work to the, efficient completion of the artist's task;

to Jorge R. Navas, who suggested ideas and discussed aspects of the work, contributing his proffesional experience and providing valuable ornithological material from the Museo Argentino de Ciencias Naturales Bernardino Rivadavia.

to Rosendo M. Fraga, who participated in the first stages, generously offering his knowledge on bird behavior, specially in the subject of calls;

to the group which, with alternations and variations, was the team of collaborators that gave its enthusiasm and youthful experience. This group included: Diego Gallegos (text elaboration); Javier Beltrán and Horacio Rodríguez Moulin (revisions of museum skins); ornithological guides Alejandro Di Giácomo (families), Horacio Aguilar (index) and Marcelo Betinelli (revision of skins);

to the young and distinguished conservation leader Juan Carlos Chébez for his contribution to the subject of common names;

to the naturalists Mauricio Rumboll and Justo Herrera, who without draw-backs offered their vast knowledge on the birds of the Paranense humid forest;

to Rodolfo Escalante (Uruguay), our advisor on the sea birds sector and to Philip Humphrey

(U.S.A), equally efficient in the enlightment on problems with *Tachyeres* genus;

to Francisco Erize, Juan Klimatis, Pablo Canevari, Guillermo Vassina, Horst Hethke (Germany), Juan Cuello (Uruguay), Carlos Saibene, Miguel A. Castelino, Andrés Johnson, José Santos Biloni, Miguel Woites, Gustavo Siegenthaler, Eduardo Casas, Tomás Sheridan, Miguel A. Fiameni, Víctor Pulido (Perú), Sergio Goldfeder, David B. Wilson, Ada Azategui, Giovanna Crispo, Carlos A. Cancelo (Uruguay), Norberto Montaldo, Laura Rozenberg, Mateo R. Zelich, Bernabé López Lanús, and Miguel Blendinger, who have made varied contributions;

to Raúl Carman, notable naturalist and predilect friend, who contributed with his usual generosity to enhance this work;

to Estela Alabarce and to Nelly Bo who, with friendly diligence went beyond their duties, put at our disposal the work material under their custody, in the Miguel Lillo Institute of Tucumán and the Museum of La Plata, respectively;

to Haydée Teggi, support without substitute in the exhausting days of text elaboration and whose enthusiasm and capacity helped solve many of the difficulties arising during those years;

to Adelino Narosky, my brother, who, as always, was an indispensable assistant in multiple tasks, seconded in this occasion by Omar González, Roberto Hermo, Javier Ospital and Pablo Losardo;

to José Luis Vázquez, the ideal publisher for a complex work that requires creative contributions and whose human and professional quality was decisive in the result obtained. And to his work group composed by: Marisa, Cristina, and Fernando Vázquez Mazzini, Miguel, Pablo and Diego Dente, Verónica Balotta, Alberto Rodríguez, María Cristina Melendi, Juan Carlos Augenti, Luis Vázquez Mansilla, and Raúl Lasarte;

to the veteran and capable bird watcher Maurice Earnshaw, for his efficient translation of part of the work into English, to Carlota de Roberts who contributed her professionalism, and to Pablo Rovner who carried out the delicate task of homogenizing the text;

to María Onestini who contributed with her learning knowledge of the English language and personal style to this edition;

to Montserrat Carbonell who for months helped with the editing of the English version with her usual generosity and knowledge, foward the completion of this work of which she is also a promoter;

to Roberto Cinti, who in the difficult stage of diffusion presented with usual honesty his undisputed knowledge;

to William Belton, former President and of the International Council for Bird Preservation, Pan American Section, for the generous and warm impulse given to our work and for his invaluable personal contribution to the translation revision;

to the honesty and efficiency of Elsa M. de Stein, collaborator of José Leiberman, Publications Director of the Asociación Ornitológica del Plata, and in charge of the technical and financial scheme which produced this "childbirth." For him, these last but perhaps deepest words of recognition, since he took with pleasure the responsibility and stoically supported the difficulties, which led to this end and give him the leading role.

T. Narosky - D. Yzurieta

INTRODUCTION

This is not a scientific book -it is a work tool. It is dedicated to the growing number of amateur birdwatchers who require improved facilities of the kind available in the more developed countries of the world. There are already a substantial number of ornithological works on both sides of the Rio de la Plata. In spite of this, they have been outpaced by the increasing interest in nature, and especially in birds. The intense activity of the Ornithological Association of the Plata and the courses it has organized for birdwatchers during the past decade are not unrelated to this surge. Their first fruits are now being felt. Better understanding of nature brings respect for life in its various manifestations and produces conservation measures inspired by public opinion. The final result justifies the investment: man, in addition to finding a new route toward peace and happiness through birds, applies intelligent measures to halt deterioration of the environment -a deterioration that drags him with it, for he is an integral part of the magic process we call life.

For this reason the Ornithological Association of the Plata has played a central role in publishing this book, which is basically for Argentina because its authors and collaborators are Argentine, as are those who have participated in the many other aspects of its publication. The distribution maps, number of races, ornithogeographic data and information on abundance all relate to our country. Nevertheless, because it was possible also to cover Uruguay by adding a few more species, these have been included as a contribution to the work of our sister country's naturalists, though we are aware that they have excellent books of their own.

When one first obtains a field guide it is useful, before testing it in the field, to come to an understanding with its authors. The abbreviations, symbols, and method of presenting the information should be learned at once so as to expedite its effective utilization. This requires that some of these items be memorized. Given that the guide is a more or less complex instrument, the sooner the birdwatcher discovers its little secrets, the sooner he will improve his knowledge of the birds.

Our effort has really been one of synthesis. It is impossible to display or describe all the possibilities, so selection, rather than inclusion, has been the dominant motif. Limited space requires permanent elimination of much data which might eventually prove useful. This makes it essential to be rigorously selective so as to incorporate a mountain of information in the small space assigned to each heading in a pocket-size book. Thus we have had to use telegraphic language and a series of symbols and abbreviations. But too many of these would have been equally disturbing. In general we have adhered to the same criteria used in "Aves Argentinas, A Field Guide to the Birds of Buenos Aires Province", but the experience of nine years and various editions of that work, and the inclusion of colored illustrations, distribution maps and many other diverse and varied factors, some quite subtle, make this "A Field Guide to the Birds of Argentina and Uruguay" more complex and, we hope, a more useful work.

The reader may be assured that no word, symbol or space is present or absent by chance, although this may not be apparent at the first reading. Doubtless there may be errors. The text emphasized in **boldface** may be used for an initial run-through that sometimes will prove to be sufficient. For this reason we have stressed these factors so they may be read isolated from the rest of the text.

The book follows the systematic order. Nevertheless, we have tried to group the most similar species of the same family on each page to emphasize their distinctive marks by comparison.Terminology with decreasing values is used "very similar...", "similar...", "resembles..", "somewhat resembles...".

The same scale is used for the illustrations on each page in order that sizes may be compared. Nevertheless, occasionally the artist has not adhered to this, so the meassurements in centimeters are more reliable than the illustrations.

Description of coloration continues to be a difficult problem. Although there are color charts of high quality, these are not useful in the field nor are they generally available to amateurs. We believe that the practice used in the guide will facilitate the solution. Certain very well known birds can serve as a basis. The tail of the Rufous Hornero, for example, will be "rufous". The collar of the Rufous-collared Sparrow "cinnamon", and in this way the personal criteria of the reader may adapt to that used in this work, which, of course, is also subjective.

We ask the indulgence of experienced birdwatchers when, for didactic purposes, we use redundant phraseology. Example: "mountains, not plains". We do this, although it appears unnecessary, to make perfectly clear a fact that is essential for separating one species from another similar one.

In the text, with few variations, an orderly sequence has been followed: common, English and scientific names, number of races in Argentina, natural measurements, behavior, voices, general aspect, descriptions of the male, female and young, distribution in the Americas, habitat, and probability of finding the bird.

Common name: In 1991, the Asociación Ornitológica del Plata edited the 'Lista Patrón de los Nombres Comunes de las Aves Argentinas' by Navas, Narosky, Bó and Chebez. In this way, a with born in 1916 was performed. Since the present eddition of his guide, each species will have as it's common Spanish name the one given in the 'Lista Patrón...'.

The ornithologists that were in charge of that work, offer us an "official" name. Nevertheless,

18

the bidwatcher will find in the field plenty of denominations whose folkloric value cannot be ignored.

Scientific Name: Taking into account the diversity of opinion among ornithologists, the lack of a definitive formula, and the fact that this is not a treatise on systematics, we have chosen to follow modern studies freely, while also bearing in mind established usage and rules, especially when the proposed change does not appear to be unarguable. Furthermore, where two equally valid possibilities exist, we have selected the name most likely to help the observer. A few times our own field experience has tilted the decision.

As an additional aid, the index includes a long series of synonyms with their equivalents. We feel we have thus solved, pragmatically, a difficult problem which, like any other criterion, is sure to encounter some objections.

In the section entitled "Ornithogeographic Regions of Argentina" some names have been modified to adapt them to the general standard of the book.

Geographic Races or Subspecies: Because an observer is generally unable to see in the field the slight differences of coloration or size that identify subspecies, the book does not give these special attention, except in those few cases where they are well known and ignoring them might create confusion. Thus, only rarely are subspecific characteristics mentioned along with the corresponding geographic area. However, in every case a symbol (2R, 3R, etc.) has been included together with the scientific name to indicate the number of races recognized for Argentina. If this symbol does not appear, it is because only one race is recognized.

Natural Measurement: The figure in centimeters given at the beginning of each species account represents not the total length of the bird, but the approximate size the observer will note for its most normal posture. Thus, the natural length of a grebe is calculated while it is swimming, and that of a woodpecker in a vertical position, from head to tail, not from the tip of the bill with the body stretched flat. In spite of the lack of precision of this figure, it is of practical importance and the observer will find it convenient to use it for comparison. In certain cases information is given on measurements of bill, tail, or wing span. When the size is emphasized in **boldface**, we wish to emphasize its special importance.

Behavior: Field experience has shown that it is often easier to recognize a bird by its behavior than by color. When this is the case, emphasis has been placed on this characteristic. Behavior typical of families or genera has been described in the paragraphs dedicated to these groupings. We have frequently attempted to describe voices, knowing how subjective this matter is. Nevertheless, it may help when similar birds have characteristically different voices, or in forests when the ear is often the only means of contact with species that live in hiding.

Migration: In order to summarize what is known, and although there are different processes and some exceptions, we have divided migratory species into three categories:

Migrant A: Birds that nest in the northern hemisphere and then fly to our country. They are found here in spring and summer. Example: sandpipers, various terns, some plovers and swallows, etc.

Migrant B: Birds that nest in Argentina (in spring and summer) and migrate northward during the winter. Example: various tyrannids such as the Fork-tailed Flycatcher, the Vermilion Flycatcher, the Tropical Kingbird, etc.

Migrant C: Birds that nest in Patagonia during the spring and appear in the center of the country and even further north during the winter. Example: some plovers, the Rufous-backed Negrito, other tyrannids, etc.

All the other species about which nothing is said as to migration are assumed to be resident during the entire year, although there may be important seasonal changes in numbers, altitudinal movements in mountainous areas, and, in many cases, certain movements are little known. It may also be that in some species one race may be resident and the other migratory, as happens with the Bar-winged Cinclodes, or that certain populations may be Migrant B and others resident. Example: the Vermilion Flycatcher. It should be noted that it is not unusual in winter to find Migrant A birds that should have returned to their breeding places in the northern hemisphere.

General Aspect: Customarily before the description some factor is mentioned that characterizes the bird, such as "showy coloration", "enormous", "drab". This characterization refers to the first impression, and is inmediately followed by details.

Description: The book does not provide minute details of the bird, being limited to only those data that the amateur can see with a binocular from a reasonable distance and after some experience. This latter will increase as the observer-field guide relationship is intensified. It is here that the greatest advantage is gained from memorizing the termilogy included in the Topograpy of a Bird. If the male and female are identical, nothing is said about it, the same as when there is no seasonal plumage change. If the contrary is the case, the non-breeding plumage of the male is described (RP) (PI in plates) and the differing features of the female or of the nuptial plumage (NP) (PN in plates) are mentioned. Only a few words have been said about the young, and this only when they are clearly different than the adults. We know that in some cases, such as that of certain Accipitridae, this information is insufficent. Specialized literature and much experience will be needed for their identification, not to mention information on silhouette, behavior, distribution, habitat, etc. The proximity of adults can also be useful.

Distribution: Information is lacking on the exact ranges of the majority of Argentine birds.

Nevertheless, we did not want to neglect an item of this importance whose true value can only be appreciated by critical use of the information. The text includes the area of distribution of the species within the Neotropics, but without mention of any range in other parts of the globe. Without any explanation, at the end of the description and before habitat, are listed the countries covered, except Argentina. Example: ... Ecuador, Peru and Bolivia; or perhaps ... from Mexico, except Paraguay ... Thus it is only an informative item. A different criterion has been followed regarding Uruguay. It is always mentioned separately and in capitals. Example: ... South America, except Chile - URUGUAY ... The reader may thus, at a glance, know if the bird is found in that country. Failure to mention it, even if the range is given as "Western Hemisphere", means that it is not known for Uruguay.

Maps with political subdivisions replace mention in the text of Argentine distribution. For this purpose we have done extensive research in the literature and use unpublished data of our own and of others. Areas of low density for the species and where it does not breed have been lightly shaded, and an arrow shows the direction of migration. It will be helpful for the future if users of the guide will contribute information on this subject.

Occasionally we duplicate information by including the Argentine distribution range in the text, when only one or two words suffices. Example: Misiones, NW, NE, etc.

Once in a while a locality is mentioned in parenthesis. This refers to places where the birdwatcher is most likely to find certain uncommon species.

Habitat: This is a factor to which the new birdwatcher usually pays little attention, but which nevertheless, in many instances, becomes essential. More species than one supposes are closely linked to certain habitats.

The breeding area given for marine birds relates exclusively to Argentina.

Chance of Finding: The likelihood of finding any given species is much more important than its abundance as such. Thus the Roman numerals from I to VI, found separate from the text at the end of each species account, indicate if there is a large or small chance of finding it.

: Hypothetically present. Included in this category are those species that, in spite of at least two or three reliable sightings, are highly unlikely to be found here because they are not found in neighboring countries with similar habitats. We also include under this heading species from bordering countries and continuous habitats where there is only one recent (less than 10 years) sighting or various earlier ones. Cases which in our opinion do not qualify for this category are included on pages 292 and 294.

I: Rare or very difficult to find.

II:Scarce or difficult to find.

IV:Relatively common or easy to find.

V:Abundant or very easy to find.

VI:Very abundant. Seen on practically every outing.

Due to the nature of this simple table, and given that in such an extensive country very important quantitative variables appear from one locality to another, the data is merely advisory. But the importance we give it is demonstrated by the long time we took to devise it, in consultation with the most distinguished field ornithologists of the country. In the event an observer finds species in group II, and even more so in group I, it will be useful to inform the A.O.P. by a simple note or any other means. It should be unnecessary to mention the importance of discoveries of birds listed at the back of the book as "Species requiring confirmation of occurrence" or as "Species of doubtful occurrence".

Families: Early in the text summary information similar to that in the species accounts is pro vided on the 82 families represented among the avifauna of Argentina and Uruguay Alongside each description are one or more silhouettes.

Genera: Within the general text, but with criteria identical to those used for families, data on generic characteristics appear at the beginning of each group. In these cases the silhouettes are in black. When the common name is for some reason more logical than the scientific one we have opted for it.

In 1978, writing in "Aves Argentinas, A Field Guide to the Birds of Buenos Aires Province", we said we aspired to contribute modestly to the dissemination of ornithology as a science and as a passionate hobby, thereby providing an outlet for longings that otherwise might remain unfulfilled. We also expressed the hope of bringing a handful of friends into the circle of those whose lives are elevated by the flight of birds. Our hopes continue the same but Argentina has changed. The handful of birdwatchers we dreamed of has been converted into a multitude. Young people and adults are constantly joining the group of those who admire or study birds in their natural setting. For that reason this new guide, to which we have devoted almost five years, is more mature. It also has another purpose. It will doubtless be useful to those taking their first steps in the field, but we hope it will also be the tool, the companion of the bird-lover, as Olrog's old, esteemed, 1959 guide was for us.

We are certainly no longer so modest in our aspirations. Argentina, as a paradise for birds, and enthusiasts on both shores of the Plata deserve all we can offer.

TOPOGRAPHY OF A BIRD

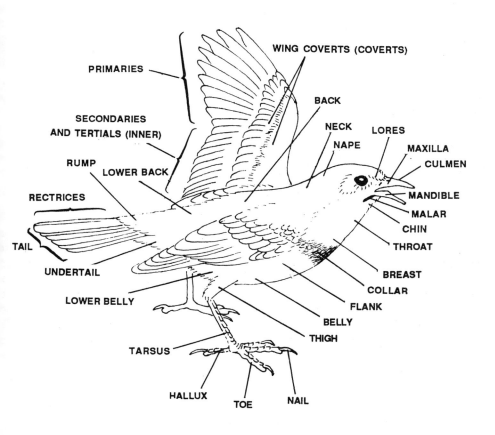

PRIMARIES

SECONDARIES
AND TERTIALS (INNER)

RUMP

LOWER BACK

RECTRICES

TAIL

UNDERTAIL

LOWER BELLY

TARSUS

HALLUX

TOE

NAIL

THIGH

BELLY

FLANK

COLLAR

BREAST

THROAT

CHIN

MALAR

MANDIBLE

CULMEN

MAXILLA

LORES

NAPE

NECK

BACK

WING COVERTS (COVERTS)

or the birdwatcher: Do not forget this is a work tool. Write, underline, critizice
nd make corrections on it. Thus, ornithologically speaking, both will profit and
ow.

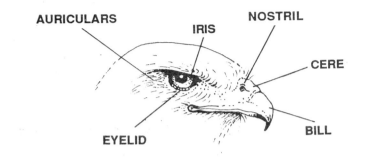

AURICULARS
IRIS
NOSTRIL
CERE
BILL
EYELID

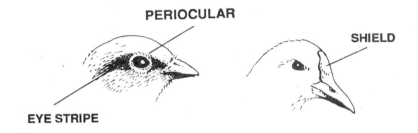

PERIOCULAR
SHIELD
EYE STRIPE

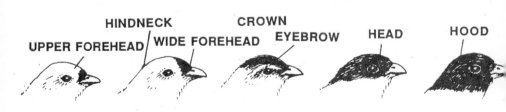

UPPER FOREHEAD
HINDNECK
WIDE FOREHEAD
CROWN
EYEBROW
HEAD
HOOD

MEASUREMENTS GIVEN ON TEXT (NATURAL SIZE)
WERE TAKEN THE FOLLOWING WAY:

24

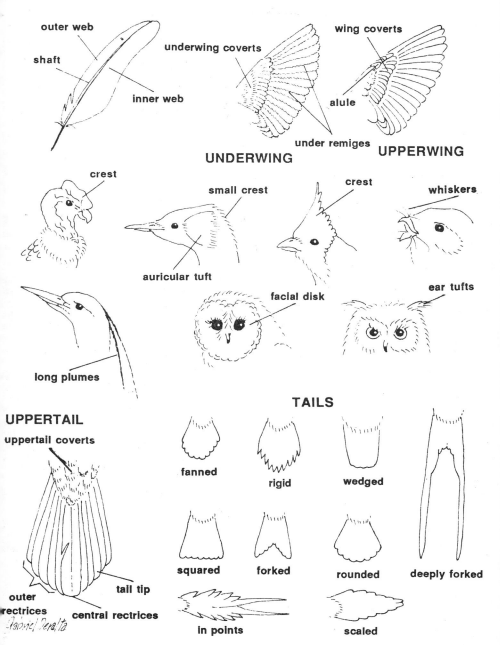

outer web

shaft

inner web

underwing coverts

wing coverts

alule

under remiges

UNDERWING

UPPERWING

crest

small crest

crest

whiskers

auricular tuft

facial disk

ear tufts

long plumes

UPPERTAIL

uppertail coverts

outer rectrices

tail tip

central rectrices

TAILS

fanned

rigid

wedged

squared

forked

rounded

deeply forked

in points

scaled

THE ARTIST'S PAGE

After having looked through this book, admiring the variety and beauty of Argentina's avifauna, it will be noted that there has not been an absolutely uniform treatment on all the plates. There are cases where only one figure is shown per species and in others two, three, four, or even five. Since this work aims to turn itself into a work tool to be used as a field guide, special emphasis is put on the identification of birds, not on artistic brilliance.

The intention is to show the most complete visual record, illustrating the majority of options: male (in the foreground), female, juvenile, seasonal plumages, design on flight, and in some cases subspecies. When some of these aspects are not shown, the text's brief description will be a substitute for the drawing's visual forcefulness.

On the other hand, we have allowed ourselves to introduce a novelty: birds in color and the habitat in black-and-white. The lively contrast between the chromatic figures and their surrounding allows to visualize the bird with clarity, although the environment is precisely detailed. In any case each species has been drawn in the place it frequents with greater assiduity, be it, forests, mountains plains, marine coasts, etc. This effort to suit the illustration to reality should not be neglected by the amateur, since it will be useful as a complement for identification in the field. Nevertheless, life --and that of birds, specially-- is dynamic and nothing can be definite in it. Thus, the watcher can find situations not foreseen here.

I want to bring- out the contribution of Mercedes Gutiérrez and Gustavo Haro of the National University of Córdoba, for the loan of skins to be studied, as a base for the illustrations. Also, would very specially like to thank Arturo L. Jaccard, Director of Renewable Natural Resources, and to Cristina Rendel for their suggestion to experiment with black-and-white surroundings; and to Roberto Straneck, Oscar Salzgeber, Carlos Bazán, Gustavo Haro, Gabriel Peralta, Rodolfo Miatello, and Lucio and Sergio Salvador for their loan of photographic silhouettes, and to those who in one way or another collaborated with their contributions and whose names I could have inadvertently omitted.

At last to Martha, my wife, and to my children who I "abandoned" during very long days in which I remained drawing, secluded in my studio. To all of them, my most profound gratefulness.

Dario Yzurieta

"If men would not throw stones at them I would have liked to be a bird;
of course, if they would not throw stones at them, I would have liked to be a man."

BIRD FAMILIES OF ARGENTINA AND URUGUAY

Collaborator: Alejandro Di Giácomo

Order Sphenisciformes

Fam. SPHENISCIDAE: **Penguins** (Pingüinos) - Southern Hemisphere (one in Galapagos Islands) - 17 species, 8 in Argentina, 2 in Uruguay - **Pelagic** - **Flightless** - Excellent swimmers and divers - On land only to breed or when exhausted - Erect posture reminiscent of cormorants - Gregarious - Breed in colonies - 1 or 2 white eggs - Wings modified into fins - Skin-like plumage - Thick bill - Legs and necks short - Web include 3 toes - ♂ & ♀ alike   Page 43

Order Rheiformes

Fam. RHEIDAE: **Rheas** (Ñandúes) - South America - 2 species, both in Argentina, 1 in Uruguay - **Flightless** - Great runners - In groups - Polygamous - ♂ incubates - Nest on ground - Many creamy eggs - Enormous - **Legs and neck long** - Small head - Wings and tail without rigid feathers - 3 toes - ♂ & ♀ somewhat different   Page 45

Order Tinamiformes

Fam. TINAMIDAE: **Tinamous** (Inambúes) - Western Hemisphere - 41 species, 15 in Argentina, 2 in Uruguay - Terrestrial - Fly little - Walkers - Polygamous - ♂ incubates - Shiny colorful eggs - Often **hunted** - Mimetic - Compact plumage - Resemble chickens - Small head - Short tail - ♂ & ♀ alike   Page 46

Order Podicipediformes

Fam. PODICIPEDIDAE: **Grebes** (Macáes) - Cosmopolitan - 18 species, 6 in Argentina, 4 in Uruguay - Aquatic - Plunge often - Good **divers** - Fairly gregarious - Fly little by day after long run - When they rarely walk, erect - Floating nest - Several whitish eggs that take on color - Resemble ducks - Satiny compact plumage - **Conical bill** - Rudimentary tail - Web include 4 toes - ♂ & ♀ alike - Seasonal dimorphism   Page 50

Order Procellariiformes

Fam. DIOMEDEIDAE: **Albatrosses** (Albatros) - Cosmopolitan - 13 species, 7 in Argentina, 4 in Uruguay - Pelagic - Excellent low **gliders** - Swimmers - On land only when breeding, often in colonies - One white egg - Look like enormous gulls - **Very long and narrow wings** - Thick **bill with a tube on each side** - Web include 3 toes - ♂ & ♀ alike   Page 51

Fam. PROCELLARIIDAE: **Petrels**, shearwaters, prions, fulmars (Petreles) - Cosmopolitan - 57 species, 21 in Argentina, 17 in Uruguay - **Pelagic** - Mainly migrants - Smaller than albatrosses and glide less - On land only to breed - One white egg - Look like gulls - **Double tube on culmen** - Web include 3 toes - ♂ & ♀ alike   Page 53

27

Fam. HYDROBATIDAE: **Storm-Petrels** (Paíños) - Cosmopolitan-
23 species, 5 in Argentina, 3 in Uruguay - **Pelagic** - Look like small
petrels with erratic flight - **Flutter over waves** with hanging legs -
Do not glide - Often appear in stormy weather - On land only to breed,
at night - One white egg - Thin bill with apical hook - **Only one tube
on culmen** - Web include 3 toes - ♂ & ♀ alike   Page 59

Fam. PELECANOIDIDAE: **Diving-Petrels** (Yuncos) - Southern
Hemisphere - 4 species, 3 in Argentina, 1 in Uruguay - **Coastal** -
Look like **small and stocky** petrels - Low and rapid flight - Excellent
plungers - Divers - One white egg - Short wings - Short and thick
bill with **2 tubes on base, open upwards** - Short legs - Web include
3 toes - ♂ & ♀ alike   Page 60

Order Pelecaniformes
Fam. SULIDAE: **Boobies** (Piqueros) - Cosmopolitan - 9 species, 1
in Argentina and Uruguay - Coastal - Dive from average heights - Fly
in file - Gregarious - Do not breed in our area - Long narrow wings-
Wedged tail - Thick bill, almost straight, **sharp** - Web inlude 4 toes
- ♂ & ♀ alike   Page 61

Fam. PHALACROCORACIDAE: **Cormorants** (Cormoranes) -
Cosmopolitan - 30 species, 6 in Argentina, 2 in Uruguay - Coastal (2
also in inland waters) - Gregarious - Plunge and dive - **Erect posture
- Sometimes bask in sun with extended wings** - Nest in colonies-
4 light blue eggs - Straight bill, somewhat long, with apical hook -
Long neck - Long tail, somewhat rigid - Web include 4 toes - ♂ &
♀ alike   Page 62

Fam. ANHINGIDAE: **Darters** (Aningas) - Western Hemisphere - 2
species, 1 in Argentina and Uruguay - Swamps and rivers surrounded by trees - Plunge following fish, that they spear with **long
straight and sharp bill - Swim semisubmerged** - Often glide high
up - Breed in colonies - 4 light blue eggs - Look like cormorants with
longer **necks and tails** - Web include 4 toes - ♂ and ♀ different
          Page 61

Fam. FREGATIDAE: **Frigatebirds** (Fragatas) - Tropical - 5 species,
1 in Argentina and Uruguay - Coastal - Agile flight - **Pursue birds-**
Do no swim - Gregarious - Do not breed in our area - Long narrow
wings - Long forked tail - Long bill with apical hook - Web include
4 toes - ♂ : Inflatable gular pouch - ♂ & ♀ somewhat different
28   Page 61

Order Ardeiformes

Fam. ARDEIDAE: **Herons** (Garzas) - Cosmopolitan - 60 species, 13 in Argentina, 11 in Uruguay - Palustrine - Slow **flight with folded-in neck** - Gregarious - Waders - Majority breeds in colonies - 3 or 4 eggs, often greenish blue - Long sharp bill - Long legs with unwebbed toes - ♂ & ♀ alike   Page 64

Fam. CICONIIDAE: **Storks** (Cigüeñas) - Cosmopolitan - 17 species, 3 in Argentina and Uruguay - Resemble herons - Larger and stockier-Less gregarious & less palustrine - **Neck stretched in flight** - Often breed in colonies - 2 to 4 white eggs - Head and neck featherless in 91) & 93) and only face in 92) - **Long & thick bill** - Long legs with unwebbed toes - ♂ & ♀ alike   Page 68

Fam. THRESKIORNITHIDAE: **Ibises,** spoonbills (Bandurrias) - Cosmopolitan - 28 species, 7 in Argentina, 5 in Uruguay - Resemble storks - Much smaller - Gregarious - Somewhat palustrine - Rapid **flight with extended neck;** sometimes fly in V - **formation** - Generally breed in colonies - 2 to 5 eggs - Neck and legs long - **Unwebbed toes - Long bill,** thin and **curved** (except 100) - ♂ & ♀ alike   Page 69

Order Phoenicopteriformes

Fam. PHOENICOPTERIDAE: **Flamingos** (Flamencos) - Cosmopolitan - 5 species, 3 in Argentina, 1 in Uruguay - In fresh and salty waters - Gregarious - Fly in file with stretched neck - Breed in colonies - Mud nest - 1 white egg - **Pink - Legs and neck very long-**Webbed toes - **Bill abruptly curved** - ♂ & ♀ alike   Page 71

· Order Anseriformes

Fam. ANHIMIDAE: **Screamers** (Chajáes) - South America - 3 species, 1 in Argentina and Uruguay - In or near wetlands - Sometimes gregarious - Slow flight - Gliders - **Scream** - 4 to 6 whitish eggs-Stocky - Chicken-like bill - Small head with **nape crest** - **Wings** long and wide, **with spurs** - Thick tarsi - Long toes unwebbed - ♂ & ♀ alike   Page 72

Fam. ANATIDAE: **Ducks,** swans, geese (Patos) - Cosmopolitan - 144 species, 38 in Argentina, 21 in Uruguay - **Aquatic** - Good **swimmers and fliers** - Plunge - Walk - Gregarious - Rapid and beaten flight - Many whitish eggs - One duck parasite - Often hunted - **Shiny speculum - Wide, flat bill with apical nail-** Short legs - Web include 3 toes - Some species, ♂ & ♀ different   Page 72

Order Falconiformes

Fam. CATHARTIDAE: **American Vultures** (Jotes) - Western Hemisphere - 7 species, 5 in Argentina, 3 in Uruguay - **Carrion eaters**- Often glide high up - Fairly gregarious - Sometimes settle with open wings - 1 to 2 eggs, white or spotted - Resemble Accipitridae - Large - **Featherless head,** often with color - Bill with apical hook - Long and wide wings - Thick legs - Weak nails - ♂ & ♀ alike   Page 82

Fam. ACCIPITRIDAE: Eagles, **hawks,** kites (Gavilanes) - Cosmopolitan - 210 species, 40 in Argentina, 18 in Uruguay - Diurnal - Rapid flight - Erect posture - 1 to 4 eggs, often spotted - Dull plumage - Often difficult to identify (phases, JJ, etc.) -**Short bill,** very curved, **without toothed border** - Sometimes tarsi feathered - Curved strong nails - Iris, cere, and legs colored - Long wings - ♀ larger   Page 83

Fam. PANDIONIDAE: **Ospreys** (Sanguales) - Cosmopolitan - 1 species, that visits Argentina and Uruguay - **Fisher** - Coastal - Rather solitary - **Flies over water** - Do not breed in our area - Hawk-like - **Wings longer and angled** - ♂ & ♀ alike   Page 93

Fam. FALCONIDAE: **Falcons,** caracaras (Halcones) - Cosmopolitan - 57 species, 15 in Argentina, 6 in Uruguay - Diurnal - Look like Accipitridae - **Bill** same but **with toothed border** - Tarsi featherless - Long tail - 2 to 4 eggs very spotted - ♀ larger - ♂ & ♀ alike   Page 94

Order Galliformes

Fam. CRACIDAE: **Guans** (Pavas de Monte) - Western Hemisphere- 43 species, 6 in Argentina, 1 in Uruguay - Terrestrial and arboreal - Hunted often - Nest in trees - 2 to 4 white eggs - Resemble turkeys- Large - Small head **Gular area and face featherless, colored -** Chicken-like bill - Wide wings - **Long tail** - Tarsi and toes strong - ♂ & ♀ alike   Page 98

Fam. PHASIANIDAE: **Quails** (Codornices) - Outside of our area includes chickens, partridges and pheasants - 177 species, 2 in Argentina - Terrestrial - In thickets - Nests on ground - Up to 14 spotted eggs - Stocky - Resemble chickens - Short bill, chicken-like - Wings, legs, tail and neck short   Page 100

Order Gruiformes

Fam. ARAMIDAE: **Limpkins** (Caráus) - Western Hemisphere - 1 species, that also lives in Argentina and Uruguay - Screamer - In wetlands - **Flies with spread primaries** - Nest hidden in marshes - Up to 7 spotted eggs - Blackish - **Long, somewhat curved bill** - Neck and legs long - Long wide wings - Short tail - ♂ & ♀ alike

Page 100

Fam. RALLIDAE: **Rails,** crakes, coots (Gallinetas, gallaretas) - Cosmopolitan - 120 species, 25 in Argentina, 15 in Uruguay - In wetlands - Fly little in daylight - Loud call - Several spotted eggs - Sometimes with shield - Short round wings - **Short tail often erect** - Long toes - (**Coots:** Aquatic, **lobbed toes**) - ♂ & ♀ alike

Page 101

Fam. HELIORNITHIDAE: **Sungrebes** (Aves de Sol) - Cosmopolitan - 3 species, 1 in Argentina - Aquatic - Difficult to see - Nest in trees near water - 2 to 6 eggs a little spotted - **Thin** conical **bill** - Wings and legs short - Long tail - **Lobbed toes** - ♂ & ♀ alike   Page 107

Fam. CARIAMIDAE: **Seriemas** (Chuñas) - South America - 2 species, both in Argentina - **Terrestrial - Runners** - Strong scream- Nest in trees - 2 to 3 spotted eggs - Lax plumage - Chicken-like bill- Neck, **legs and tail long** - Wings somewhat short and rounded - Short toes - ♂ & ♀ alike   Page 108

Order Charadriiformes

Fam. JACANIDAE: **Jacanas** (Jacanas) - Cosmopolitan - 7 species, 1 in Argentina and Uruguay - In wetlands - Walk over floating vegetation - Polyandric - 4 eggs with black designs, on aquatic plants - Colorful plumage - Short **bill with frontshield** - Rounded wings, with spurs - Short tail - Toes and nails very long - J: Very different- ♂ & ♀ alike   Page 108

Fam. ROSTRATULIDAE: **Painted-Snipes** (Aguateros) - Cosmopolitan - 2 species, 1 in Argentina and Uruguay - In wetlands - Hide during day - Polyandric - Nest on ground - 2 spotted eggs - Mimetic- Long **bill, curved on apex** - Wide wings - Short tail - Long toes - ♂ & ♀ alike   Page 108

31

Fam. HAEMATOPODIDAE: **Oystercatchers** (Ostreros) - Cosmopolitan - 7 species, 3 in Argentina, 2 in Uruguay - Coastal - Strong whistles - Low flight - Nest on ground - 2 or 3 spotted eggs - Compact plumage, blackish or black-and-white - **Red bill, long** and narrow - Wings and legs long - Short tail - ♂ & ♀ alike   Page 109

Fam. CHARADRIIDAE: **Plovers,** lapwings (Chorlos) - Cosmopolitan - 63 species, 12 in Argentina, 8 in Uruguay - Resemble Scolopacidae - Not so gregarious nor so coastal - Rapid flight - Nest on ground - 2 to 4 spotted eggs - Often seasonal dimorphism - Slender- **Short bill with thick apex - Large head** - Not very long legs - 3 toes and 1 absent or rudimentary - (Lapwings: Non coastal - Noisy - Rounded wings with spurs) - ♂ & ♀ alike   Page 110

Fam. SCOLOPACIDAE: **Sandpipers,** snipes (Playeros) - Cosmopolitan - 82 species, 22 in Argentina, 17 in Uruguay - **Migrants** with seasonal dimorphism, except *Gallinago* - More **gregarious,** coastal and with smaller head than Charadriidae - Rapid flight - Nest on ground - 3 to 4 spotted eggs - Slender - Bill and legs sometimes very long - Sharp wings - 4 toes - ♂ & ♀ alike   Page 113

Fam. RECURVIROSTRIDAE: **Stilts,** avocets (Teros Reales) - Cosmopolitan - 8 species, 2 in Argentina, 1 in Uruguay - coastal in inland waters - Gregarious - Nest on ground - 2 to 4 spotted eggs - **Slender-** Black and white plumage - **Long thin bill, straight or curved upward** - Short tail - **Legs very long** - Somewhat webbed toes - ♂ & ♀ alike   Page 110

Fam. PHALAROPODIDAE: **Phalaropes** (Falaropos) - Cosmopolitan - 3 species that visit Argentina, and 1 or 2 Uruguay - Migrants - Look-like Scolopacidae - **Swimmers** - 2 pelagic - Gregarious - Do not breed in our area - Seasonal dimorphism - **Long thin straight bil-** Long sharp wings - **Lobbed toes** - ♀ larger; more colorful in NP   Page 119

Fam. THINOCORIDAE: **Seedsnipes** (Agachonas) - South America-
4 species, all in Argentina, 1 in Uruguay - Terrestrial - Walkers-
Neither coastal nor in wetlands - Sitting look like pigeons and in flight
like plovers - Nest on ground - 4 spotted eggs - Stocky - **Mimetic -
Short thick bill - Legs** and tail **short** - ♂ and ♀ alike or slightly
different   Page 120

Fam. CHIONIDIDAE: **Sheathbills** (Palomas Antárticas) - In Antarctica - 2 species, 1 in Argentina and Uruguay - Coastal - **Look like
white pigeons** - Tame - Terrestrial - Lazy fliers - Nest among rocks
or in hollows - 2 to 3 spotted eggs - **Thick short bills, with horn
sheath at base** - Short tail - ♂ & ♀ alike   Page 121

Fam. STERCORARIIDAE: **Skuas,** jaeggers (Salteadores) - Cosmopolitan - 5 species, all in Argentina, 3 in Uruguay - Coastal and pelagic
- **Chase other species** to rob prey - Swimmers - Nest on ground - 2
to 3 spotted eggs - **Look like gulls** - Rather brownish - **Thick bill with
apical hook** - Long **wings,** sharp **with white spot** -**Central tail
rectrices longish** - Webbed toes - ♂ & ♀ alike   Page 121

Fam. LARIDAE: **Gulls** (Gaviotas) - Cosmopolitan - 48 species, 7 in
Argentina, 4 in Uruguay - Diverse aquatic environments - Gregarious
- Noisy - Breed in colonies - Up to 4 spotted eggs - Seasonal
dimorphism (except 296) - **Rather white** - Apical hook less notable
than in Stercorariidae - Wings long and sharp - Webbed toes - ♂ &
♀ alike   Page 122

Fam. STERNIDAE: **Terns** (Gaviotines) - Cosmopolitan -42 species,
12 in Argentina and Uruguay - Diverse aquatic environments -
Resemble gulls - More slender - **Plunge** - Do not swim - Gregarious-
Breed in colonies - 2 to 3 spotted eggs - Seasonal dimorphism -
Straight bill, sharp without hook - Wings short and narrow - Tail
often very long and forked - Legs very short - Webbed toes - ♂ &
♀ alike   Page 124

Fam. RYNCHOPIDAE: **Skimmers** (Rayadores) - Cosmopolitan - 3
species, 1 in Argentina and Uruguay - Coastal - **Skim water** - Gregarious - Look like terns - Breed in colonies, in sandy beaches - 3 to
4 spotted eggs - Slight seasonal dimorphism - **Long and strange bill,
with maxilla shorter** - Long and thin wings - Legs very short -
Webbed toes - ♂ & ♀ alike   Page 127

Order Columbiformes
Fam. COLUMBIDAE: **Pigeons,** doves (Palomas) - Cosmopolitan - 284 species, 23 in Argentina, 9 in Uruguay - Unmistakable - Walkers-Sustained and noisy flight - **Cooing** - 1 or 2 white or creamy eggs - Stocky - Small head, rounded - Thin **bill**, short, **with cere at base** - Short neck - Long sharp wings - Short legs, often reddish - ♂ & ♀ alike ⠀⠀⠀⠀⠀⠀⠀⠀⠀⠀⠀⠀⠀⠀⠀⠀⠀⠀Page 128

Order Psittaciformes
Fam. PSITTACIDAE: **Parrots,** macaws, parakeets (Loros) - Cosmopolitan - 327 species, some 24 in Argentina, 5 in Uruguay - Unmistakable - **Noisy** - Climbers - Rapid and beaten flight - Rather gregarious - Nest in trees, except 349) - 2 to 6 white eggs - **Green** - Large head - Thick, **very curved bill** - Long sharp wings - Short legs- **2 toes forward and 2 backward** - ♂ & ♀ alike ⠀⠀⠀Page 134

Order Cuculiformes
Fam. CUCULIDAE: **Cuckoos** (Cuclillos) - Cosmopolitan - 125 species, 12 in Argentina, 8 in Uruguay - Climbers - Several parasitize - Nests in trees - Egg color and number variable, some with calcium mesh (369) - Slender - Dull plumage - Bill somewhat curved - Short wings - **Long tail, graded - 2 toes forward and 2 backward** - ♂ and ♀ alike ⠀⠀⠀⠀⠀⠀⠀⠀⠀⠀⠀⠀⠀⠀⠀⠀⠀⠀Page 140

Order Strigiformes
Fam. TYTONIDAE: **Barn-Owls** (Lechuzas de Campanario) - Cosmopolitan - 9 species, 1 in Argentina and Uruguay - Nocturnal - Strong call - Nest in buildings or trees - Several white eggs- Look like Strigidae - Slender - **White face with facial disk heart-like** - Bill straight and longish - Legs long and feathered - **Toes covered by "bristles"** - ♂ & ♀ alike ⠀⠀⠀⠀⠀⠀⠀⠀⠀⠀⠀⠀⠀Page 143

Fam. STRIGIDAE: **Owls** (Lechuzas) - Cosmopolitan - 121 species, 16 in Argentina, 8 in Uruguay - Mostly nocturnal - Slow and silent flight - Nest in hollows or on the ground - 2 to 7 white eggs, spherical- Large head, sometimes with "ears" - **Rounded facial disk - Curved and short bill** - Legs, rather short and toes feathered - Long and curved nails - ♂ & ♀ alike ⠀⠀⠀⠀⠀⠀⠀⠀⠀⠀Page 143

Order Caprimulgiformes

Fam. NYCTIBIIDAE: Potoos (Urutaues) - Western Hemisphere - 5 species, 1 in Argentina and Uruguay - Nocturnal - Still by day - Catch insects on flight or from a look-out point - 1 spotted egg, on trunk ends- Incubate in **vertical position** - Mimetic - Look like Caprimulgidae-Head and eyes large - Bill very small - **Enormous mouth without whiskers** - Wings and tail long - Short legs - ♂ & ♀ alike
Page 147

Fam. CAPRIMULGIDAE: Nightjars, nighthawks (Atajacaminos) - Cosmopolitan - 67 species, 14 in Argentina, 5 in Uruguay - Nocturnal or **crepuscular** - In daytime still on the ground or on branches, in **horizontal position** - Broken and silent flight - 2 spotted eggs, on the ground - **Mimetic** - Large head - Legs, bill and neck short - **Large mouth surrounded by whiskers** - Red eyes at night -Wings and tail long - ♂ & ♀ somewhat different
Page 148

Order Apodiformes

Fam. APODIDAE: Swifts (Vencejos) - Cosmopolitan - 80 species, 7 in Argentina, 1 in Uruguay - **Gregarious - Permanent flight,** rapid and sinuous, generally at great heights - Alight vertically on rocky walls, where they nest - Several white eggs - **Resemble swallows** Often dark coloration - Short bill - Large mouth - **Wings very long, narrow, curved** - Short legs - Strong nails - ♂ & ♀ alike
Page 152

Order Trochiliformes

Fam. TROCHILIDAE: Hummingbirds (Picaflores) - Western Hemisphere - 319 species, 28 in Argentina, 7 in Uruguay - Unmistakable - Often tame - **Flight very fast**, agile and sonorous, even backward- **Hover** in the air **in front of flowers** - Polygamous - Nests low - 2 white eggs, cylindrical - Small - Resemble insects - **Showy plumage with metallic sheen - Bill thin** and long, at times curved - Diminutive legs - ♂ & ♀ rather different
Page 154

Order Trogoniformes

Fam. TROGONIDAE: Trogons (Surucuáes) - Cosmopolitan - 35 species, 3 in Argentina - In humid forests - Arboreal - Short and slow flight - Breed in trees or in termite holes - 2 to 4 whitish eggs - **Showy plumage - Short, thick and toothy bill** - Wings and legs short - **Long, wide and graded tail** - 2 toes forward and 2 backward - ♂ & ♀ different
Page 161

Order Coraciiformes

Fam. ALCEDINIDAE: **Kingfishers** (Martín-pescadores) - Cosmopolitan - 86 species, 3 in Argentina and Uruguay - Passive - Sit on branches or posts near water - **Plunge** to capture fish - Rapid and undulated flight - Nest in caves - Several white, shiny eggs - Showy plumage - Short body - Large head - Small crest - **Straight, long, thick and sharp bill** - Short and rounded wings - 3 toes forward, 2 of them united, and 1 backward - ♂ & ♀ somewhat different

Page 162

Fam. MOMOTIDAE: **Motmots** (Burgos) - Western Hemisphere - 8 species, 2 in Argentina - In humid forests - Arboreal - Passive - Slow and undulated flight - Nest in caves - 2 white eggs, shiny - **Showy plumage, rather green** - Thick bill, saw-edged - Short wings - Long tail, graded - ♂ & ♀ alike

Page 163

Order Piciformes

Fam. BUCCONIDAE: **Puffbirds** (Chacurúes) - Western Hemisphere - 31 species, 4 in Argentina - Passive - **Tame** - In visible sites - Short and slow flight - Nest in caves or tree cavities - 2 to 4 white eggs, shiny - Resemble kingfishers - Large head, rounded - **Thick bill, with whiskers at base** - Short legs - 2 toes forward and 2 backward- ♂ & ♀ alike

Page 165

Fam. RAMPHASTIDAE: **Toucans** (Tucanes) - Western Hemisphere - 37 species, 5 in Argentina - Arboreal - Noisy - Rather in groups - Flight high, slow and undulated - Nest in tree cavities - 2 to 4 white eggs, shiny - Showy plumage - **Very large and colorful bill,** compressed, saw-edged - Short wings - **Long tail bent over back while sleeping** - Long toes, 2 forward and 2 backward - ♂ & ♀ alike, except 449)

Page 163

Fam. PICIDAE: **Woodpeckers** (Carpinteros) - Cosmopolitan - 210 species, 30 in Argentina, 7 in Uruguay - **Climbers** - Arboreal - Some terrestrial - Strong call - Undulated flight - Drum - Nest in tree cavities or cliffs - Several white eggs, shiny - Large head - **Strong bill, straight and sharp** - Stiff tail, that they use as support - Short tarsi - 2 toes forward and 2 backward - ♂ & ♀ slightly different

Page 166

36

Order Passeriformes

Fam. DENDROCOLAPTIDAE: **Woodcreepers** (Trepadores) - Western Hemisphere - 48 species, 12 in Argentina, 2 in Uruguay - Arboreal - **Climb** in a spiral, **without using** long, rigid, pointed **tail as support** - Rapid flight, from one trunk to the next to land vertically - Loud call - 2 to 4 white eggs, in tree holes - Resemble Picidae and Furnariidae - Brown - **Bill often curved** - Tarsi short - 3 toes forward and 1 backward, as with all passerines - ♂ & ♀ alike   Page 174

Fam. FURNARIIDAE: **Horneros,** miners, spinetails (Horneros) - Western Hemisphere - 218 species, 76 in Argentina, 26 in Uruguay- Weak flight - Strong calls, not very melodious, sometimes duets - Often large **closed nests of sticks** - Also caves, etc. -2 to 5 white eggs (rarely greenish) - **Dull plumage often brown** - Thin bill, without apical hook - Wings short and rounded - ♂ & ♀ alike   Page 177

Fam. FORMICARIIDAE: **Antbirds,** antshrikes (Bataráes) - Western Hemisphere - 227 species, 23 in Argentina, 3 in Uruguay - **Hidden** - Fly little - **Loud calls - Tame** - Nest at low heights - 2 to 3 spotted eggs - Resemble Furnariidae - More colorful - **Thick bill with apical hood** - Short and rounded wings - ♂ & ♀ different
          Page 196

Fam. RHINOCRYPTIDAE: **Gallitos,** tapaculos (Gallitos) - Western Hemisphere - 28 species, 10 in Argentina - Terrestrial - Sometimes hidden - Run rapidly - Strong calls - Nest at low heights - 2 to 3 white eggs - Stocky body - Large head - Short wings - **Erect tail, often bent over back** - Long tarsi - ♂ & ♀ alike   Page 202

Fam. COTINGIDAE: **Cotingas,** becards, bellbirds (Anambés) - Western Hemisphere - 77 species, 10 in Argentina, 2 in Uruguay - Arboreal - Rapid flight - Often strong calls - 2 to 4 spotted eggs - Some resemble Tyrannidae - Wide bill, with apical hook - Wings and tail rather long - Showy plumage - ♂ & ♀ different   Page 205

Fam. PIPRIDAE: **Manakins** (Bailarines) - Western Hemisphere - 55 species, 6 in Argentina - In humid forests - Arboreal - Powerful calls - Complicated nuptial displays - Nest at low heights - 2 spotted eggs- Resemble Cotingidae and Tyrannidae - **Small** -Stocky - Showy plumage - Large head - **Short and wide bill** - Tail rather short - Wings short and rounded - ♂ & ♀ different   Page 207

37

Fam. TYRANNIDAE: Monjitas, **tyrants,** flycatchers, tyrannulets, elaenias (Viuditas) - Western Hemisphere - 380 species, 122 in Argentina, 36 in Uruguay - Often hunt on sallying flight - Some agressive - Calls, nests, and eggs varied - **Bill** often thin, **with whiskers and apical hook** - Wings and tarsi long - ♂ & ♀ generally alike

Page 209

Fam. PHYTOTOMIDAE: **Plantcutters** (Cortarramas) - South America - 3 species, 2 in Argentina, 1 in Uruguay - **Call hoarse, bleating-like** - Eat buds - Nest in bushes at low heights - 2 to 4 greenish eggs, spotted - Look like Emberizidae - **Bill short, thick, saw-edged** - Short and rounded wings - ♂ & ♀ different   Page 240

Fam. HIRUNDINIDAE: **Swallows** (Golondrinas) - Cosmopolitan - 79 species, 14 in Argentina, 11 in Uruguay - **Rapid flight, agile with much gliding** - **Gregarious** - Drink on flight - Sit on cables and wire fences - Mostly migrants - Nest in cavities, sometimes in colonies - Several white eggs or a little spotted - **Neck, bill and legs short** - Wings long and sharp - ♂ & ♀ often alike   Page 240

Fam. CORVIDAE: **Jays** (Urracas) - Cosmopolitan - 102 species, 3 in Argentina, 2 in Uruguay - **Groups - Noisy** - Restless - Nest in trees - Several spotted eggs - **Large** - Showy **plumage, bluish** - Thick bill, with "bristles" over nostrils - **Long** and rounded **tail** - ♂ & ♀ alike

Page 244

Fam. CINCLIDAE: **Dippers** (Mirlos de Agua) - Cosmopolitan - 5 species, 1 in Argentina - Aquatic - Plunge using short wings as oars - **Walk submerged** - Low flight - Closed nest of moss on rocky walls over water - Several white eggs - **Stocky** - Straight bill - **Short tail** - Tarsi and toes thick - ♂ & ♀ alike   Page 245

Fam. TROGLODYTIDAE: **Wrens** (Ratonas) - Cosmopolitan - 59 species, 3 in Argentina, 1 in Uruguay - Restless - Short flight - Varied calls - Nest in cavities - Several spotted eggs - (768: closed nest, in grasslands, white eggs) - **Small** - Dull plumage - **Thin bill**, rather long and somewhat curved - Wings rounded - **Straight tail, erect** - Tarsi and toes thick - ♂ & ♀ alike   Page 245

Fam. MIMIDAE: **Mockingbirds,** mockingthrushes (Calandrias) - Western Hemisphere - 31 species, 5 in Argentina, 2 in Uruguay - Conspicuous - Low flight - Melodious and varied song - **Imitate** - Semispherical nest, at low heights - 3 to 5 greenish eggs, spotted - Slender - Thin bill, somewhat curved - Wings short and rounded - **Long tail,** often erect - ♂ & ♀ alike   Page 246

Fam. TURDIDAE: **Thrushes** (Zorzales) - Cosmopolitan - 303 species, 11 in Argentina, 3 in Uruguay - Rather terrestrial - **Flick tail** with fallen wings - Melodious song - Do not imitate - Semispherical nest, at low heights, of mud and vegetable matter - 3 greenish eggs, spotted - Resemble mockingbirds - More hidden and stocky - Bill almost straight - Long and sharp wings - Tarsi strong - ♂ & ♀ often alike   Page 247

Fam. MOTACILLIDAE: **Pipits** (Cachirlas) - Cosmopolitan - 53 species, 8 in Argentina, 4 in Uruguay - Tame - Terrestrial - **Walk much** - Mimetic - In display **soar high,** emitting typical song and **falling in glide** - Nest on ground - 3 or 4 spotted eggs - Similar among themselves - Striated - Thin and straight bill - Sharp and long wings - Tail dark with outer rectrices light - **Hallux nail very long,** except 787) - ♂ & ♀ alike   Page 250

Fam. SYLVIIDAE: **Gnatcatchers** (Tacuaritas) - Cosmopolitan - 370 species, 2 in Argentina, 1 in Uruguay - Arboreal - Acrobatic - **Active** - Pleasant and varied song - Imitate sometimes - Nest fluffy, in trees, at medium height - 3 or 4 light blue eggs, spotted - **Small - Slender** - Thin and straight bill - **Long tail**, often erect - ♂ & ♀ somewhat different   Page 252

Fam. VIREONIDAE: **Vireos,** peppershrikes (Chivíes) - Western Hemisphere - 37 species, 3 in Argentina, 2 in Uruguay - Arboreal - **Strong call, continuous and musical** - Nest in trees, semispherical - 3 to 4 spotted eggs - Back greenish - ♂ & ♀ alike   Page 252

Fam. PLOCEIDAE: **Sparrows** (Gorriones) - Cosmopolitan - 156 species, 1 introduced in Argentina and Uruguay - **Associated to man** - Bold - Noisy - Gregarious - Rather terrestrial - Closed nest in diverse cavities, also in trees - Several spotted eggs - Short, thick and conical bill - ♂ & ♀ different   Page 253

Fam. PARULIDAE: **Warblers** (Arañeros) - Western Hemisphere 117 species, 9 in Argentina, 5 in Uruguay - Arboreal - **Active - Acrobatic** - Pleasant voice - Nest in trees or thickets - Up to 4 spotted eggs - **Showy plumage** - Small - Resemble Tyrannidae - Thin straight bill - Rounded tail - Sometimes ♂ & ♀ different   Page 253

Fam. COEREBIDAE (Probably not valid): **Bananaquit**, dacnis (Saíes) - Western Hemisphere - 36 species, 4 in Argentina - Forest dwellers - Arboreal - Acrobatic - Nest on trees - 2 or 3 spotted eggs - Small - Showy plumage - Resemble Parulidae - ♂ & ♀ alike, except 810)   Page 255

Fam. TERSINIDAE: **Swallow-Tanagers** (Tersinas) - Western Hemisphere - 1 species, also in Argentina - In humid forests - Arboreal - Rather passive - Often hunts insects on flight - Strong whistle - Erect posture - Nest in cavities - 3 to 4 white eggs - **Showy plumage** - Resemble tanagers - **Bill wide, flat,** with slight apical hook - Long sharp wings - ♂ & ♀ different   Page 256

40

Fam. THRAUPIDAE: **Tanagers** (Fruteros) - Western Hemisphere - 222 species, 26 in Argentina, 6 in Uruguay - Arboreal - Generally gregarious - Melodious calls - Often **frugivorous** - Nest in trees - 2 to 4 spotted eggs - **Showy plumage** - Resemble Emberizidae - **Bill rather thick and conical** - Wings sharp - ♂ & ♀ different   Page 257

Fam. CATAMBLYRHYNCHIDAE: **Plush-capped Finches** (Diademas) - South America - 1 species, also in Argentina - Little known-In humid forest - Frugivorous and insectivorous - Nest unknown - Showy plumage - Resemble Thraupidae and Emberizidae - **Frontal tuft rigid - Short bill, thick and flat** - Scaled tail - ♂ & ♀ alike   Page 263

Fam. EMBERIZIDAE: Cardinals, seedeaters, **finches** (Cardenales)- Cosmopolitan - 315 species, 80 in Argentina, 24 in Uruguay - Rather **granivorous and gregarious** - **Pleasant** varied **song** - White or spotted eggs - **Thick, short and conical bill** - ♂ & ♀ generally different - ♂ showy plumage   Page 264

Fam. FRINGILLIDAE: **Siskins** (Cabecitasnegras) - Cosmopolitan - 112 species, 7 in Argentina, 3 in Uruguay (2 introduced) - **Gregarious - Noisy - Delicate pleasant song** - Nest in trees or cavities - 2 to 4 eggs - Small - Resemble Emberizidae - Bill somewhat longer and sharp - Showy plumage - ♂ & ♀ different   Page 284

Fam. ICTERIDAE: **Cowbirds,** caciques, blackbirds (Tordos) - Western Hemisphere - 88 species, 23 in Argentina, 15 in Uruguay - Often **gregarious** and noisy - Active - Nest variable, sometimes very large and hanging - Some breed in colonies and others parasitize - Several spotted eggs - Showy plumage, rather black - **Conical straight and sharp bill,** in general long - Tarsi and toes thick - ♀ somewhat smaller   Page 286

Symbols and abbreviations

♂	male
♀	female
J	juvenile
♂♂	males
♀♀	females
JJ	juveniles
RP (PI in plates)	rest plumage
NP (PN in plates)	breeding/nuptial plumage
NP (next to a geographic location)	National Park
R	race or subspecies
F	phase
ξ	endemic (to Argentina)
I,II,III,IV,V,VI	indicate the lower or higher probability of being seen
WS	wingspan
[ ]	squarebrackets mean information inside may not happen
( )	bracket used in usual sense
In bold types	shows most important or special characteristics of a species or information worth paying attention to
+	sea birds which may be found dead along our coasts. Higher probability with higher number of +
N, S, E	cardinal points
W, NW (O or NO in plates)	west, north west
C	center of country
South Atlantic Islands	**South Sandwich, South Georgias, South Orkneys and South Shetlands**
C. America	**Central America**
N. America	**North America**
S. America	**South America**

Fam. Spheniscidae, see page 27

1)EMPEROR PENGUIN (Pingüino Emperador) *Aptenodytes forsteri*

90 cm - Black hood - Grey blue back - **Large auricular patch white & yellow;** with yellow **continued on breast-** Long curved bill with prolonged base of mandible rosy - Feet partially feathered J: Auricular patch whitish ... Chile ... Breeds in Antarctica in winter
II

2) KING PENGUIN (Pingüino Rey) *Aptenodytes patagonicus*

75 cm - Similar to 1) - More colorful - Hood blackish brown - **Large oval auricular patch & breast orange,** separated - Tarsus .not feathered - J: Yellowish auricular patch ... Chile ... Breeds in Malvinas & Georgias III

PYGOSCELIS: Usually swim with semi-erect tails - Often sympatric - Longish tails-Thick bills - Different distribution of black & white on heads (3 species)

3) BEARDED PENGUIN (Pingüino de Barbijo) *Pygoscelis antarctica*

48 cm - **Crown and** ear to ear **chinstrap black,** around white face - Black bill - Rosy feet - J: Throat & face spotted with black - Breeds in Antarctica & South Atlantic Islands IV

4) ADELIE PENGUIN (Pingüino Ojo Blanco) *Pygoscelis adeliae*

48 cm - **Black hood** - Conspicuous **white iris and periocular patch** - Bill (looks short) reddish with black tip-Rosy feet - J: Looks like 3) - Without periocular patch - White throat - Bill without red - Breeds in Antarctica & South Atlantic Islands IV

43

5) GENTOO PENGUIN (Pingüino de Vincha) *Pygoscelis papua -2R*

48 cm - Black hood speckled with white-**White supraocular patch continued in band over crown,** looking like ear-phones - Red bill with black culmen-Orange feet - J: Less white on crown ... Breeds in Antarctica, South Atlantic Islands, Malvinas & Staten Islands IV

6)MACARONI PENGUIN (Pingüino Frente Dorada) *Eudyptes chrysolophus*

45 cm - Longish tail - Black hood with end pointing downwards on throat - **Gold on forehead continued as a tuft** - Thick chestnut **bill with rosy colored wedge at base** - J: Tuft smaller & paler... Chile & Brazil - [URUGUAY] ... Breeds in Antarctica, [Malvinas] & South Atlantic Islands - + III

7) ROCKHOPPER PENGUIN (Pingüino Penacho Amarillo) *Eudyptes crestatus*

40 cm - Hops when on land - Small crest- Similar to 6) - **Yellow eyebrow continued as a tuft,** not meeting on forehead - Black on throat not pointed - Bill more orange - J: Almost without tuft - Pale throat ... Chile & Brazil - URUGUAY... Breeds in Malvinas & Staten Islands - +++ IV

8) MAGELLANIC PENGUIN (Pingüino Patagónico) *Spheniscus magellanicus*

44 cm - Short tail - **White eyebrow continued as gular line between black chin & collar** - Black line on flanks - Rosy loral & periocular patches - J: Without black or white lines ... Brazil & Chile - URUGUAY - **Breeds in Chubut** (Punta Tombo, Camarones), **& Santa Cruz,** T. del Fuego & Malvinas - +++ V

44

♀

9) GREATER RHEA
(Nandú)   *Rhea americana*

1.50 m - Often in semiliberty in estancias - Does not fly - Runs swiftly - In groups - Small head & **back uniform ashy grey** - Long & strong **tarsi not feathered** - **Crown, base of long neck & breast, black** - ♀: 1.30m - With less black ... Brazil, Paraguay & Bolivia- URUGUAY ... Savannas, forests, steppes & rural areas   III

10) LESSER RHEA
(Choique)   *Pterocnemia pennata-2R*

1.10 m - Appearance & behavior like 9)- Shorter bill-Head, neck & **back** brownish grey to chestnut, **speckled white-** Underparts whitish, including **feathered upper tarsi** - Southern race: upperparts more ochre & speckling more conspicuous - (Tarsus with 16 to 18 scutes) - NW race: head & neck more ochre - Long scapulars & darker coverts with white tip - (Tarsus with 8 to 10 scutes) ... Peru, Bolivia & Chile ... High Andean steppes (I) also Patagonia
III

CRYPTURELLUS: Walk in dense vegetation - Heard more than seen - Almost never fly - Look like pigeons - Brown colored (4 species)

11) UNDULATED TINAMOU
(Tataupá Listado)
Crypturellus undulatus
27 cm - Melancholic, almost human whistle *hoo..hooee..hooeehoo* - Dark crown - **Back, neck & breast rufous finely barred** - Coverts more greyish - Rest of underparts ochraceous - Thighs & lower belly cinnamon barred dark - **Legs greenish** - Bill blackish ... From Venezuela, except Chile ... Forests in the Eastern Chaqueño District   II

12) BROWN TINAMOU   (Tataupá Rojizo)
Crypturellus obsoletus
26 cm - Series of rising guttural notes - Uniform back & grey head unlike 11) - Similar to 13) - **Rufous breast** changing to **ochraceous barred dark on legs & lower belly** - Orange iris - Dark **bill & legs, not reddish** ... From Venezuela, except Chile ... Humid forest in **Misiones**   II

13) TATAUPA TINAMOU   (Tataupá Común)
Crypturellus tataupa
22 cm - Occasionally seen crossing footpaths - Swift & short series of harsh descending trills *prrr.. prr.. prrr.. prrrr* - **Purple back - Head, neck & breast plumbeous** turning ochraceous on rest of underparts - White throat-**Thighs & belly scaled** with ochraceous & brown - Brown iris - **Bill & legs reddish** ... Brazil, Paraguay, Bolivia & Peru ... Forests & humid ravines   IV

14) SMALL-BILLED TINAMOU
(Tataupá Chico)
Crypturellus parvirostris
19 cm - Clear notes start very separate, then accelerate ascending & end with descending trills - Similar to 13 - **Bill & feet red**der & shorter - Back rufous less purple - Throat ochraceous - Breast ochraceous grey (not plumbeous) - Lower belly blackish & ochraceous - Thighs ochraceous marked with cinnamon - **Undertail coverts cinnamon spotted with blackish** - Iris chestnut... Brazil, Paraguay, Bolivia & Peru ... Forests in **Misiones**   III

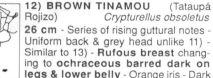

15) SOLITARY TINAMOU
(Macuco)   *Tinamus solitarius*

42 cm - Tame - Passive - Three long, clear & melancholic whistles - Roosts in shrubs - **Nearly half a meter in height** - Longish tail - Head & hindneck chestnut spotted - **Ochre line in slender neck** - **Back olive grey barred blackish** ... Brazil & Paraguay ... Forests in **Misiones**   II

16) RED-WINGED TINAMOU
(Colorada)   *Rhynchotus rufescens-3R*

38 cm - Loud single whistle, followed by additional mournful ones - Longish curved bill - Crown & ocular line blackish- **Head, neck & breast cinnamon** (or cinnamon grey) (spotted in NW) - **Black barred - Rufous remiges** conspicous in flight - Legs whitish grey... Brazil, Paraguay & Bolivia - URUGUAY... Tall pastures in savannas, hills and rural areas-(El Palmar NP)   III

17) ORNATE TINAMOU
(Inambú Serrano) *Nothoprocta ornata*

30 cm - Similar to 18) - Different habitat- Longer bill - **Speckled on** head & **neck-** Back more ochraceous - Grey **breast** [slightly barred] **without white dots - Cinnamon flanks** ... Peru, Bolivia & Chile ... Prepuna zones & **High Andean steppes** in NW   II

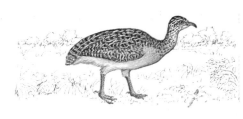

18) BRUSHLAND TINAMOU
(Inambú Montaraz)
          Nothoprocta cinerascens-2R

28 cm - Song of 7 or 8 whistled notes - Tamer & larger than 19) - **Does not whistle on taking flight** - Back darker & more contrasting than in 17) - **Erectile blackish small crest** more conspicuous· than in 17) & 19) - **Breast with white specks** - Rest of underparts whitish - **Greyish legs** ... Bolivia & Paraguay ... Forests, savannas & steppes with bushes   IV

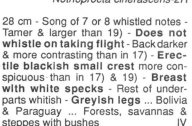

47

19) ANDEAN TINAMOU (Inambú Silbón) *Nothoprocta pentlandii-3R*

24 cm - Similar to 18) - Smaller - Less tame - Similar song of only 2 or 3 notes- **Anxious whistle on taking flight - Head, neck & breast plumbeous** spotted white-Rest of underparts cinnamon - Flanks not barred - **Yellow legs**... Ecuador, Peru, Bolivia & Chile ... Grasslands & wooded hills   III

20) SPOTTED TINAMOU (Inambú Común) *Nothura maculosa-7R (.)*

25 cm - Noisy & sudden flight, low, parabolic & short - Hunters' most common quarry - Crosses roads unhurriedly - Flutelike whistles, accelerating at the end - Typical non-forest tinamou-like coloring - Head, neck & breast ochre, striated - White throat - **Underparts cinnamon** or ochre - Flanks barred - **Primaries spotted on both webs** (see road kills) ... Brazil, Paraguay & Bolivia - URUGUAY ... Low pastures, savannas & rural areas   V

21) DARWIN'S TINAMOU (Inambú Pálido) *Nothura darwinii-2R*

22 cm - Fast whistles followed by flutelike ones, contrary to 20) - Alike but somewhat **smaller, paler &** more **uniform** - Striations on breast more conspicuous-Underparts ochraceous - **Inner web of external primaries not spotted** (see road kills) ... Peru & Bolivia ... Steppes with bushes & savannas   IV

48   (.) The *chacoensis* form is here considered as within *N. maculosa*

22) ELEGANT CRESTED-TINAMOU (Martineta Común) *Eudromia elegans-8R*

39 cm - Groups - Flies little - Conspicuous - Elegant-**Dappled** - **Long** slender **crest** - **Two white lines descending along neck,** from eye - White throat - Underparts ochraceous [**striated & barred** with black] - Both webs of primaries spotted - **J:** Similar but **smaller than adult** ... Chile ... Savannas, grasslands, bush & Patagonian steppes, & rural areas IV

23) QUEBRACHO CRESTED-TINAMOU (Martineta Chaqueña) *Eudromia formosa*
39 cm - Similar to 22) - Flies more - Crest does not curve forward - Somewhat **cinnamon** - **Back with spaced ochre dots** - Underparts ochraceous, spotted - Inner webs of primaries not spotted ... Paraguay ... Chaco type savannas & **forests** (Reserva de Copo, Santiago del Estero) III

24) PUNA TINAMOU
(Quiula Puneña) *Tinamotis pentlandii*
41 cm - Looks like 22) - Without crest - Similar behavior - Tame - Less elegant-**White lines on neck** longer - White throat more conspicuous - Plumbeous dorsal striations - Lower back olivaceous - Cinnamon coverts - **Thighs & lower belly rufous** - Allopatric with 25) - Brown iris ... Peru, Bolivia & Chile ... High Andean steppes in the NW (above 4000 meters) II

25) PATAGONIAN TINAMOU
(Quiula Patagónica) *Tinamotis ingoufi*
35 cm - Looks like 24) - Sympatric only with 22) - Conspicuous **white lines on head & neck** - **Back cinnamon** - Striated throat - Scaled breast - **Reddish remiges** conspicuous in flight (like in 16) - Thighs & lower belly cinnamon (not rufous) - Yellow iris ... Chile ... Patagonian steppes (E of Santa Cruz) III

26) LEAST GREBE   (Macá
Gris)   *Podiceps dominicus*

19 cm - Looks like 30) & 27) in RP-**Ashy
grey** to plumbeous - Darker crown -
Without auricular tuft - **Yellow iris** - NP:
Black throat - From N. America, except
Chile - [URUGUAY] - Wetlands in the N
III

27) WHITE-TUFTED GREBE
(Macá Común)   *Podiceps rolland-2R*

23 cm(In Malvinas 33 cm) - Back dark
brown - White face with blackish lines -
Neck & breast brown - Underparts
white - Red iris - **NP**: Small crest - Head,
neck & back black - **White auricular
tuft - Underparts rufous** - J: Striated
neck ... Bordering countries and Peru -
URUGUAY ... Wetlands   V

28) SILVERY GREBE   (Macá
Plateado)   *Podiceps occipitalis-2R*

25 cm - Often in large flocks - Small crest-
White - Head & back plumbeous
(grey in NW) - **Black nape** - Red iris -
NP: Golden auricular tuft (whitish in
NW) - From Colombia along the W - High
Andean & Pampas Lakes, & Patagonian
wetlands   IV

29) HOODED GREBE   (Macá
Tobiano)   *Podiceps gallardoi*

28 cm - ♂ - **White, including fore-
head-** Looks like 28)-**Hood & line on
hindneck black** - Erectile **rufous
small crest** - Back blackish - Bill black
with sky blue tip - Iris red - Yellow region
around eye - Lakes, with *Myriophyllum,*
in Patagonian plateau in **Santa Cruz** II

30) PIED-BILLED GREBE (Macá Pico Grueso) *Podilymbus podiceps*

28 cm - **Stocky** - Without auricular tuft or small crest - **Thick bill** - Brownish- Lighter on underparts- **NP**: Crown & back blackish - **Throat black - Pale bill with black ring** - Underparts silvery grey, speckled - All Western Hemisphere ... URUGUAY.. Wetlands   IV

31) GREAT GREBE
(Macá Grande)   *Podiceps major-2R*

44 cm - The largest - Elegant - Melancholic & sonorous call - **Long neck** which sometimes rests on back - **Long pointed bill** - Hindneck grey - Underparts white - **NP**: Small crest & back blackish - **Neck rufous** - **J**: Streaked white ... Brazil, Paraguay, Peru & Chile-URUGUAY ... Wetlands and seashores   IV

● *Fam. Diomedeidae, see page 27*

32) WANDERING ALBATROSS
(Albatros Errante)
Diomedea exulans-2R

WS: 3.20 m - **Enormous - White, including mantle & underwing** - Primaries & tip of inner remiges [& outer rectrices] black - [Coverts mottled] - Long **bill rosy** with horn-colored tip - Eyelids rosy or grey - **J**: Much more common (95%) than adults - Various plumages - Brown with varying proportions of white ... Chile & Brazil - [URUGUAY] ... Breeds in Georgias [& Malvinas]   IV

33) ROYAL ALBATROSS
(Albatros Real) *Diomedea epomophora*

WS: 3 m - Very **similar to adult 32)**- **Bill** more **yellowish - Black line between mandibles** - Black eyelids - **J**: **Similar to adult,** not as J 32) ... Chile, Peru & Brazil - URUGUAY ...   IV

51

SMALL ALBATROSSES 34 to 36: Much smaller than the Wandering & Royal (32 & 33) - Similar to each other - Look like large - gulls Long wings bordered with black un- - derneath White - Upperwing, mantle & tail black- JJ: Less white on underwing - - Blackish bill (3 species) (.)

34) GRAY-HEADED ALBATROSS
(Albatros Cabeza Gris)
Diomedea chrysostoma

WS: 2m - **Head & neck grey** [with large white forehead] - **White half-circle behind eye - Bill black with yellow upper & lower borders** ... Peru & Chile ... Breeds in Georgias   III

35)YELLOW-NOSED
ALBATROSS   (Albatros Pico Fino)
Diomedea chlororhynchos

WS: 1.90 m - Slightly black ocular zone- Slender **black bill, only with upper-part of maxilla yellow** & orange tip - J: Grey on crown ... Brazil - URUGUAY +
III

36)BLACK-BROWED ALBATROSS
(Albatros Ceja Negra)
Diomedea melanophrys

WS: 2.20 m - Somewhat gregarious - **Often seen from shore** - Large black ocular patch - **Yellow bill** ... Ecuador, Peru, Chile & Brazil - URUGUAY ... Breeds in Malvinas, Georgias & Staten Islands - ++ -   V

(.) *D. cauta* has been captured in Argentine waters

Fam. Diomedeidae, see page 27

37) SOOTY ALBATROSS
(Albatros Oscuro)   *Phoebetria fusca*

WS: 2m - Very elegant - Narrow wings - **Large wedgeshaped tail** - Looks **blacker than 38)** - Brown with darker head - **White half-circle behind eye- Black bill-** Yellow line on mandible - J: Ochraceous collar - Whitish nape ... Chile - [URUGUAY]   I

38) LIGHT-MANTLED ALBATROSS
(Albatros Manto Claro)   *Phoebetria palpebrata*

WS: 2.10 m - Similar to 37) - **Back & underparts ashy grey contrasting with rest blackish - Black bill** - Sky blue line on mandible - J: Mantle & breast barred with ochraceous ... Brazil & Chile ... Breeds in Georgias   III

 Fam. Procellaridae, see page 27

39) SOUTHERN GIANT PETREL
(Petrel Gigante Común)
                     Macronectes giganteus

WS: 2.15 m - Looks like *Phoebetria* - Less elegant - Tail less pointed - More flapping - Swims well - Daring - Often on shores & in ports - **Dark brownish grey** (all white phase in Antarctica)- **Whitish on head**, often extended - **Thick yellowish bill with olive tip** - J: Browner - Less white - Variable plumage ... Peru, Chile & Brazil - URUGUAY... Breeds in Antarctica, Malvinas & South Atlantic Islands   VI

40) NORTHERN GIANT PETREL
(Petrel Gigante Oscuro)
                     Macronectes halli (.)

WS: 2.10 m - Almost indistinguishable from 39) even in behavior - Darker - **Without all white phase - Head not entirely whitish** - White restricted to face & throat (like subadult of 39) - **Bill** olive yellow **with reddish tip** - J: Like J 39) - Bill with reddish tip - URUGUAY   II

(.) Sometimes considered as race of *M. giganteus*

53

41) WHITE-CHINNED PETREL (Petrel Barba Blanca)*Procellaria aequinoctialis*

50 cm - WS: 1.35 m - Low flight - Often seen from seashore - Feet extend beyond tail - Larger than 42) & 43) & much smaller & **dark**er than the Giant (39) - **White chin** barely visible - Conspicuous **ivory bill**... Peru, Chile & Brazil - URUGUAY ... Breeds in Malvinas & Georgias   IV

42) SOOTY SHEARWATER (Pardela Oscura)   *Puffinus griseus*

45 cm - WS: 95 cm - Undulating flight with rigid wings - Dives - Does not follow ships - Gregarious - Resembles 41) - Back black or **blackish brown** - More **slender bill** (character of genus) **black** - Underparts paler - Pale chin - **White underwing coverts** - [Lilac feet] ... Migrant C to Central America - URUGUAY...Breeds in Malvinas - ++ IV

43) KERGUELEN PETREL (Petrel Pizarra)
          Pterodroma brevirostris (.)

32 cm - WS: 70 cm - Often soars high up- **Plumbeous -** [Silvery sheen, more so underwing] - Slightly white on shoulders & quills of remiges - Thick bill (character of genus) & feet black ... URUGUAY III

44) HOODED PETREL   (Petrel Cabeza Parda)   *Pterodroma incerta*

41 cm - WS: 1 m - Back, underwings, undertail coverts & breast **brown**, **contrasting sharply with rest of white underparts** - [Throat & nape pale] - Thick black bill - Lilac feet ... Brazil - [URUGUAY]   III

54   (.) *P. macroptera* & *P. externa* have been cited for the SW Atlantic

45) CORY'S SHEARWATER
(Pardela Grande)   *Puffinus diomedea*

50 cm - WS: 1.20 m - Robust - **Bigger than 46)** - **Upperparts blackish brown,** without darker crown - Grey face & flanks - **Underparts,** including underwing coverts, **white** - [Slightly white rump] - **Yellowish bill** - Lilac feet - Migrant A ... Brazil - URUGUAY - + ... II

46) GREATER SHEARWATER
(Pardela Cabeza Negra)
Puffinus gravis

44 cm - WS: 1.10 m - Gregarious - Bill slightly slender - **Crown & tail black** - Back & half-collar brownish - **Band on nape, rump,** [wing band] **& underparts white** - Underwing white with black border - Lilac feet ... Venezuela & Brazil - URUGUAY ... [Breeds in Malvinas]   IV

47) CAPE PETREL
(Petrel Damero)   *Daption capense*

35 cm - WS: 90 cm - Gregarious - Robust - **Striking black & white dorsal pattern** - Black hood - Spot on remiges and all underparts white - White tail with black terminal band ... Irregular Migrant C to Ecuador along the W & N. America along the E - URUGUAY ... Breeds in Antarctica & South Atlantic Islands - +   IV

48) WHITE-HEADED PETREL
(Petrel Cabeza Blanca)
Pterodroma lessonii

45 cm - WS: 1 m - Wings arched in flight- Greyish **white** on back - Ocular zone black - **Wings & upperback plumbeous** - **Dark underwing** - Thick black bill - Lilac feet ... Chile & Brazil ... [URUGUAY]   II

49) SOFT-PLUMAGED PETREL
(Petrel Collar Gris)   *Pterodroma mollis*

35 cm - WS: 85 cm - Timid & solitary - Looks like 48) - Striated forehead - **Upperparts & collar** (incomplete) **grey** - Black ocular zone - Face, throat & rest of **underparts white** (or greyish) - **Underwing blackish** - Black bill - Lilac feet - Some melanic individuals ... Brazil- [URUGUAY]   III

50) MANX SHEARWATER
(Pardela Boreal)   *Puffinus puffinus*

35 cm - WS: 85 cm - Gregarious - Does not follow ships - **Back, including cheek, black** - **Underparts·white** - Underwing with black border - Slender black bill - Lilac feet - Migrant A ... Brazil- URUGUAY ... +   III

51) LITTLE SHEARWATER
(Pardela Chica)   *Puffinus assimilis*

27 cm - WS: 55 cm - Gregarious - Dives- Low flight with rapid flapping like diving petrels - Similar to 50) - Upperparts plumbeous - **Cheek & underparts white** -Bill & feet sky blue - [Chile]   I

52) GRAY PETREL
(Petrel Ceniciento) *Adamastor cinereus*

48 cm - WS: 1.20 m - Rapid flapping - Ascends to dive - Follows ships & whales- Gregarious - Robust - Ashy grey (or brown) including **underwing, tail & undertail coverts, contrasting with rest of white underparts** - In color pattern resembles a cormorant - Greenish bill - Greenish lilac feet ... Peru, Chile & Brazil - URUGUAY   III

53) SOUTHERN FULMAR
(Petrel Plateado) *Fulmarus glacialoides*

45 cm - WS: 1.10 m - Gregarious - Looks like a gull - **White, grey back** - Black **primaries with** conspicuous **white basal zone** - Tip of inner remiges blackish - **Rosy bill with tip & nostrils black** -Lilac feet ... Ecuador, Peru, Chile & Brazil - URUGUAY ... Breeds in Antarctica & South Atlantic Islands - ++   III

54) ANTARCTIC PETREL
(Petrel Antártico)*Thalassoica antarctica*

40 cm - WS: 1 m - Gregarious - Settles on floating ice - Looks slightlly like Cape Petrel (47) - Striking pattern - Two contrasting areas: **hood, back, tail tip & front half of wing brown - Underparts & rest of wing & tail white** ... Breeds in Antarctica   II

55) SNOW PETREL
(Petrel Blanco)   *Pagodroma nivea*

34 cm - WS: 80 cm - Gregarious - Erratic high flight - Quick flapping - Settles on floating ice - Looks like a pigeon - **White- Iris & bill black** - Feet plumbeous ... Breeds in Antarctica & South Atlantic Islands   III

57

56) BLUE PETREL
(Petrel Azulado)   *Halobaena caerulea*

30 cm - Resembles prions, with which it associates - Less agile flight with much gliding - Forehead speckled - **Crown &** half-collar **blackIsh** - Back & wings gre- yish blue with blackish open M visible in flight - Square **tall wIth whIte tIp** - Underparts white - Black bill - Feet sky blue ... URUGUAY ... Breeds in Geor- gias - +   II

*PACHYPTILA (Prions): Gregarious - Agile & erratic flight - Do not follow ships Alike- Resemble 56) in color & **wing pattern** - Wedgeshaped tail with black tip - Sky blue bill & feet - (3 species) (.)*

57) DOVE PRION
(Prion Pico Grande) *Pachyptila desolata*

28 cm - Slightly bigger & darker - White eyebrow less conspicuous than in 58) - Black ocular band - Dark lores - Bluish half-collar & white throat more conspicuos - **Bill** (2.8 cm) **strong**, wide at base: 1.4 cm ... Peru, Chile & Brazil - URUGUAY ... Breeds in South Atlantic Islands   II

58) SLENDER-BILLED PRION
(Prion Pico Fino)   *Pachyptila belcheri*

26 cm - Somewhat paler - **Lores & long broad eyebrow whIte** - Black ocular band - **Bill** like 57) **narrow**er **at base:** 1 cm - In flight dorsal M some- what less conspicuous & outer rectrices whiter than in 57) & 59) ... Peru, Chile & Brazil - URUGUAY ... Breeds in Malv- inas - +++   IV

59) FAIRY PRION
(Prion Pico Corto)   *Pachyptila turtur*

25 cm - Smaller - More sky blue - Dorsal M more conspicuous - Eyebrow & ocular band less conspicuous - **Black taIl- band very wide** - **Short bIll** (2.3 cm)... Chile- Breeds in Beauchene, near Malvinas   II

(.) *P. forsteri=P. vittata*, with a very wide bill, has been cited for Malvinas

60) GRAY-BACKED STORM-PETREL
(Paíño Gris)　　　*Garrodia nereis*

17 cm - WS: 35 cm - Smaller & paler than 64) - **Hood,** back, coverts **& breast blackish - Remiges & tip of tail black** - [Pale wingbars] - **Rump & tail ashy grey,** not white - Rest of under-parts, including underwing coverts, white ... Chile ... Breeds in Malvinas & Georgias　　　III

61) WILSON'S STORM-PETREL
(Paíño Común)
　　　　　Oceanites oceanicus-2R

18 cm - WS: 40 cm - Gregarious - Dances on the wake of ships - **Blackish, including underwing** - Con-spicuous **white rump [continued on lower belly]** - [Pale wingbars] - Incon-spicuous yellow feet ... Coasts of Amer-ica - URUGUAY... Breeds on South Atlantic Islands [& Malvinas] - +　　　V

62) BLACK-BELLIED STORM-PETREL
(Paíño Vientre Negro)　*Fregetta tropica*

20 cm - WS: 48 cm - Follows ships - [Whitish throat] - Upperparts, **breast &** undertail coverts **blackish** - [Pale wing bars] - **Rump & underwing coverts white** - Rest of **underparts white with longitudinal black band** (if lack-ing, like 63; could be forms of a single species) ... Peru & Chile - URUGUAY ... Breeds in South Atlantic Islands　　　II

63) WHITE-BELLIED STORM-PETREL
(Paíño Vientre Blanco)
　　　　　Fregetta grallaria

Like 62) without black ventral band - There are intermediate forms ... Chile　　　I

59

64) WHITE-FACED STORM-PETREL
(Paíño Cara Blanca)

Pelagodroma marina
20 cm -WS: 45 cm - Pendular dancing over waves - Does not follow ships - Flight similar to that of Spotted Sandpiper. 264) - Larger than 60) - **Crown & ocular band black - Forehead & eyebrow white** - **Tail** (not the tip) **black** - **Rump grey - Underparts from chin,** including almost all wing, **white** - Feet like 61) ... URUGUAY I

● *Fam. Pelecanoididae, see page 28*

*PELECANOIDES (.) (Diving-Petrels): At sea almost indistinguishable between them - Continuous flapping & little gliding over waves - **Dive abruptly from a certain height & emerge flying** - Small - Robust - Short wings - Black back - Underparts white- Along the continental shelf & coast - (3 species)*

65) MAGELLANIC DIVING-PETREL
(Yunco Ceja Blanca)

Pelecanoides magellani
20 cm - **Scapulars with white margin forming a dorsal V in flight -** [**Internal remiges**, coverts & rump, also **with white margin**] - Only one with **postocular white line** which descends joining in underparts - Dark halfcollar - J: Almost without white margins... Chile ... Breeds in Staten Island & T. del Fuego II

66) COMMON DIVING-PETREL
(Yunco Común)

Pelecanoides urinator-3R
19 cm - **Wide grey collar - Underwing** more **grey** than white - **Without white** eyebrow or **margins** ... Chile - URUGUAY ... Breeds in Malvinas & Georgias - In Winter farther N - Rare in Patagonian lakes (Puelo) - + II

67) SOUTH GEORGIAN DIVING-PETREL
(Yunco Geórgico)

Pelecanoides georgicus
19 cm - ξ - Sympatric with 66) - **Scapulars greyish** like 65) - **White tip in inner remiges** - Underwing white - Grey on face & neck without forming a collar ... Breeds in Georgias III

(.) *P. exsul*, from Georgias considered race of *P. urinator*

Fam. Sulidae, see page 28

68) BROWN BOOBY
(Piquero Pardo)   *Sula leucogaster*

60 cm - WS: 1.40 m - Groups flying in line- Undulating flight over waves - Dives from air - Swimmer - Hood, back, **pointed tail & breast blackish brown** - Rest of underparts white - **Underwing white** with blackish border- **Robust conical yellowish bill** - J: More uniform - Underparts pale without clear separation from breast ... From N. America to Colombia and along Atlantic to Brazil - Seacoasts -**URUGUAY** - Accidental in B. Aires   I

Fam. Anhingidae, see page 28

69) ANHINGA
(Aninga)   *Anhinga anhinga*

66 cm - Often on shrubs or posts - Rests with open wings - More elegant than a cormorant - While swimming only **long snakelike neck** emerges - **Straight pointed bill** - Glossy **black - Silvery patch on coverts** - Long rounded tail with ochre tip - ● : **Head, neck & breast cinnamon** in clear contrast with rest black - J: Browner ... From N. America, except Chile - URUGUAY ... Rivers, lakes & marshes   III

Fam. Fregatidae, see page 28

70) MAGNIFICENT FRIGATEBIRD
(Ave Fragata)   *Fregata magnificens*

65 cm -WS: 2.30 m (weight 1.5 kg) - Much **gliding** - Groups - Dives without submersion - Audacious - Pirates - Unmistakable silhouette in flight: **narrow angled wings & long deeply forked tail** - Glossy **black** - Red gular pouch - ♀: Collar & breast white - J: Often seen - Head & underparts white ... From N. America to Colombia & along Atlantic to URUGUAY & **B. Aires** - Seacoasts   II

61

Fam.. Phalacrocoracidae, see page 28

PHALACROCORAX: Long neck, held extended in flight - Gregarious - Dive - While swimming straight hooked bill points up - On land stretch wings out to dry- Erect posture resembles that of penguins - Long rigid tail - (6 species)

71) NEOTROPIC CORMORANT
(Biguá) . *Phalacrocorax olivaceus-2R*

63 cm - **Blackish,** with gloss - Iris pale green - NP: White feathers at base of bill- J: Brown - Underparts pale ... From N. America - URUGUAY ... Seacoasts & wetlands including inhabited areas   V

72) RED-LEGGED CORMORANT
(Cormorán Gris)
Phalacrocorax gaimardi

50 cm - Unmistakable - Dark **grey** - Coverts very spotted silvery - **White patch on neck** - **Yellow bill** with red base - Conspicuous **red legs** ... From Peru, along the Pacific ... Seacoasts in **S. Cruz** (Puerto Deseado)   III

73) ROCK CORMORANT
(Cormorán Cuello Negro)
Phalacrocorax magellanicus

57 cm - Like 74), 75) & 76), black back & white underparts - **Neck & upper breast black** - **Auricular patch white** - Often white gular spot [spread along throat] - **Periocular & iris red** - J: Brown - White gular [& lower belly] ... Chile ... Seacoasts & shores of Lago Fagnano in T. del Fuego   IV

74) GUANAY CORMORANT
(Guanay) *Phalacrocorax bougainvillii*

62 cm - Looks like intermediate between 73) & 75) or 76) - Only **periocular red-Green iris** - Without white auricular - **Wedgeshaped** white gular patch **extends down to middle of neck**, not linked with **white underparts** - Yellowish bill ... Chile, Peru [& further N] - Seacoasts in **Chubut** (Punta Tombo) II

75) KING CORMORANT
(Cormorán Real)
　　　　　Phalacrocorax albiventer

60 cm - Resembles 73 & 74) - Perhaps conspecific with 76) - Without white on back - Crown & **cheeks** (head) **black** - Small crest & caruncle yellow, absent in RP - **White shoulders**, reduced or absent in RP - **All underparts white** - Blue eyelids - J: Brown back ... Chile - URUGUAY ... Seacoasts　　　　　V

76) BLUE-EYED CORMORANT
(Cormorán Imperial)
　　　　　Phalacrocorax atriceps-3R

60 cm - Very similar to 75) - White of underparts reaches face arc shaped - **White cheeks** - Shoulders & conspicuous **dorsal patch white**, smaller or absent in RP - Eyelids also blue - J: Like J 75) ... Chile ... Southern seacoasts & Lake Nahuel Huapi (Isla Victoria)　　　　　IV

63

77) WHITE-NECKED HERON
(Garza Mora)   *Ardea cocoi*

75 cm - Shy - Solitary - Largest of herons- Back **grey** - Crown, long nape plumes, two discontinued lines on neck & **pectoral flanks black** - Rest of underparts white - J: Without black flanks ... From Panama - URUGUAY ... Wetlands   IV

78) RUFESCENT TIGER-HERON
(Hocó Colorado)   *Tigrisoma lineatum*

62 cm - Often on trees - Passive - **Rufous** - Back appears brown because slightly vermiculated - Conspicuous **white lines from chin to breast** - Underparts cinnamon - J: Often seen - Like J 79) - Looks like 85) & J 89) - Blackish & cinnamon barring ... From Honduras - URUGUAY ... Wetlands on edge of forests & savannas   III

79) FASCIATED TIGER-HERON
(Hocó Oscuro)   *Tigrisoma fasciatum-2R*

56 cm - Resembles 78) - Curved maxilla- Dark - **Without rufous** - Crown & band on hindneck black -Back thinly barred ochraceous - J: Very similar to J 78) - (Observe maxilla) - From Mexico along W - Rivers & streams in forests   II

80) WHISTLING HERON
(Chiflón)   *Syrigma sibilatrix*

48 cm - In flight wings not above body line - Flutelike whistle - **Striking coloration** - Crown & long plumes on nape blue black - Back blue grey - **Neck & breast yellowish** - Cinnamon coverts striated - Bill rosy with black tip - J: Paler- Colombia, Venezuela, Brazil, Paraguay & Bolivia - URUGUAY ... Wetlands, nearby areas & plantations - Expanding   IV

81) GREAT EGRET
(Garza Blanca)   *Casmerodius albus*

65 cm - Groups - Sometimes on trees - **White - Yellow bill - Blackish feet** - NP: Long plumes on back & breast ... From N. America - URUGUAY ... Wetlands & nearby areas, & in S also seacoasts   **V**

82) SNOWY EGRET
(Garcita Blanca)   *Egretta thula*

40 cm - Groups - Often with 81) - Similar- **Black bill - Black legs with yellow feet** - NP: Plumes on nape, breast & back - J:Legs greenish yellow ... From N. America - URUGUAY ... Wetlands & nearby areas   **V**

83) CATTLE EGRET
(Garcita Bueyera)   *Bubulcus ibis*

35 cm - In **flocks** - **Around or perched on cattle** - Follow ploughs - Smaller than 81) - **Yellow bill thicker** than 82) -Shorter neck - Legs greenish black - **NP: Cinnamon on crown, back & breast**- Legs yellow or orange ... From N. America - URUGUAY ... Rural zones & wetlands - Recent colonist - Expanding   **VI**

84) LITTLE BLUE HERON
(Garza Azul)   *Florida caerulea (.)*

40 cm - Dark - **Plumbeous - Head & neck lilac rufous** - Bluish bill with black tip & greenish legs (or both blackish) - NP: Plumes on crown, back & breast - **J: Often seen - Resembles 82) - White Bill like adult** - Greenish legs - Intermediate plumages ... From N. America, except Bolivia, Paraguay, Chile & Argentina ... Wetlands & nearby areas ... Rare in **URUGUAY**

(.) Cited very occasionally for Argentina

65

Fam. Ardeidae, see page 29

BITTERNS: Reclusive - Short & ungainly flight with legs hanging - When alarmed, **point bill upwards simulating dead reeds** *- (3 species)*

85) PINNATED BITTERN
(Mirasol Grande) *Botaurus pinnatus*

55 cm - Deep call, like bellowing - Looks like J 78), J 79) & J 89) - Ochraceous - Blackish crown - **Variegated back (more striated than barred) with black** - Underparts white striated with cinnamon on neck, breast & flanks - **Thick tarsi & long toes greenish** ... From Mexico, except Peru, Bolivia & Chile - URUGUAY ... Marsh vegetation

II

86) STRIPE-BACKED BITTERN
(Mirasol Común) *Ixobrychus involucris*

28 cm - Ochraceous - Striated - Long black band on crown - **Back black,** rufous & white - J: A little more contrasted ... S. America - URUGUAY ... Marsh vegetation

III

87) LEAST BITTERN
(Mirasol Chico) *Ixobrychus exilis*

25 cm - Similar to 86) - Darker - Crown **& back black, without striations -** Face **& hindneck rufous - Long black gular stripe - ●** : Chestnut back - J: Sparsely striated ... From N. America, except Chile ... Marshes in NE

II

66

88) STRIATED HERON
(Garcita Azulada)   *Butorides striatus*

34 cm - Not as reclusive as bitterns - Crouches when moving - Waggles tail rapidly - Sudden loud cry - **Bluish** - Crown & plumes on nape black - Coverts reticulated with white - **Thick cinnamon striations on throat** - Yellow legs (orange in NP) - J: Brownish grey striated on underparts ... From Costa Rica - URUGUAY ... Wetlands with vegetation
IV

89) BLACK-CROWNED NIGHT-HERON
(Garza Bruja)   *Nycticorax nycticorax-3R*

47 cm - Gregarious - Perches on trees - Crepuscular - Loud *kuak* - Looks hunched - Robust bill - **Grey** - **Black crown & back** - Long plumes on nape & forehead white - Underparts whitish (S race plumbeous, some melanic specimens occur) - Yellowish legs - J: Often seen - Brown, speckled & striated with white ... From N. América - URUGUAY ... Wetlands & seacoasts
IV

90) BOAT-BILLED HERON
(Garza Cucharona)
            Cochlearius cochlearius (.)

43 cm - Similar to 89) in habits, appearance & voice - Strange **bill, very large & flat** - Forehead & face white - Crown, long crest & upper back black - Rest of **upperparts & breast pale grey** - **Rest of underparts rufous** & black - J: Brown - Black crown - Underparts pale... From Mexico, except Chile ... Marshes in NE
I

(.) Sometimes included in Fam. Cochlearidae   **67**

91) WOOD-STORK
(Tuyuyú) *Mycteria americana*

65 cm - Groups - Often on trees - **White- Head & neck blackish** - **Remiges & tail black** conspicuous in flight - **Bill** horn color **with curved tip** - J: Splashed with brown ... From N. America - URUGUAY - Flooded savannas, lakes & marshes IV

92) MAGUARI STORK
(Cigüeña Americana)
Euxenura maguari

85 cm - Standing, **rear third of body black** - In flight **tail** appears **white with sides black** - Periocular & legs red - **Straight bill** violaceous horn color - Yellow iris - J: Black with gloss ... S. America, except Ecuador & Peru - URUGUAY ... Wetlands & rural zones IV

93) JABIRU
(Yabirú) *Jabiru mycteria*

1.10 m - Erect posture - **White, including wings & tail** - Head & neck black - Wide **red collar** - Strong **black bill slightly curved upwards** - J: Splashed with brown - Rosy collar ... From Mexico, except Chile - URUGUAY Flooded savannas & marshes II

Fam. Threskiornithidae, see page 29

IBISES 94 to 96: Groups - On trees & ground-Loud calls - Curved bill - (3 species)

94) PLUMBEOUS IBIS
(Bandurria Mora)
Harpiprion caerulescens

62 cm - Trumpets while walking - **Ashy grey** - Olivaceous sheen - **White forehead** - Conspicuous ruffled **crest on nape** & neck striated whitish - Iris & legs reddish - J: More opaque ... Brazil, Bolivia & Paraguay - URUGUAY ... Marshes & flooded savannas in N   II

95) BUFF-NECKED IBIS
(Bandurria Baya)
Theristicus caudatus-2R

57 cm - Nasal & repeated call, like car horn - In flight looks like a large lapwing- Crown & hindneck cinnamon - **Neck ochre yellow - Back ashy grey - Coverts white** - Periocular, gular, remiges, tail & **underwing coverts black -** Rest of underparts black (ashy grey in N) - Legs reddish ... From Panama - URUGUAY ... Lakes, water-courses, marshes, flooded savannas & tall pastures - S population Migrant C in rural areas   IV

96) GREEN IBIS
(Tapicurú) *Mesembrinibis cayennensis*

47 cm - Hides in trees - Heard more than seen - Sometimes in shallow waters - Loud & melodious *kro..kro* at dusk - **Olivaceous** - Long **metallic green plumes on hindneck** - Wings & tail with bronze sheen - Bill & short legs greenish... From C. Rica, except Chile ... Rivers, streams & marshes in **humid forests** of **Misiones**   II

IBISES 97 to 99: *In wetlands - Resemble "bandurrias" but more terrestial - B i l l s also curved - Smaller & blackish - Quiet - (3 species)*

97) BARE-FACED IBIS
(Cuervillo Cara Pelada)
Phimosus infuscatus

40 cm - Groups or small flocks - In shallow waters - Sometimes with 99) - Similar - Stockier - Looks **black**er & more opaque - Green sheen - **In flight rosy legs barely extend beyond tail** - Bare face rosy - **Ivory bill** (rosy in NP) - S. America, except Peru & Chile - URUGUAY - Marshes, flooded savannas & lakes   IV

98) PUNA IBIS
(Cuervillo Puneño)   *Plegadis ridgwayi*

50 cm - Resembles allopatrics 97) & 99)- Larger -Legs shorter than 99) - Tail a little longer - Blackish - Head & neck chestnut - Upperparts with green sheen- **Reddish bill** - Black legs - J: Paler - Head & neck finely striated white... Peru, Bolivia & Chile - **High Andean lakes** in NW   II

99) WHITE-FACED IBIS
(Cuervillo de Cañada)   *Plegadis chihi*

40 cm - **Large flocks** flying in V - In flight legs extend considerably beyond tail - Often follows ploughs - Similar to 97) & 98) - Resembles Limpkin (212) - Smaller - Darker bill - Looks blackish - Slight green & violet sheen - Striated white on neck - **NP: Chestnut** - Crown,wings & tail with green sheen - [White line around bare face] - Bordering countries & Peru - URUGUAY - Wetlands & **rural areas**   V

70

Fam. Threskiornithidae, see page 29

100) ROSEATE SPOONBILL

(Espátula Rosada) *Ajaia ajaja*
55 cm - Flocks - Feeds moving **long flat bill** from side to side while wading in shallow water - Also perches on trees - **Rosy** - Resembles flamingos in color - **Coverts,** rump, spot on breast & undertail coverts **crimson** - Tail ochraceous - J: Whitish ... From N. America - URUGUAY ... Wetlands & nearby areas III

Fam Phoenicopteridae, see page 29

FLAMINGOS: In wetlands - Flocks (mixed in NW) - Rosy - Slight seasonal color variation - In flight indistinguishable from each other -Thick bent bill - JJ: [Apart from adults] - Swim more - Whitish stained with brown - (3 species)

101) CHILEAN FLAMINGO

(Flamenco Austral)
Phoenicopterus chilensis
70 cm - Salmon coloring - **Red coverts** hide black remiges - **Bill rosy white** with tip black - Legs greyish blue - **Knees** & feet **crimson** ... From Ecuador & Brazil - URUGUAY - Fresh or brackish lakes & estuaries IV

102) ANDEAN FLAMINGO

(Parina Grande)
Phoenicoparrus andinus
75 cm - Whiter - Coverts deep rosy - **Violet patch in** upper **breast** (lacking in J) - Standing, **rear third of body black** (inconspicuous in NP) - Black bill with yellowish base & red mark - **Legs yellow** ... Peru, Bolivia & Chile ... High Andean lakes in NW III

103) PUNA FLAMINGO

(Parina Chica) *Phoenicoparrus jamesi*
63 cm - Bill, neck & legs shorter (difficult to identify by size) - **Inconspicuous rosy in coverts** - Rear third of body black, less noticeable than in 102) - Slight rosy striations on breast - **Bill orange yellow** with pointed black tip - **Lores,** periocular & **legs red** ... Peru, Bolivia & Chile ... High Andean lakes in NW II

● *Fam. Anhimidae, see page 29*

104) SOUTHERN SCREAMER
(Chajá)   *Chauna torquata*

85 cm - Terrestrial- Sometimes in flocks; when gliding high look like eagles - Sometimes perch - **Loud bisyllabic scream** - Stocky - **Ashy grey** - Visible **crest on nape - Black & white neck collars** - Periocular & thick legs reddish- **Underwing coverts white & remiges black**, conspicuous in flight- Brazil, Paraguay & Bolivia - URUGUAY... Marshes, flooded savannas & lakes   IV

● *Fam. Anatidae, see page 29*

105) MUSCOVY DUCK
(Pato Real)   *Cairina moschata*

65 cm - Shy & decreasing due to hunting pressure - Perches on trees - Quiet snort - Resembles its domestic descendant - Small crest - **Black** - Green sheen on upperparts - **White spot on wing** conspicuous in flight & when folded - Red caruncle & periocular - ♀ : 53 cm - Without caruncle - J: With slight or no white on wing ... From Mexico, except Chile - URUGUAY ... Marshes, rivers & swamps, often in forests   II

106) COMB DUCK
(Pato Crestudo) *Sarkidiornis melanotos*

60 cm - Shy & decreasing - Perches on trees - Flocks - Fly single file - Unmistakable - **Head & neck white speckled with black - Upperparts black** with strong sheen - **Underparts white - Black caruncle** very conspicuous in NP - ♀ : 48 cm - Without caruncle ... From Panama, except Chile - [URUGUAY] ... Marshes, flooded savannas & rivers   II

107) ORINOCO GOOSE

(Ganso de Monte) *Neochen jubatus*
58 cm - Tame - Flies little - **Erect posture** - .Resembles *Chloephaga* - **Ochraceous** - Back brown & chestnut - Wings & tail black with green sheen - Speculum & undertail coverts white - **Belly chestnut** - Reddish legs ... S. America, except Chile ... Rivers, streams & wooded river islands .in N (upper River Bermejo) II

DENDROCYGNA: Gregarious -Whistle, even in nightflights - Erect posture - Long necks - Long legs extend beyond tail in fligh (3 species)

108) FULVOUS TREE-DUCK

(Sirirí Colorado) *Dendrocygna bicolor*
38 cm - Bisyllabic rapid nasal whistle - **Cinnamon** - Black line on hindneck - Back blackish with undulating cinnamon markings - **White rump - Barred cream on flanks** - Plumbeous legs ... From N. America - URUGUAY ... Wetlands & nearby areas IV

109) BLACK-BELLIED TREE-DUCK

(Sirirí Vientre Negro)
 Dendrocygna autumnalis
38 cm - Whistle of 4 or 5 syllables - **Face & throat ashy grey** - Neck like 108) - Upperparts chestnut - **Wingband white,** more visible in flight - Rump, **belly & lower belly black** - White periocular - Reddish bill - Rosy legs - J: Lack white wingband & black underparts- From N. America, except Chile ... Marshes swamps & flooded areas II

110) WHITE-FACED TREE-DUCK

(Sirirí Pampa) *Dendrocygna viduata*
38 cm - Trisyllabic rapid & sharp whistle- **Throat & front of head white, rear black -** Rufous neck - Wings, rump, & center of belly black - **Flanks finely barred black & white - J: Cinnamon** (instead of white) **on head** - From C. Rica, except Chile - URUGUAY ... Wetlands & rural areas IV

111) COSCOROBA SWAN
(Coscoroba) *Coscoroba coscoroba*

65 cm - Gregarious - Elegant - Looks like a swan - Call: *coscoroba* - **White** - Black on primaries visible in flight - **Red bill** - Rosy legs - J: Marked brown ... Brazil, Paraguay & Chile - URUGUAY ... Wetlands IV

112) BLACK-NECKED SWAN
(Cisne Cuello Negro)
Cygnus melancoryphus

80 cm - Behavior & aspect like 111) - Unmistakable - **Head & long neck black** - Rest white - Red caruncle - J: Head & neck brownish grey - Rest spotted brown ... Paraguay & Brazil - URUGUAY ... Wetlands & seashores - In winter further N V

CHLOEPHAGA (Sheld geese): On migration 114, 116 [& 117] mix in large flocks - Erect-Resemble geese - Short bill -Conspicuous wing pattern in flight: white, with dark primaries, tertiaries & central band (not in ♂ 113) - Black tail (except 113)-(5 species)

113) KELP GOOSE
(Caranca) *Chloephaga hybrida-2R*

52 cm - Whistle like 114) - Not very gregarious - Strong sexual dimorphism- **White** - Black bill - Yellow legs - ● : Resembles ♀ 114) - More contrasting - **White periocular & tail** - Coarsely barred white & black on underparts - **Rosy bill** ... Chile ... **Southern seashores** - In winter further N IV

114) UPLAND GOOSE (Cauquén Común) *Chloephaga picta [3R]*

54 cm - **White, barred black** on back, flanks, [neck & underparts] - Black bill & legs - ♀: Chestnut - [Head ochraceous]- Upperback & breast barred black - Belly barred black & white - Undertail coverts brownish grey - Yellow legs ... Chile - [URUGUAY] ... Migrant C - Water courses in woods, meadows & Patagonian marshes V

74

115) ANDEAN GOOSE
(Guayata)   *Chloephaga melanoptera*

60 cm - Shy - Allopatric with other-*Chloephaga* - Thick neck - **White** - Purple wing band - **Reddish bill & legs**- Peru, Bolivia & Chile ... High Andean lakes - Winter in lower areas - (Pozuelos NP)   III

116) ASHY-HEADED GOOSE
(Cauquén Real)
Chloephaga poliocephala

53 cm - Looks like ♀ 114) - Call: like short bark - Sometimes perched on branches- **Head & neck ashy grey** - Upperback & breast chestnut somewhat barred - Black rump (not white as in 114) - Flanks heavily barred white & black - Rest of underparts white - Undertail coverts cinnamon - Periocular white - Black bill - Orange legs ... Chile ... Migrant C - Wetlands & near Araucano Forest   IV

117) RUDDY-HEADED GOOSE
(Cauquén Colorado)
Chloephaga rubidiceps

50 cm - Looks like ♀ 114) - **Smaller** - More defined **chestnut head & neck**- Upper & underparts more finely barred - Whitish periocular - Undertail coverts chestnut, not barred white - Legs more orange [with some black] ... Chile ... Migrant C - Meadows & open fields in general near water - Seriously decreasing on mainland   I

118) CRESTED DUCK   (Pato
Crestón)*Lophonetta specularioides-2R*

42 cm - Shy - Harsh bark-like call - Pointed tail - Splashed ochraceous brown - Rump & underparts paler - **Wide crown** (except forehead) **& slight crest on nape dark** -Dull plumage; except in flight: purple & **white speculum** - Red iris - ♀ :Tail less pointed ... Peru, Bolivia & Chile ... Andean & Patagonian lakes, rivers & seacoasts   III

75

119) SPECTACLED DUCK
(Pato de Anteojos)　　*Anas specularis*

40 cm - Flies following watercourses in woods - Characteristic bark - Blackish back - Scaled upperback - Conspicuous **white patch in front of eye** & large halfmoon on throat - Purple sheen, black & white speculum - Underparts brownish - Flanks spotted - J: Without white marks ... Chile -Lakes, rivers & streams in Araucano Forest & occasionally on Patagonian plateau　　III

120) SOUTHERN WIGEON
(Pato Overo)　　*Anas sibilatrix*

37 cm - Erratic flight - Often in groups - Long trilling whistle - **Wide white forehead & malar region** - Rest of **head & neck black with green sheen** - Back feathers black with white edges - **Rump & spot on wing white, conspicuous in flight** - Cinnamon flanks - Underparts white - ♀ & J: Paler ... Brazil, Paraguay & Chile - URUGUAY ... The southern population is Migrant C - Wetlands　　IV

121) BROWN PINTAIL
(Pato Maicero)　　*Anas georgica-2R*

39 cm - Very gregarious - Resembles 122) - Nests in open fields - Longer neck - Forehead smaller - **Pointed tail - ochraceous** brown - **Cinnamon crown** - Back, breast & **flanks speckled** - Throat, neck & rest of underside almost whitish - Speculum: black between ochre bands - Bill yellow with black culmen - ♀: Less pointed tail ... S. America, except Venezuela & Guianas - URUGUAY ... Wetlands & nearby areas, & rural areas　　V

122) SPECKLED TEAL
(Pato Barcino)　　*Anas flavirostris-2R*

33 cm - Nests on trees - Bill like 121) - Neck & tail shorter - Higher forehead & slight crest (less conspicuous in ♀) - **Dark head & neck** - Speculum black between cinnamon bands - **Uniform flanks - NW race:** 37 cm - Well defined contrast between dark upperparts & **whitish underparts** ... S...America except Guianas - URUGUAY ... Wetlands　　IV

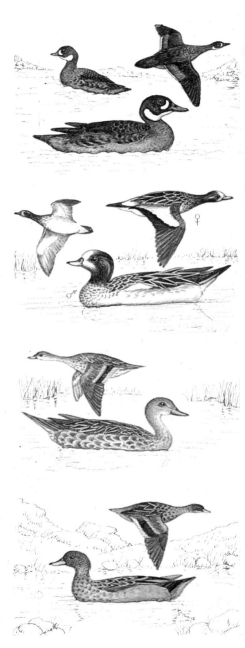

123) RED SHOVELER
(Pato Cuchara)   *Anas platalea*

36 cm - **Cinnamon chestnut - Head & neck pale** - Black dots on back, breast & flanks - **Coverts sky blue with white** band, conspicuous in flight (as in 124 & 125) - Undertail coverts black with white spot - **Bill** (6 cm) **long, high & widened,** which carries almost touching water - **White iris** - ♀: Without chestnut - Dark iris - Bill like ♂ ... Bordering countries & Peru - URUGUAY ... Wetlands   IV

124) BLUE-WINGED TEAL
(Pato Media Luna)   *Anas discors*

30 cm - Brown, speckled & dotted with black - Wing pattern like 123) - **Head & neck dark ashy grey** - Conspicuous **white spot on flanks & halfmoon on face** - ●: Without conspicuous markings- **Pale lores** & slight eyebrow - URUGUAY ... Irregular Migrant A - Wetlands   II

125) CINNAMON TEAL
(Pato Colorado)   *Anas cyanoptera-2R*

36 cm - Looks like 123) including wing pattern - Smaller bill - Much more **rufous - Red iris -** ♀: Similar to ♀♀ 123) & 124) - A little more cinnamon ... From N. America, more common in W - URUGUAY... Wetlands   III

126) WHITE-CHEEKED PINTAIL
(Pato Gargantilla)   *Anas bahamensis*

35 cm - Resembles 121) - Cinnamon - **White face & throat** well defined - Back & underparts dotted black - Green & cinnamon speculum - **Pointed creamy tail - Red base on** plumbeous **bill** ... Caribbean & S. America, mostly along W - URUGUAY ... Wetlands, often brackish   IV

127) PUNA TEAL
(Pato Puneño)   *Anas puna*
38 cm - Very similar to 128) even wing pattern (may be conspecific) - Paler - Big black crown, not brown - Less conspicuous bars & dots on breast & flanks-**Bill bluish,** without yellow ... Peru, Bolivia & Chile ... **High Andean lakes** in NW   II

128) SILVER TEAL
(Pato Capuchino)   *Anas versicolor-2R*
31 cm - Wide crown & nape dark brown - Face & throat ochraceous- Back splashed black-ish- Green & white speculum - **Rear third silvery grey** finely barred black-Underparts with black dots - Flanks barred - **Bluish bill with yellow base-** Bordering countries ... URU-GUAY ... Wetlands [with floating vegetation]   IV

129) TORRENT DUCK
(Pato de Torrente)
             Merganetta armata-2R
30 cm - Swims & dives even up **rapids-** Alights on emergent stones - Flies low, following water courses - Striking - Elegant - Tail broad, long & rigid - **Head & neck white** with black lines - **Back blackish with long white stria-tions- Red bill -** ♀: Plumbeous crown-Blackish back with ashy grey striations - Conspicuous cinnamon **rufous un-derparts** - J: Grey head - Underparts white - Streaked flanks ... From Vene-zuela along the W ... Fast Andean rivers & streams   III

130) BRAZILIAN MERGANSER
(Pato Serrucho)   *Mergus octosetaceus*
42 cm - Shy - Dives - Alights on stones or branches over water - Slender - Looks like a cormorant - **Long crest on nape** - Head & thin neck blackish - Dark brown back - **Large white speculum** more conspicuous in flight - Underparts barred with ochraceous brown - **Long & slender** black bill - Reddish legs ... Brazil & Paraguay ... Streams in humid forests of **Misiones** (River Uruguaí) - Endangered   I

78

_TACHYERES: Flightless (except 133), al-
though sometimes they try - Swim & dive
**Run over water kicking violently &
flapping wings** - Indistinguishable from
each other in the field, but different in bone
structure & size - **Allopatric distribution**
except for 133) - **Robust - Large heads -
Bills high & wide - Scaled - Ashy grey
Underparts & speculums white** - Orange legs - Plumage variations between
sexes, molts (3 per year) & age - Heads &
necks whitish, ashy grey or brown [with
white periocular and postocular lines] (4
species)_

131) FLIGHTLESS STEAMER-DUCK
(Quetro Austral)   *Tachyeres pteneres*

80 cm - NP: ♂ y ♀ orange yellow bill,
unlike sympatric 133) ... Chile -
Seacoasts in S. T. del Fuego   III

132) FALKLAND STEAMER-DUCK
(Quetro Malvinero)
                      Tachyeres brachypterus

80 cm - ξ - Very tame - NP: Orange bill -
♀ : Yellowish bill, unlike sympatric 133)-
Seacoasts in Malvinas   V

133) FLYING STEAMER-DUCK
(Quetro Volador)
                      Tachyeres patachonicus

65 cm - Long wings - Reluctant to **fly** but
can do it well & for **long distances**
NP: Orange yellow bill - ♀ : Greyish bill
unlike ♀ 131) & ♀ 132) - ♀ in RP: Brown
head with fine & interrupted postocular
line, unlike ♀ in RP of 134) ... Chile ...
Only one in far inland **Patagonian
lakes** ... Sympatric with 131) & 132), &
rarely with 134) on seacoasts   III

134) CHUBUT STEAMER-DUCK
(Quetro Cabeza Blanca)
                      Tachyeres leucocephalus

80 cm - ξ - NP: Yellow bill - ♀: Greyish
bill - ♀ in RP: Brown head with full white
postocular band ... Almost only one in
seacoasts of Chubut   III

135) ROSY-BILLED POCHARD
(Pato Picazo) *Netta peposaca*
43 cm - Large flocks - Robust - **Black** with sheen - Conspicuous **white wing band, undertail coverts & underwing** - **Flanks ashy grey** - Rosy bill - Caruncle & iris reddish - ♀: Brown - Back darker - Periocular & throat whitish - Blackish bill ... Brazil, Paraguay & Chile-URUGUAY ... Wetlands   V

136) SOUTHERN POCHARD
(Pato Castaño) *Netta erythrophthalma*

35 cm - Similar to 135) without caruncle- **Dark brown,** purple - Less conspicuous **white wingband** - Underwing dark -**Chestnut flanks** (not ashy grey) - Bluish bill - Red iris - ♂: Brown - Darker on head - **Lores, postocular & sides of throat white** ...   From Venezuela & Brazil through the W [to Chile]... **High Andean lakes** in NW   II

137) BRAZILIAN DUCK
(Pato Cutirí) *Amazonetta brasiliensis*
35 cm - Tame - Whistles - Brown - Black crown & hindneck bands - Rump, wings & tail shiny black - Face & sides of neck pale - Blue speculum - **White triangular patch** on tip of inner remiges **visible in flight** - **Red bill & legs** - ♀: Flies in front of ♂ - **Loral & supraocular spots** & throat **white** - Plumbeous bill... S. America, except Ecuador, Peru & Chile - URUGUAY ... Marshes, flooded savannas & lakes   IV

138) RINGED TEAL
(Pato de Collar) *Callonetta leucophrys*
28 cm - Perches on trees - Striking - **Head & neck whitish** - Black crown & hindneck bands - Rufous scapulars - **Circular white patch on wing conspicuous in flight - Breast rosy with black dots** - Finely barred on flanks - ♀ : Browner - Eyebrow & spots on head & neck white - Flanks slightly barred brown ... Brazil, Paraguay & Bolivia - URUGUAY ... Marshes, flooded savannas & lakes   III

139) BLACK-HEADED DUCK
(Pato Cabeza Negra)
Heteronetta atricapilla

34 cm - Shy - Often hidden - Very aquatic Looks like 141) - Thinner neck - Longer bill - Tail not visible - Brown, not chestnut **Black hood** - Slight white **tip on inner remiges** visible in flight - **Bill** plumbeous **with red basal spot** - ♀: Without hood - Whitish eyebrow & throat - Pale bill... [Bordering countries] ... URUGUAY ... Wetlands   III

OXYURA: Dive often - Do not usually walk Stiff rectrices - Stocky - Necks short & thick - Chestnut - Black hoods - Sky blue bills - ♀: Brown - Dark bills - (3 species)

140) ANDEAN RUDDY DUCK
(Pato Zambullidor Grande)
Oxyura ferruginea

37 cm - Often raises tail - Similar to 141) Bill wide at tip and stronger - [**White chin**] - ●: **Uniform face** [very slight subocular band] - Cinnamon belly somewhat barred black... From Colombia along the W to Chile... Andean & W Patagonian plateau lakes.   II

141) LAKE DUCK
(Pato Zambullidor Chico) *Oxyura vittata*

31 cm - Raises tail like 140) - Bill narrower at tip - ●: Conspicuous **whitish subocular band & throat** ... Brazil, Paraguay & Chile - URUGUAY ... Lakes & marshes   III

142) MASKED DUCK
(Pato Fierro)   *Oxyura dominica*

30 cm - Resembles 141) - Less shy but reclusive - Floats half submerged in vegetation - **Does not usually raise tail** -Flies more, showing **white patch in center of wing - Black crown, face & chin,** no hood - **Back spotted with black** - ●: **Two conspicuous ochraceous bands in blackish face**... From N. America, except Chile - URUGUAY... Marshes, flooded savannas & lakes   III

Fam. Cathartidae, see page 30

143) ANDEAN CONDOR
(Cóndor Andino)   *Vultur gryphus*

95 cm - **WS: 3 m** - Flies at great height with wings horizontal & **primaries open** like fingers - Excellent glider - Black- Head reddish with crest - **Collar & large patch on upperwing white**- ♀: Smaller - Without crest - J: Brown-Without white ... From Venezuela along W ... Andes & high elevations - (Pampa de Achala, Cordoba)   III

AMERICAN VULTURES: Much gliding - Black -White legs - (3 species from page 82)

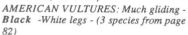

144) TURKEY VULTURE   (Jote
Cabeza Colorada)   *Cathartes aura-3R*

55 cm - **WS: 1.75 m** - Not very gregarious - Flight profile in open V, legs do not extend beyond tail - Silhouette sleeker than 146) - **Head & neck reddish** - (**White nape** in N) - Conspicuous **whitish underside of remiges** -J: Head & legs blackish ... From N. America -URUGUAY ... Various habitats   IV

145) LESSER YELLOW-HEADED VULTURE   (Jote Cabeza
Amarilla)   *Cathartes burrovianus*

51 cm - WS: 1.60 m - Like 144) - **Head yellow,** rosy & greenish - **Underside of remiges** also **whitish** - Slight **pale patch on upperside of primaries** visible in flight ... From Mexico, except Bolivia & Chile - URUGUAY ... Forests & savannas   III

146) BLACK VULTURE
(Jote Cabeza Negra) *Coragyps atratus*

53 cm - **WS: 1.40 m** - Tamer & more gregarious - **Groups** flying or perched on trees - Flaps wings often & strongly - Horizontal flight profile, legs do not extend beyond **short tail** - **Blackish head** - Conspicuous **white patch on primaries** ... From N. America - URUGUAY ... Almost every habitat   V

Memorize the symbols

147) KING VULTURE
(Jote Real)   *Sarcoramphus papa*
76 cm - WS: 1.90 m - Striking color -
Flight profile like 146) or 148) - **White** -
Wide wings with creamy coverts -
Remiges & short tail black - Head
highly colored - Orange neck & caruncle-
Plumbeous collar - White iris - **J: Black-
ish** - Brown iris ... From Mexico, except
Chile ... Forests & savannas in N (El Rey
NP)   III

Fam. Accipitridae, see page 30

148) BLACK-CHESTED
BUZZARD-EAGLE   (Aguila
Mora)   *Geranoaetus melanoleucus-2R*
♂: 60 cm - ♀: 70 - Glides high in **open
areas** - Perches on posts - **Shape in
flight: triangular**, due to long broad
wings & short tail - **Remiges, tail &
breast plumbeous, contrasting
with underwing coverts & belly**
[finely barred] **white** - Coverts silvery
grey - J: Often seen - Longer tail much
barred - Eyebrow & underparts striated
& barred brown, cinnamon ... S. America
mostly along W - URUGUAY ... Various
habitats   IV

149) BLACK-AND-WHITE
HAWK-EAGLE
(Aguila Viuda) *Spizastur melanoleucus*
54 cm - Glides & perches high up -
**White, including long feathered
tarsi** - Periocular, **crest on nape &
back black** -**Tail barred black** -
Underwings white with barred remiges -
Black bill with cere orange - J: Browner ...
From Mexico, mostly along E, except
Chile ... Forests & nearby areas in NE (II)
& NW   III

150) MANTLED HAWK
(Aguilucho Blanco)
               Leucopternis polionota
50 cm - Sharp whistles - Robust -
Rounded wings - **White**, even underwing - Resembles 149) without crest -
Black tail with end half white -
Blackish back - Tip of remiges & **base of
primaries white,** conspicuous in
flight... Brazil & Paraguay ... Humid forests in **Misiones**   II

KITES: Do not hide - Resemble falcons - Narrow pointed wings - Long tails - (4 species from page 84)

151) SWALLOW-TAILED KITE
(Milano Tijereta)
Elanoides forficatus - [2R]
50 cm - Slow gliding over tree tops, often in groups - Looks like an enormous Fork-tailed Flycatcher (677) - **White**, even underwing coverts - Upperback, **wings & long deeply forked tail black** - J: Head & breast striated ... From N. America, except Chile - [URUGUAY] ... Migrant B [One Migrant A race] ... Forests in N   III

152) WHITE-TAILED KITE
(Milano Blanco)   *Elanus leucurus*

35 cm **- Hovers -** Resembles a gull- **White** - Upperparts grey - Ocular patch, **coverts**, primaries, & patch on underwing coverts **black** - J: Flicks tail - Spotted cinnamon brown ... From N. America- URUGUAY ... Savannas, steppes & rural zones - In slow expansion   V

J

153) MISSISSIPPI KITE
(Milano Boreal)
Ictinia mississippiensis

35 cm - Resembles 154) - Flocks - Black **primaries without rufous - inner remiges tip whitish,** visible in flight- Tail black **without bars** - [J]: Underparts striated with chestnut - Tail barred- Migrant A ... Forests & savannas   II

154) PLUMBEOUS KITE
(Milano Plomizo)   *Ictinia plumbea*

35 cm - Perches on higher dead trees - **Grey - Pale head - Rufous primaries** - Underside of **tail** black **with 2 white bars** - Red iris - Legs golden yellow - **J:** Similar to J 153) - **Plumbeous striations on underparts -** Wings (without rufous) & tail whitish on edges - Migrant B in flocks ... From C. America, except Chile ... Forests in N IV

155) GREAT BLACK HAWK
(Aguila Negra) *Buteogallus urubitinga*
♂: 58 cm - ♀: 64 - Call flute-like -Wide rounded wings - **Black - Tail white with wide black band** - Long yellow legs - J: Back mottled with cinnamon - **Long eyebrow & hindneck ochraceous - Dark half-collar** - Underparts striated & barred - Tail barred with black & cinnamon ... From C. America, except Chile - URUGUAY ... Wetlands & wooded habitats   III

156) BAY-WINGED HAWK
(Gavilán Mixto) *Parabuteo unicinctus*
♂: 46 cm - ♀: 54 - Glides high - Often terrestrial - Looks like 157) - More slender - Different flight profile - **Blackish - Coverts,** underwing coverts **& thighs rufous - Long tail with base (like rump) & tip white** - Undertail coverts ochraceous - J: Ochre, striated - Wide eyebrow - Back mottled with cinnamon - **[Chestnut on coverts]** - Undertail barred ... From N. America - URUGUAY... Forests & savannas   III

157) SNAIL KITE
(Caracolero) *Rostrhamus sociabilis*
38 cm - In swamps - Gregarious - Slow flight looking at water or gliding high - Invisible & low sites - Nasal *ke..ke..* - Thin hooked bill - Looks **blackish - Rump & undertail coverts white** - Orange legs - ♀: Dark brown - Underparts, even underwings, speckled - Face ochraceous - J: Like ♀ - **White eyebrow** - Back mottled ... From C. America, except Chile - URUGUAY .... Wetlands   V

158) HOOK-BILLED KITE
(Milano Pico Garfio)
Chondrohierax uncinatus
♂: 39 cm - Tame - Musical whistle - Very hooked bill - **Plumbeous** - Black tail with two pale bands - **Finely barred underparts** white - White iris - **Underside of remiges barred black & white** - (Or black-Tail band & dots on primaries white) - ♀: 43 cm - Brown back - **Nape & ventral bars cinnamon - J:** Tail barred - **Underparts whitish** ... From N. America except Chile ... Forests in N   II

159) GRAY-HEADED KITE
(Milano Cabeza Gris)
Leptodon cayanensis
♂: 50 cm - ♀: 55 - Slow glides - Wings broad & rounded - Legs short - **Grey head** - Black back - **Long barred tail-Underparts white** - Underwing coverts black & remiges reticulated & barred - J: Like 149) without crest - (Or: black head, light striations on underparts & rufous collar) ... From Mexico, except Chile ... Forests in NE   II

160) LONG-WINGED HARRIER
(Gavilán Planeador)   *Circus buffoni*
♂: **50 cm** - Often in marshes - **Glides low, wings slightly** pointing **upwards** & primaries open - Longuish - Upperparts & **tip of remiges black** - Eyebrow & **underparts white** (Or: underparts black, lower belly & thighs rufous) - **White rump** & thin yellow legs as in 161) - ♀: 55 cm - Brown - White nape -Underparts slightly striated ... S. America - URUGUAY ... Wetlands & rural areas   IV

161) CINEREOUS HARRIER
(Gavilán Ceniciento)
Circus cinereus [2R]
♂: **40 cm** - Resembles 160) in aspect & behavior - More terrestrial - Also **white rump - Grey** - Underwings white - **Tip of remiges & tail black-** Inconspicuously **barred cinnamon underparts** - ♀: 48 cm - Resembles ♀ 160) - Grey tail barred blackish - Underparts barred chestnut - J: Underparts striated cinnamon ... S. America except N - URUGUAY ... Same habitats as 160)- More common in Patagonia   III

162) GRAY HAWK
(Aguilucho Gris)   *Buteo nitidus*
36 cm - Soars high - Flicks short tail on alighting - Longer call than 169) - Wings broad with narrow base - **Grey - Underparts with thin white bars** - Black tip on primaries - Broad black & white bars on tail - **J:** Blackish [spotted cinnamon] - Ochraceous eyebrow- **Throat** & malar **stripes** blackish - Underparts speckled ochraceous - Tail slightly barred ... From N. America, except Chile ... Forests in N   II

*ACCIPITER: Shy - Rapid flight between trees - Sometimes soar high - **Short rounded wings** reticulated ventrally - Long tails barred - Long legs - Thighs more feathered than in Micrastur - Backs brown to black - ♀♀ much larger than ♂♂- (4 species)*

163) GRAY-BELLIED HAWK (Esparvero Grande) *Accipiter poliogaster* ♂: **40 cm - ♀: 48** - Looks like 164) without rufous on thighs & like 195) without band on nape - **Black crown - Underparts white** or greyish - J: Looks like a small 185) without crest - (Was considered different species: *A. pectoralis*) ... S. America, except Chile ... Humid forests in **Misiones** II

164) BICOLORED HAWK (Esparvero Variado) *Accipiter bicolor-3R* ♂: 32 cm - ♀: 40 - Less hidden - Plumage variations - Sympatric with 168) in N - **Thighs rufous - Underparts grey barred brown & white** in S, **or belly barred rufous & white** in N - Underwing coverts rufous, cinnamon or white - J: Browner - White nape - Underparts striated or splashed - Thighs ochre spotted with rufous ... From Mexico - URUGUAY ... Yungas, Chaco, Araucano & humid forests III

165) SHARP-SHINNED HAWK (Esparvero Común) *Accipiter striatus* ♂ 23 cm - ♀: 28 - Looks like 164) - Slender- **Underparts finely barred white - Cinnamon thighs** - Golden iris- J: White nape - Throat & underwing coverts ochraceous - Underparts barred & striated cinnamon ... From N. America, except Chile - URUGUAY ... Forests, savannas & plantations - (Cerro Colorado, Cordoba) IV

166) TINY HAWK (Esparvero Chico) *Accipiter superciliosus* ♂: **20 cm - ♀: 26** - Size of a thrush - Short tail - Resembles 165) - Black crown - Thighs barred (not uniform cinnamon) - **Red iris** - Rufous phase: tail & wings rufous barred with black - J: Ventrally barred cinnamon ... From Nicaragua, except Bolivia & Chile ... Humid forests in **Misiones** I

167) PEARL KITE

(Milano Chico) *Gampsonyx swainsonii*
22 cm - Looks like a **small** hawk - Soars high - Perched flicks tail - **Wide forehead, cheeks & thighs cinnamon - Upperparts & half-collar blackish-** White & chestnut bands on nape - **Underparts white -** J: Cinnamon flanks ... Nicaragua & S. America, except Chile ... Forest, savannas & palm groves in N **II**

168) RUFOUS-THIGHED KITE

(Milano de Corbata) *Harpagus diodon*
29 cm - Very similar to Misiones race (grey underparts) of 164) - **Bill** a little blunt **with 2 "teeth"** - Slight & half-hidden white patch on back - **White throat with black central stripe - J:** Also like J 164) - **Rufous thighs - Throat stripe** like adult ... Guianas, Brazil, Bolivia & Paraguay ... Higher trees in humid forests of NW & NE **II**

169) ROADSIDE HAWK

(Taguató Común)
Buteo magnirostris-3R
34 cm - Tame - Flight with much flapping - Rounded wings - Erect, at medium height, near roads - Vociferous - Loud harsh call - **Dark** brown **hood - Rufous patch on** upper **wing conspicuous in flight** - Underparts striated & finely barred inconspicuous - Tail barred - Blackish - **J: Forehead, wide eyebrow & throat ochraceous** - Back mottled with ochre - Ventral striations more conspicuous ... From Mexico, except Chile - URUGUAY ... Forests, humid forests edges, savannas & plantations **V**

170) WHITE-RUMPED HAWK

(Taguató Negro) *Buteo leucorrhous*
33 cm - Flies above tree tops - Waggles tail while perched - Looks like Everglade Kite (157) - **Black - Rump & undertail coverts white - Rufous thighs - Tail with 2 or 3 white bars** - Underwing cream with black primaries - J: Blackish spotted with rufous ... S. America, except Chile ... Forests in N **II**

Reread the Glossary

HAWKS (171 to 177): In open spaces - Much soaring - Diving flight - Hover - Robust - Wide wings & tails - Different color phases (In text ♂♂ & ♀♀ not treated differently) - (7 species)

171) WHITE-TAILED HAWK (Aguilucho Alas Largas)   *Buteo albicaudatus* ♂: 48 cm - ♀: 58 - Resembles 173) - **Perched, wings extend beyond black-banded white tail - Hood,** back **& sides of breast blackish - Rufous shoulders** - White throat & underparts (Or: blackish with dark wings & tail normal) - J: Eyebrow & thighs ochraceous - Belly spotted blackish ... From N. America - URUGUAY ... Forests, savannas, hills & rural areas   III

172) SWAINSON'S HAWK (Aguilucho Langostero) *Buteo swainsoni* ♂: 44 cm - ♀: 52 - **Flocks** with many JJ- Often **terrestrial - Blackish brown** upperparts **& breast** - White throat & underparts - Grey tail more barred than 171), band less conspicuous - **Underwing coverts white & blackish remiges** - (Or: blackish with dark wings & tail normal) - J: Browner - Half-collar - Thick striations on underparts - Migrant A ... URUGUAY ... Savannas, plantations & rural areas - (Villa Maria & San Francisco, Cordoba)   III

173) RED-BACKED HAWK (Aguilucho Común)   *Buteo polyosoma* ♂: 44 cm - ♀: 52 - **Tail like 171**), extends beyond wings when perched - **Grey back - Underparts white** except wings barred - (Or: all plumbeous, or rufous back with flanks & belly barred, or with grey breast & rufous belly, etc.) - **J:** More cinnamon than J 172) - Without half-collar or tail band - **Dark malar** - (Or: blackish, auricular cinnamon) ... From Colombia to Chile - URUGUAY ... Andes, Patagonia & hills   IV

174) PUNA HAWK   (Aguilucho Puneño)   *Buteo poecilochrous* ♂ : 48 cm - ♀: 58 cm - Very similar to 173) (3rd primary shorter than 5th) - Also various plumages - Commonest pattern: rufous back - **Underparts barred rufous & grey** [rufous on breast] ... From Colombia along W to Chile ... Puna in NW   I

89

175) RUFOUS-TAILED HAWK
(Aguilucho Cola Rojiza)*Buteo ventralis*
♂: 45 cm - ♀: 53 - Like J 173) - More rufous - Blackish back mottled - **Upper-tail rufous, barred** - White throat - Underparts ochraceous striated & spotted black - **Rufous thighs** & underwing barred white - Undertail greyish - (Or: all black, with wings & undertail dotted grey) - **J:** Much barred grey tail - Black malar - **Throat & center of breast white** - Rest of underparts striated ... Chile ... Araucano Forest   II

176) WHITE-THROATED HAWK
(Aguilucho Andino)   *Buteo albigula*
♂: 38 cm - ♀: 41 - Similar to 177) - Longer tail with inconspicuous bars - **Underparts white,** except wings barred - **Chestnut striations on flanks** - J: Underparts striated blackish ... From Venezuela along W to Chile ... Araucano Forest [& NW]   II

177) SHORT-TAILED HAWK
(Aguilucho Cola Corta)
    Buteo brachyurus
♂: 36 cm - ♀: 39 - Even smaller than 176)- **Upperparts blackish - Tail short** slightly barred - **Forehead & underparts (except remiges) white** - Flanks lack striations - Thighs lack rufous - (Or: blackish even underwing coverts - Nape & forehead white-Tail & wings normal) - J: Pale mottled back -Tail more barred - [Underparts striated]- Ochraceous thighs ... From N. America, except Chile ... Not far from water in N humid forests   II

178) CRANE HAWK
(Gavilán Patas Largas)
    Geranospiza caerulescens
46 cm - Tame - Jumps among branches- Short flights - Lanky - Pretty **sky blue grey - Long narrow tail** blackish barred with cinnamon & white - Ventral finely barred - **Long orange legs** - In flight, conspicuous **white halfmoon, at base of** black **primaries** ... From Mexico, except Chile - URUGUAY ... Forests & savannas   III

90

179) HARPY EAGLE
(Harpía)   *Harpia harpyja*

♂: **70 cm** - ♀: 90 - The most **powerful** eagle - Very thick legs (claw 7 cm) - Wings broad & rounded - Conspicuous & erectile **divided** black **crest - Ashy grey hood** - Blackish back & breast - Rest of underparts white - Broad tail barred whitish & black - Thighs & underwing barred - **J: Head, neck & breast white** - Back mottled ... From Mexico, except Chile ... Forests in N   I

180) CRESTED EAGLE
(Aguila Monera)   *Morphnus guianensis*

♂: 65 cm - ♀:78 - Resembles 179)- Smaller & more elegant - Legs longer & thinner - **Breast grey**, not blackish - Erectile crest with white, not divided - Blackish back slightly speckled with brown & white - **Long**er **tail** barred - Underparts white [with slight cinnamon or black bars] - **Underwing coverts white** - J: Head & breast white - Coverts pale ... From Honduras, except Chile ... Humid forests in **Misiones**   I

181) BLACK-AND-CHESTNUT EAGLE
(Aguila Poma)   *Oroaetus isidori*

♂: **65 cm** - ♀: 78 - Larger than 185- Long crest, thin & erectile - Feathered legs - Conspicuous coloration - Shorter **tail with** only **apical band black - Black hood,** back & **thighs - Underparts chestnut,** slightly striated black - Underwing coverts chestnut; **base of primaries** & rectrices, **whitish**, all conspicuous in flight - **J:** More **whitish** - Crest dotted with black - Back splashed with brown - Tail barred ... From Venezuela along W, except Chile ... Montane forests in NW   I

Fam. Accipitridae, see page 30

182) CROWNED EAGLE
(Aguila Coronada)
Harpyhaliaetus coronatus
♂: 62 cm - ♀: 72 - Shrill cry - **Not in humid forests** - Tame - **Crest on nape** - **Brownish grey** - Darker back- **Tail black with white band** - J: Head more ochraceous - Breast splashed with brown - Rest of underparts ochraceous striated ... Brazil, Paraguay & Bolivia - [URUGUAY] ... Forests, savannas & steppes with bushes   III

183) SOLITARY EAGLE
(Aguila Solitaria)
Harpyhaliaetus solitarius
♂: 65 cm - ♀: 70 -Soars high - Hovers Small crest - Short thick legs - **Black** - **Tail** shorter than in 155) **with central band white** - ♀: Browner - J: Like J 182)- Crown, ocular band & breast dark brown- Rest of underparts spotted ... From Mexico along W, except Chile... Yungas in **Salta**   II

184) BLACK HAWK-EAGLE
(Águila Crestuda Negra)
Spizaetus tyrannus
♂: 60 cm - ♀: 66 - **Black** - Long angular wings which in flight resembles 160) - **Remiges reticulated on underparts- Long tail barred** with greyish- Resembles a melanic 185) - Crest with white on nape - Lower belly, thighs & feathered tarsi barred & spotted white - J: More like a 185) - Without rufous - White superciliary - Black face - Underparts striated & splashed, not barred ... From Mexico, except Chile ... High strata in humid forests of NE   II

185) ORNATE HAWK-EAGLE
(Águila Crestuda Real)
Spizaetus ornatus
♂: 58 cm - ♀: 63 - Elegant - Striking - Like a large J 163) - **Black** crown, malar & **erectile crest** - Looks like 184) - **Rufous head, neck & pectoral flanks** - White throat - **Underparts barred black & white** - J: **White crest, hood**, feathered tarsi & **underparts** - Thighs barred ... From Mexico except Chile ... Forests in N   II

186) BLACK-COLLARED HAWK
(Aguilucho Pampa)*Busarellus nigricollis*

♂: 46 cm - ♀: 50 - Perches near water-
Mournful long whistle of 2 or 3 different
notes - Resembles 187) - Long & broad
wings - **Rufous - Whitish hood** - Conspicuous **black collar** - Black remiges
conspicuous in flight - Short barred tail
with broad black tip - Whitish legs - J:
Paler - Striated - Ochraceous breast ...
From Mexico, except Chile - [URU-
GUAY]... Marshes, forests & savannas
in N   III

187) SAVANNA HAWK
(Aguilucho Colorado)
                    Heterospizias meridionalis

♂: 46 cm - ♀: 50 - In open - Tame - Flight
low & reluctant - A little terrestrial - Long
whistle - **Cinnamon** - Brownish back -
Rufous coverts - **Black tail with central band & tip white** - Underparts
finely & inconspicuously barred - **Wings**
long, broad & rounded **with black tips**
on all remiges, like 186) - Long yellow
legs - **J:** Resembles J 186) - Conspicuous **white eyebrow** - Dark brown back
with shoulders splashed rufous -
Ochraceous underparts striated &
barred - **Thighs barred** ... From Panama, except Chile - URUGUAY ... Savannas, marshes & nearby areas, & rural
areas   IV

Fam. Pandionidae (.), see page 32

188) OSPREY
(Águila Pescadora)   *Pandion haliaetus*

50 cm - Hawk-like - **Slow flapping at
medium height over water** - Perches
on trees - Hovers - **Dives from height
to fish** with claws - Long angular wings-
Small crest - **White** - Blackish brown
back - **Black ocular band** -
Barred tail-Breast slightly striated -
Underwing: **coverts white, remiges
reticulated, black spot on bend** - J:
Mottled with whitish - Breast more
striated - Migrant A ... Western
Hemisphere- URUGUAY ... Lakes,
dams, rivers & streams   II

(.) Sometimes included as Subfamily Pandioninae in Family Accipitridae   **93**

Fam. Falconidae, see page 30

POLYBORUS: Scavengers - Fairly terrestrial - Often run - Small crests - Wings long & rounded - Long tails - Yellow legs - JJ: Look like large Chimango Caracara (193)- (4 species)

189) MOUNTAIN CARACARA

(Matamico Andino)
Polyborus megalopterus
47 cm - Shy - **Black including breast- Rump, tips of tail** & inner remotes, **underwing coverts & rest of underparts white - Orange face** - J: Brown - Wingbars, base of primaries, wide rump, tip of tail & undertail cinnamon , conspicuous in flight ... Peru, Bolivia & Chile ... Prepuna & High Andean steppes   IV

190) WHITE-THROATED CARACARA

(Matamico Blanco) *Polyborus albogularis*
47 cm - Resembles 189) - Probably allopatric - **All underparts white** (including breast) - **Yellow face** - J: Similar to J 189) - Forehead & auriculars blackish - **Crown - Neck & breast striated ochre** - Rest of underparts dotted Chile ... Araucano Forest & nearby areas - (Lake Belgrano, Santa Cruz)   III

191) STRIATED CARACARA

(Matamico Grande) *Polyborus australis*
55 cm - Very tame - Curious - Hoarse *kaa* - **Black - Neck & breast white finely striated** - Lower belly, **underwing coverts & thighs chestnut** - Orange face - Tip of tail (but not rump) white - White patch on base of primaries, visible in flight - **J:** Similar to J 190)-**Neck & breast speckled with cinnamon**, not ochre - **Chestnut tail** ... Chile ... Meadows, forests & seacoasts in extreme S   II

192) CRESTED CARACARA

(Carancho)   *Polyborus plancus-2R*
55 cm - Guttural *krrok* .. with head thrown backward - Conspicuous **blackish** lower belly & **crown** - Back & breast barred - Ochraceous throat - **Whitish tail with black tip - Large white patch at base of primaries** -In flight neck longer than 193) - Reddish face - J: Browner & more striated, not barred - Grey legs ... From N. America - URUGUAY ... Various habitats   V

193) CHIMANGO CARACARA
(Chimango)   *Milvago chimango-* [3R]
37 cm - **Often along roads scaveng-
ing** - Hoarse call, loud & sharp - Smaller
than 192), paler, lacks crest & in flight
neck looks shorter - **Brown** - Underparts
ochraceous (barred in S) - Whitish tail
with slight barring & blackish band on tip-
Ochraceous patch on wing - Whitish
legs - J: Whitish wing-bars - Feet sky
blue ... Brazil, Paraguay & Chile - URU-
GUAY ... Various habitats   IV

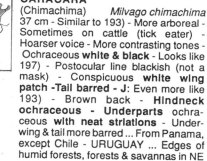

194) YELLOW-HEADED CARACARA
(Chimachima)   *Milvago chimachima*
37 cm - Similar to 193) - More arboreal -
Sometimes on cattle (tick eater) -
Hoarser voice - More contrasting tones -
Ochraceous **white & black** - Looks like
197) - Postocular line blackish (not a
mask) - Conspicuous **white wing
patch -Tail barred** - J: Even more like
193) - Brown back - **Hindneck
ochraceous - Underparts** ochraceous **with neat striations** - Underwing & tail more barred ... From Panama,
except Chile - URUGUAY ... Edges of
humid forests, forests & savannas in NE

195) COLLARED FOREST-FALCON[III]
(Halcón Montés Grande)
Micrastur semitorquatus
53 cm - Behavior & aspect of *Accipiter*
(163) - Reclusive - Heard more than
seen - Passive - Wings short & rounded-
Bill short & thick - Long legs - **Crown,
"sideburns" & back blackish - Band
on nape & all underparts white** (or
blackish or rufous) - **Long black tail
with 3 or 4 spaced white lines** - J:
Brown back somewhat barred with
cinnamon - **Underparts & tail very
barred** ... From Mexico, except Chile ...
Forests in N   II

196) BARRED FOREST-FALCON
(Halcón Montés Chico)
*Micrastur ruficollis-*2R
35 cm - Behavior & aspect of 195) -
Same bill, legs & tail - Back & throat
brown, grey or rufous - Rest of
underparts very barred with black - J:
Brown - Underparts ochraceous barred
irregularly - [Throat & neck white] ...
From Mexico, except Chile ... Medium
strata in forests in N   II

197) LAUGHING FALCON

(Guaicurú) *Herpetotheres cachinnans*
40 cm - Shy - Perches on high dead trees - Passive - Erect - Call: repeated laugh, often in duet - Looks like an owl - Large head - Wings short & round - **Ochraceous white** - Conspicuous **black mask** - Upperparts brown - **Ochraceous patch at base of primaries** conspicuous in flight - Black tail barred - J: Wings mottled with rufous ... From Mexico, except Chile ... Forests & savannas in the Eastern Chaqueño District   II

198) SPOT-WINGED FALCONET

(Halconcito Gris)
Spiziapteryx circumcinctus
♂: 25 cm - ♀: 28 - ⚤ - Tame - In open - Flies reluctantly with much flapping - Nasal clucking while flicks white barred black tail - **Rounded wings,** not pointed like 203) - Back **brownish grey**, striated - **Long eyebrow, malar streak,** throat, lower belly & **rump white**- Wings with white dots - Underparts with neat fine striations ... [Paraguay] ... Savannas & dry forests   III

FALCO: Swift flight, powerful & even acrobatic - Erect - Long pointed wings-Tails rather long - Short legs - Black moustaches - (5 species)

199) PEREGRINE FALCON

(Halcón Peregrino)
Falco peregrinus-2R
♂: 37 cm - ♀: 42 - Hunts on wing with swift dives - **Perches** high **on** trees, rocks or **buildings** - Robust - **Black head** (or only **crown & "sideburns" with white auriculars**) - Plumbeous back - Tail barred with grey & black - Underparts white with breast slightly striated & rest barred - Pale phase (in S): striated ochre hood & upperparts grey barred (*) - J: Brown back, striated in crown - One race Migrant A, another Migrant B to Colombia ... URUGUAY ... Open fields and inhabited areas   III

(*) Formerly considered a species & named *F. kreyenborgi*

200) APLOMADO FALCON
(Halcón Plomizo) *Falco femoralis-2R*
♂: 33 cm - ♀: 38 - In open - Hunts on wing-
Elegant - Folded wings reach middle of
long, black, white-barred **tail** - Plumbeous back - **Headband whitish
ochraceous** - Moustache & auricular
band black - Throat & cheeks whitish -
Breast slightly striated - **Black waistcoat** - Belly & thighs cinnamon - **J:** Back
brown mottled with ochraceous - **Striated breast** - Rest of underparts
ochraceous ... From N. America - URU-
GUAY ... Open & rural areas & planta-
tions   IV

201) ORANGE-BREASTED FALCON
(Halcón Negro Grande)
Falco deiroleucus
♂: **28 cm** - ♀: **34** - In open - Hunts on
wing - Tame - Bisyllabic call like 199) -
Resembles 200) - Darker & more robust-
**Without headband - Folded wings
reach tip of** black medium size **tail,**
barred finely white- Black back - Wide
ochraceous patch on throat turning
**cinnamon toward breast - Black wais-
coat barred with ochre** - Rufous belly &
thighs - J: Belly & thighs barred ... From
Mexico, except Chile ... Forests &
savannas in N   II

202) BAT FALCON
(Halcón Negro Chico) *Falco rufigularis*
♂ : **23 cm** - ♀: **26** - Perches on higher
trees - Hunts on wing - Crepuscular -
Robust - **Like 201)** - Less cinnamon on
breast - **Black waiscoat with fine
white barring** includes breast ... From
Mexico, except Chile ... Forests & sa-
vannas in N   III

203) AMERICAN KESTREL
(Halconcito Colorado) *Falco sparverius*
25 cm - In open, on posts & wires - Tame-
Hovers - Plumbeous crown - **Rufous
back & upper tail** - Moustache,
"sideburns" & nape patch black - Lacks
waistcoat - **Plumbeous coverts** with
black spots - Underparts speckled - ♀:
28 cm - All **upperparts rufous barred
with black** - Underparts striated brown
... From N. America - URUGUAY ...
Open fields, rural areas, forests,
plantations & inhabited areas   V

97

204) BARE-FACED CURASSOW
(Muitú)   *Crax fasciolata*

85 cm - Unmistakable - **Black** - White belly & tip of tail - Base of bill yellow - Conspicuous **curly crest - ♂: Black & white crest - Back, tail & breast barred** - Rest of underparts cinnamon... Brazil, Paraguay & Bolivia ... Forests in NE - (Arroyo Guaycolec, Formosa) - Decreasing   II

205) BLACK-FRONTED PIPING-GUAN
(Yacutinga)   *Pipile jacutinga (.)*

62 cm - Blackish - Striations on breast, **crest & coverts white** - Bluish sheen on wings & tail - Ocular patch sky blue - Red throat pouch ... Brazil & Paraguay... Medium & high strata near water in humid forests in NE - Decreasing   II

206) CHACO CHACHALACA
(Charata)   *Ortalis canicollis*

52 cm - Collective call *cha..cha..la..co,* loud & hoarse - **Brownish** - Head, neck & breast ashy grey - Back slightly olivaceous - Underparts ochraceous - **Undertail coverts & outer rectrices rufous** - Ocular & throat patches reddish ... Brazil, Paraguay & Bolivia ... Forests & savannas of **Chaqueño** type (not humid forests)   IV

98   (.) *P. cumanensis* from NW has been cited in the past & it might still exist in the yungas

Reread characters of genus with each species

PENELOPE: *(.) (Guans) - Noisy especially at twilight - Small crested - Blackish brown-* **Red pouches** *- Long blackish tails - (3 species)*

207) DUSKY-LEGGED GUAN
(Pava de Monte Común)
Penelope obscura-2R

68 cm - Back browner & with less olive sheen than 209) - Conspicuous **white striations on coverts** (even more so in NW where sympatric) - Light striation on crown, neck, back & breast - Underparts brown - Dark ocular patch ... Brazil, Paraguay & Bolivia - URUGUAY ... Forests - (El Rey NP)   III

208) RUSTY-MARGINED GUAN
(Yacupoí)   *Penelope superciliaris*

55 cm - Paler, more uniform, greenish & arboreal than 207) - Lacks dorsal stripes- **Eyebrow & scaled breast whitish -Rufous markings in secondaries** & scapulars - Chestnut rump & belly - Blue ocular zone ... Brazil, Paraguay & Bolivia... Medium & high strata in humid forests of NE (Iguazu NP)
III

209) RED-FACED GUAN
(Pava de Monte Alisera)
Penelope dabbenei

64 cm - Very much like 207) - More olive sheen - **Crown striated with white - Belly chestnut - Reddish ocular patch** ... Bolivia ... Montane forests in NW (Calilegua NP)   II

(.) The citation of *P. montagnii* for the NW appears to be erroneous

Fam. Phasianidae, see page 30

210) SPOT-WINGED WOOD-QUAIL
(Urú)   *Odontophorus capueira*

25 cm - Flocks - Terrestrial - More heard than seen - **Flutelike, loud & repeated** *uru* at dusk - Robust - Thick & short bill - Chestnut crown & small crest - Conspicuous **cinnamon eyebrow** - Reddish periocular patch - Brownish back spotted with black & rufous - White spots on wings - Uniform grey underparts - J: Underparts spotted with white - Reddish bill ... Brazil & Paraguay ... Humid forests in NE   II

211) CALIFORNIA QUAIL
(Codorniz de California)
Lophortyx californica

23 cm - Noisy homogeneous flocks - Walks among vegetation - Low flight - Allopatric with 210) - Plumbeous - **Slender conspicuous black crest** - Neck scaled & flanks striated white - **Black bib** bordered with white - ♀: Brown - Smaller crest - Striated bib - Introduced from N. America ... Chile ... Forests & shrubby steppes   III

Fam. Aramidae, see page 31

212) LIMPKIN
(Carau)   *Aramus guarauna*

4 cm - In marshes - After breeding in loose flocks - Terrestrial, sometimes perches on trees - Loud calls *krau* & others - Low **flight with sudden flaps from horizontal line upwards** - Reminiscent of ibises (97) - More robust Straighter neck - Blackish brown - **Yellowish bill** barely curved - **Hindneck splashed with white** ... From N. America, except Chile - URUGUAY ... Wetlands   IV

100

*ARAMIDES: Not so aquatic - Terrestrial &
on bushes - Prefer running to flying - Strong
duets or in chorus - **Look like chickens**
with long bills - Rapidly flick their short erect
black tails - Olivaceous backs - Rufous
remiges - Irises & legs reddish - Greenish
yellow bills - (3 species)*

213) GIANT WOOD-RAIL
(Ipacaá)   *Aramides ypecaha*

42 cm - The tamest - Comes out into the
open - Striden *uaikaá* - **Hindneck
chestnut** - Throat & breast grey - **Belly
rosy cinnamon** ... Brazil & Paraguay -
URUGUAY ... Marsh vegetation &
nearby areas   IV

214) GRAY-NECKED WOOD-RAIL
(Chiricote)   *Aramides cajanea*

36 cm - Strident *cheeri..cot* - Colors
darker & better defined than 213) - Hides
more - **Grey head & neck - Rufous
breast** (not rosy, grey or plumbeous) -
Rest of underparts black ... From Mexico, except Chile - URUGUAY ... Wetlands in forests   III

215) SLATY-BREASTED
WOOD-RAIL
(Saracura)   *Aramides saracura*

32 cm - Calls distinct from 213) & 214) -
Crown plumbeous - Upperparts cinnamon brown gradually turning oliva-
ceous- **Whitish throat contrasts
with remaining plumbeous underparts** ... Brazil & Paraguay ... Wetlands
& humid forests of NE   III

101

RALLUS: In swamps - Rarely fly or swim-Erect tails - Smaller than Aramides & larger than Laterallus - Loud & varied calls - Heard more than seen - Sometimes walk out of vegetation to dart back rapidly - **Fine, long, somewhat curved, green bills** *(except 218) - Reddish long legs & irises-Lack frontal shields - (4 species)*

216) PLUMBEOUS RAIL
(Gallineta Común)
Rallus sanguinolentus-4R
27 cm - Resembles a small 215) - Sometimes on top of bushes in water - Choirs at dusk - Plumbeous - Olive brown back - **Bill** (6 cm) **with red & sky blue spots** on base - J: Brown - Whitish throat - Bill & legs black ... Bordering countries & Peru - URUGUAY ... Marsh vegetation & nearby areas IV

217) BLACKISH RAIL
(Gallineta Negruzca) *Rallus nigricans*
24 cm - Similar to 216) - Distinctive call like 169) - **Whitish** or grey **throat** - Paler **bill** (5 cm) **lacking red base** ... From Colombia, except Chile ... Marshes & rivers in humid forests of **Misiones** III

218) AUSTRAL RAIL
(Gallineta Chica) *Rallus antarcticus (.)*
20 cm - Little known - **Ochraceous back dotted with black** resembling allopatric 224) - Distinguishable from crakes by long (3 cm) **red bill** [horn color in RP] - Slight ochraceous eyebrow - Chestnut coverts - Underparts plumbeous with conspicuous **black & white barring on flanks** ... Chile ... Patagonian reed beds I

219) SPOTTED RAIL
(Gallineta Overa) *Rallus maculatus*
24 cm - Striking **dappled** pattern - Head & **underparts blackish, striated & barred white** - Back brown striated & spotted with black & white - Pale **bill** (4.5 cm) **with red basal spot** ... From Mexico, except Bolivia & Chile - URUGUAY ... Marsh vegetation III

(.) Sometimes considered race of *R. limicola*

CRAKES: Fly little - Do not swim- Walk or run inside vegetation - In flight resemble minute coots - Heard more than seen - Erect tails - Short bills - (8 species)

220) BLACK CRAKE
(Burrito Cuyano)*Laterallus jamaicensis*

13 cm - Resembles 221) & 227) - **Blackish** - Head & underparts plumbeous - **Nape & hindneck cinnamon-** Brown back speckled - Flanks & undertail coverts barred black & white - J: Lacks cinnamon ... N. & C. America, Peru & Chile ... Brackish grasslands II

221) DOT-WINGED CRAKE
(Burrito Negruzco)
$\qquad$ *Laterallus spilopterus*

14 cm-Little known - Lacks cinnamon neck of 220) - **Blackish** - Back striated brownish - **Coverts with slight white barring** - Flanks & undertail coverts barred black & white ... URUGUAY ... Brackish grasslands & temporary marshes II

222) RUFOUS-SIDED CRAKE
(Burrito Común)
$\qquad$ *Laterallus melanophaius*

16 cm - Upperparts brown - Underparts white - **Sides of neck & breast cinnamon** - Flanks barred black & white - **Undertail coverts cinnamon,** unlike 223) - Legs olivaceous brown (not green) ... S. America, except Chile - URUGUAY ... Marsh vegetation III

223) RED-AND-WHITE CRAKE
(Burrito Colorado)
$\qquad$ *Laterallus leucopyrrhus*

16 cm - Similar to 222) - Sometimes together - In general more reddish - **Rufous head, sides of neck & breast - Undertail coverts white** (black & white in ♀) - **Reddish legs** ... Brazil & Paraguay - URUGUAY ... Marsh vegetation - (Magdalena, B. Aires) II

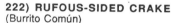
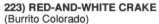

103

224) ASH-THROATED CRAKE
(Burrito Grande)　　*Porzana albicollis*

21 cm - Call *kraooo* in duet - **Upperparts brown spotted black** -Underparts grey -Flanks & undertail coverts barred blackish & white - **Bill greenish** without red ... From Venezuela aiong E & Bolivia ... Marsh vegetation - (Iguazu NP)　　II

225) PAINT-BILLED CRAKE
(Burrito Pico Rojo)　*Neocrex erythrops*

18 cm - Similar to 224) - Olivaceous **brown back** without spots - Flanks & undertail coverts very slightly barred - **Bill with red base** & yellow tip - **Reddish legs** - J: No red on bill ... From Panama, except Chile ... Marsh vegetation in NW　　II

226) YELLOW-BREASTED CRAKE
(Burrito Amarillo)　*Porzana flaviventer*

13 cm - Shrill *peep* - **Yellowish - Eyebrow & underparts white** - Blackish back spotted & striated white & cinnamon - Neck & breast ochraceous Flanks & undertail coverts barred black... From C. America through E - URUGUAY ... Marsh vegetation　　II

227) SPECKLED CRAKE
(Burrito Enano)　　*Coturnicops notata*

11 cm - Even smaller than 220) - Little known - **Blackish** - Back dotted, **breast striated**; flanks & undertail coverts barred white - **White underwing coverts & speculum** conspicuous in flight ... Venezuela, Colombia, Guianas, Brazil & Paraguay - URUGUAY ... Marsh vegetation　　II

FULICA: Great swimmers - Sometimes walk, but never far from water - Poor flyers- Chatter amongst reeds - Gregarious - Resemble ducks - Short bills - Alike - Different frontal shields - **Blackish** - Heads & necks black - Undertail coverts white - JJ: Brown- Underparts spotted white - (6 species)

228) GIANT COOT
(Gallareta Gigante) *Fulica gigantea*

45 cm - Very large - Sympatric with 229) but unmistakable - **Slender** large rosy white **frontal shield dividing crown in two swellings** - Striking **red bill** with base of maxilla & tip white - **Red legs** ... Peru, Bolivia & Chile ... High Andean lakes in NW   II

229) HORNED COOT
(Gallareta Cornuda) *Fulica cornuta*

45 cm - As large as 228) & 229) - Strange **frontal horn-like wattle** (lacking in J)-Strong yellowish **bill with black culmen** - Olivaceous legs ... Bolivia & Chile... High Andean lakes in NW   III

230) AMERICAN COOT
(Gallareta Andina) *Fulica americana*

33 cm - Sometimes with 228) & 229) - Flies frequently - Inconspicuous dark red frontal shield - **Ivory bill, high** & somewhat curved ... From N. America along W ... High Andean lakes in NW (Runtuyoc Lake, Jujuy)   IV

105

231) RED-GARTERED COOT
(Gallareta Ligas Rojas) *Fulica armillata*

35 cm - Often with 232) & 233) - **Red spot between** yellow **bill & frontal shield** - **Red garter** on thighs not always visible ... Brazil, Paraguay & Chile - URUGUAY ... Wetlands   V

232) WHITE-WINGED COOT
(Gallareta Chica)   *Fulica leucoptera*

30 cm - Walks a lot - **Flies more readily** than 231) & 233) showing **white on tip of secondaries** - Rounded **frontal shield yellow** or orange, without red ... Bordering countries - URUGUAY ... Wetlands   V

233) RED-FRONTED COOT
(Gallareta Escudete Rojo)
           Fulica rufifrons

32 cm - Shier & more reclusive than 231) & 232) - **Pointed head** - Straight back - Longer & more erect tail with **conspicuous white undertail coverts** - **Pointed dark red frontal shield** covers part of yellow bill ... Brazil, Paraguay, Perú & Chile - URUGUAY ... Wetlands with rushes   IV

234) COMMON GALLINULE
(Pollona Negra) *Gallinula chloropus-2R*

29 cm - Looks like *Fulica* in aspect & behavior - Similar to 233) - Less gregarious - Rhythmic nodding while swimming, like 237) - Clucking - Straight back, lower in front - **Discontinuous white line on flanks** - **Divided white** conspicuous **undertail coverts** - Garters & **frontal shield red- Bill red** with yellow tip - J: Brown- White throat - [Rosy bill] ... From N. America - URUGUAY ... Wetlands with vegetation   III

235) PURPLE GALLINULE

(Pollona Azul)   *Porphyrula martinica*
28 cm - Walks & flies more than 234)-
Swims little - Striking & brilliant coloring-
Violaceous blue - Back greenish -
White undertail coverts - Sky blue frontal
shield - Bill red with yellow tip - Yellow
legs - J: Resembles 236) - Brownish -
Underparts paler - Sky blue on wings -
Throat & lower belly white ... From N.
America - URUGUAY ... Wetlands with
vegetation   III

236) AZURE GALLINULE

(Pollona Celeste) *Porphyrula flavirostris*
23 cm - Less shy than 235) - Sometimes
together - Difficult to distinguish from J
235) - **Greenish sky blue**, including
face & flanks - Crown & back olivaceous
brown - **Underparts whitish** - Bill &
frontal shield pale green - Yellow legs - J:
Back more striated than J 235) - Darker
rump ... S. America, except Peru &
Chile... Marshes in NE   II

237) SPOT-FLANKED GALLINULE

(Pollona Pintada)
                 Porphyriops melanops-2R
20 cm - Tame - Swims among floating
vegetation with **rhythmical nodding**
of head like small 234) - **Plumbeous** -
Lores & forehead black - Back brown -
White dots on flanks - Short green
bill- J: Brown - White throat ... Bordering
countries, Colombia & Peru -
URUGUAY... Wetlands   IV

Fam. Heliornithidae, see page 31

238) SUNGREBE

(Ipequí)
                          Heliornis fulica
23 cm - Shy - Hidden amongst low
branches hanging over water - Swims,
dives & flies well - Repeated flute-like
whistle - Looks like a grebe - Longish -
**Crown, lateral & dorsal lines on
long neck black** - Brown back - Broad
black tail with white tip - White eyebrow,
neck & lower belly - Red bill ... From C.
America, except Chile ... Streams in
humid forests in NE   II

Fam. Cariamidae, see page 31

239) BLACK-LEGGED SERIEMA
(Chuña Patas Negras)
Chunga burmeisteri

57 cm - Flocks - Prefers running to flying - Also on trees - Shy - Loud calls - Long tail - Greyish - Hen-like **bill & long legs black** - White eyebrow - **Lacks** conspicuous **forehead tuft** of 240) ... Paraguay & Bolivia ... Savannas & Chaqueño type forests   III

240) RED-LEGGED SERIEMA
(Chuña Patas Rojas)   Cariama cristata

70 cm - Aspect & behavior of 239) - Less gregarious - **Long disheveled forehead tuft** - More ochraceous - **Bill & long legs red** ... Brazil, Paraguay & Bolivia - [URUGUAY] ... Savannas & forests, even humid - (El Rey NP)   III

Fam. Jacanidae, see page 31

241) WATTLED JACANA
(Jacana)   Jacana jacana

22 cm - Tame - Walks on floating vege- tation - Acts as sentinel - Unmistakable- Legs & **toes** (13 cm) **very long** - Up- perparts brown - **Yellow remiges** vis- ible in flight or when wings lifted - J: Up- perparts brown - **Eyebrow & under- parts white** ... From Panama, except Chile -URUGUAY ... Wetlands   V

Fam. Rostratulidae, see page 31

242) SOUTH-AMERICAN PAINTED-SNIPE
(Aguatero)   Nycticryphes semicollaris

17 cm - Crepuscular - Hides - Silent - Resembles a Common Snipe (279) but flies in straight line, short distances, low & silently - **Blackish** - Belly, eyebrow, band on crown & **dots on wing white- Ochraceous V on back -** Long green **bill, curved tip** - J: Without dots on wings ... Brazil, Paraguay & Chile - URUGUAY ... Marshes & flooded sa- vannas   III

Fam. Haematopodidae, see page 32

 *HAEMATOPUS: Coastal - Strong whistle - Aspect & behavior vaguely similar to lapwings (248) - **Very long red bills** - Legs pale rose - (3 species)*

243) AMERICAN OYSTERCATCHER (Ostrero Común) *Haematopus palliatus-2R*

35 cm - Resembles 244) - Distinctive wing pattern could aid in flight identification - Black head, neck, breast & tail - **Brown back** - Conspicuous **white zone between breast & folded wing** - Rest of underparts white - **Reddish eyelid** ... From N. America - URUGUAY ... Seacoasts   V

 244) MAGELLANIC OYSTERCATCHER (Ostrero Austral) *Haematopus leucopodus*

35 cm - Barely more robust than 243), often mixed groups - **Back black** (not brown) - **Black of breast extends farther** [without white area separating it from folded wing] - **Yellow eyelid...** Chile ... Southern seacoasts & lakes in steppes of Santa Cruz   III

 245) BLACKISH OYSTERCATCHER (Ostrero Negro) *Haematopus ater*

36 cm - **Black,** a little more brown on back - Eyelid reddish ... Peru & Chile - [URUGUAY] ... Southern seacoasts   IV

246) ANDEAN AVOCET
(Avoceta Andina) *Recurvirostra andina*

39 cm - Nasal call - Behavior of 247) - Shorter bluish legs - **White** even on underwing coverts - **Black wings,** upperback & tail - Conspicuous **bill very much curved upward** ... Peru, Bolivia & Chile ... **High Andean lakes** in NW

III

247) SOUTH AMERICAN STILT
(Tero-Real) *Himantopus melanurus*

34 cm - Flocks - Passive - Insistent *gep..gep*, like small dog - Very elegant - **Upperparts black - White** forehead, crown & **underparts** (including underwing coverts) - **Bill** (6 cm) **long & straight - Very long red legs** - J: Back brown - Crown & face blackish - Rosy legs ... Bordering countries & Peru-URUGUAY ... Shallow water   V

Fam. *Charadriidae*, see page 32

248) SOUTHERN LAPWING
(Tero Común) *Vanellus chilensis (.)*-3R

31 cm - Well known - Aggresive defending nest - Insistent *teu..teu*, harsher in S, like parrot - Back brownish - Green & purple sheen on coverts - Forehead, **slender nape crest & breast black-** Black remiges & tailband conspicuous in flight - Rest white - Reddish eyelid, iris, bill & legs ... From Panama - URUGUAY... Grasslands, rural areas, wetlands & steppes   VI

249) ANDEAN LAPWING
(Tero Serrano)   *Vanellus resplendens*

27 cm - **Paler** & smaller **than 248)** - Hoarser call - **Without crest on nape-Head, neck & breast ochraceous grey -** Violet sheen on coverts - **White wingband** ... From Colombia along the W ... High Andean fields, lakes & grasslands in NW   IV

250) BLACK-BELLIED PLOVER
(Chorlo Artico)   *Pluvialis squatarola*

25 cm - Passive - Shy - Trisyllabic melancholic whistle - More solitary than 251) - Larger bill - Looks greyish **white** - White eyebrow inconspicuous - White wingband & rump, barred tail & **black axillaries, conspicuous in flight** - Underparts white - **NP:** Rarely seen - **Back speckled black & white** - Eyebrow, sides of neck & **lower belly white** - Face & rest of **underparts black** - Also intermediate plumages - Migrant A ... URUGUAY ... Seacoasts (Punta Rasa, B. Aires)   II

251) AMERICAN GOLDEN PLOVER
(Chorlo Pampa)   *Pluvialis dominica*

22 cm - In seashores & **open fields** - More gregarious, **brownish** & tamer than 250) - **White eyebrow** - Without black axillaries - Slight wingband & pectoral striation - Rest of underparts white- **NP:** Rarely seen - **Back speckled** brown & **gold** - White in eyebrow, descending along flanks - Rest of **underparts black** - Also intermediate plumages - Migrant A ... URUGUAY ... Wetlands, rural areas & seacoasts   IV

252) TAWNY-THROATED DOTTEREL
(Chorlo Cabezón)   *Oreopholus ruficollis*

25 cm- In winter loose flocks **in open fields** - Pleasant trill in flight - Passive - Erect - Crown, hindneck & breast ashy grey - Rest of **upperparts cinnamon with broad black striations** - Eyebrow, face & wingband white - **Throat cinnamon - Black spot on belly** - Reddish legs ... From Peru along W - URUGUAY ... Andean & Patagonian steppes - Southern population is Migrant C   III

CHARADRIUS: Gregarious, although less than sandpipers - Tame - Run like marbles rolling & stop suddenly- Do not wade - Small- Short bills- Brownish backs - Foreheads slight wingbands, & underparts, white - Blackish tails with outer rectrices white - (4 species)

253) TWO-BANDED PLOVER

(Chorlito Doble Collar)
Charadrius falklandicus
16 cm - More passive than 255) - Repeated *pit..* in flight - **Two** brownish, **breast bands**, lower one wider [incomplete] - NP: Upper forehead bands, collars, bill & legs black - Hind crown cinnamon ... Chile & Brazil - URUGUAY... Seashores, lakes & marshes   IV

254) SEMIPALMATED PLOVER

(Chorlito Palmado)
Charadrius semipalmatus
14 cm - Behavior of 253) - Repeated *tweet..* - **Very short bill** - Eyebrow & **complete collar white** - Face & one pectoral band brownish - **Salmon legs**- PN: Upper forehead, face & collar black- Postocular white spot - Base of bill orange - Migrant A... [URUGUAY]... Sea & lake shores - (General Lavalle & Punta Rasa, B. Aires)   II

255) COLLARED PLOVER

(Chorlito de Collar) *Charadrius collaris*
13 cm - Fast, very active & noisy - Like 254) - Without collar on nape - Upper forehead, **eyestripe & one breast band black** (even in RP) - Hindcrown & sides of neck cinnamon - Black bill - Rosy legs - J: Brownish crown & breast band ... From Mexico - URUGUAY ... Lake , river & stream shores, marshes & **sandbanks**   III

256) PUNA PLOVER

(Chorlito Puneño)   *Charadrius alticola*
16 cm - Perhaps conspecific with 253) - Same call - Allopatric - In RP looks like Sanderling (267) - **Without breastbands,** or one or two incomplete & diffuse - Bill & legs black - NP: Black upper forehead - Hindcrown cinnamon ... Peru, Bolivia & Chile ... **High Andean lakes**   III

257) RUFOUS-CHESTED DOTTEREL

(Chorlito Pecho Canela) *Zonibyx modestus* 18 cm - Tame - Passive - Short melancholic whistle - **Upperparts & breast uniform brown** - Conspicuous **eyebrow** & rest of underparts **white** - **NP: Cinnamon breast** ending in **black pectoral band** - J: Back scaled with ochre - Without eyebrow ... Chile & Brazil- URUGUAY ... Breeds in Malvinas, Tierra del Fuego & S Santa Cruz - Migrant C ... Peat bogs & pastures, seacoasts & wetlands III

258) MAGELLANIC PLOVER

(Chorlito Ceniciento) *Pluvianellus socialis (.)* 18 cm - **Scratches ground** - Whirls - Looks like a dove - **Upperparts & breast ashy grey** - Wingband & rest of underparts white - **Iris & legs reddish-** J: Back splashed white or gold - Breast striated - Iris & legs orange ... Chile ... Lake shores - (Escarchados, Santa Cruz) III

259) DIADEMED SANDPIPER-PLOVER

(Chorlito de Vincha)*Phegornis mitchellii* 16 cm - Low & melancholic whistle - Striking pattern - Bill thin & long - **Hood blackish chestnut** - **White headband** around hindcrown & nape - **Hindneck rufous** - White collar - Underparts thinly barred brown & white - Yellow legs- J: Hindneck & collar greyish ... Peru, Bolivia & Chile ... High altitude meadows II

260) SURFBIRD

(Playero de Rompiente) *Aphriza virgata (..)* 22 cm - Tame - On tide line - Looks like 257) in RP - Short bill - Upperparts brownish - Breast brownish & rest of underparts white [slightly splashed] - **Wingband & wide rump white** - Wide tip of tail black - Base of mandible & **legs yellow** -[NP: Scaled]... Migrant A along the Pacific... **T. del Fuego** I

(.) It has been considered a separate family (Pluvianellidae)
(..)Sometimes included in Fam. Charadriidae

113

TRINGA: Passive -Wade in shallow water - Nod heads & necks, as if saluting - Whistle in flight - Elegant - Long legs - Lack wing-bands - Breasts slightly striated - Rest of underparts white - Migrants A - (3 species)

261) GREATER YELLOWLEGS
(Pitotoy Grande)   *Tringa melanoleuca*

29 cm - Successive whistles - Rather solitary - Somewhat smaller than Stilt (247) - Back brownish slightly striated - Forehead, eyebrow & **rump white** - **Bill** (5.5 cm) longer & **strong**er than 262) **[slightly curved upwards]** - **Yellow legs** ... URUGUAY ... Wetlands & seacoasts   III

262) LESSER YELLOWLEGS
(Pitotoy Chico)   *Tringa flavipes*

23 cm - Almost like 261), except for size (often seen together) & **bill** (3.5 cm) **thinner & straight**er - One or two whistles... URUGUAY ... Wetlands [& seacoasts]   V

263) SOLITARY SANDPIPER
(Pitotoy Solitario)   *Tringa solitaria-2R*

19 cm - Not gregarious - Soft & frequent *pit..wit* - **Back brown**er & more **uniform** than 262) - **Legs** shorter & **greenish** yellow - Split rump (not white) - **Tail barred** - **White periocular** (not forehead & eyebrow) ... URUGUAY ... Wetlands in forests   III

264) SPOTTED SANDPIPER
(Playerito Manchado) *Actitis macularia*

15 cm - In RP resembles 263) even voice - Typical short low **vibrating flight with wings below body-line** - Glides with arched wings - Continuous **flicking of rear third of body - White wingband** - Yellowish legs - **NP:** White eyebrow - **Underparts with black dots** -Bill rosy ... URUGUAY ... Migrant A- Same habitats as 263) & edges of humid forests   II

265) BUFF-BREASTED SANDPIPER
(Playerito Canela)*Tryngites subruficollis*

17 cm - Tame - Often with Golden Plover(251 or with 252) - Bill somewhat short - **Ochraceous cinnamon** - Back splashed black - **Whitish periocular** - Without conspicuous wingband or rump- Underwing white - **Yellowish legs** - Migrant A ... URUGUAY ... **Pastures, marshes & rural areas** - (Estancia Medaland, Pinamar, B. Aires)   II

266) RUDDY TURNSTONE
(Vuelvepiedras)   *Arenaria interpres (.)*

21 cm - Shy - Passive - Turns over stones, over shells, etc. - Short bill - In flight **unmistakable brown, black & white dorsal pattern** - Two round white spots on dark breast area - Short **red legs - NP: Rufous on back** instead of brown - Migrant A ... URU- GUAY ... Seacoasts   III

267) SANDERLING
(Playerito Blanco)   *Calidris alba*

17 cm - Shy - Runs in front of waves - Often on one leg - Sharp *tweet* - Re- sembles 268) - Seen together - Smaller- More active - **White** - Grey back with black spots, edged white - Conspicuos **white wingband** - Remiges, **central rectrices** & feet **black** - Migrant A ... URUGUAY ... Seacoasts [& lake shores]   III

268) RED KNOT
(Playero Rojizo)   *Calidris canutus*

22 cm - Very gregarious - Passive - Flies reluctantly - Chubbier than 267) - Looks **grey** - Back ashy grey - Incon- spicuous wingband - [**Flanks**] & rump **barred** - Slight striation on breast - Eye- brow & underparts white - **Olivaceous legs** - Black bill somewhat thick - **NP:** Back splashed black - **Underparts cin- namon** - White lower belly - Migrant A ... URUGUAY ...Seacoasts   III

(.) Sometimes included in Fam. Charadriidae

SANDPIPERS 269) to 272): Gregarious - Mixed groups, allowing comparison of details - Tame - Small - Inconspicuous wingbands - Throats, bellys & lower bellys whitish - Migrants A - (4 species)

269) PECTORAL SANDPIPER

(Playerito Pectoral) *Calidris melanotos* **18 cm** - Passive - [Series of] *prrip..* - Hidden **in grass** - Longish neck sometimes extended - **Back splashed black** - Split rump - White eyebrow - **Neat contrast between striated breast & rest of underparts - Bill black with yellow base** - **Yellowish legs** ... URUGUAY ... Wetlands   IV

270) BAIRD'S SANDPIPER

(Playerito Unicolor)   *Calidris bairdii* **15 cm** - Very much like 271) - Tame - Call *kreep* - Bill slightly straighter & more pointed - More **ochraceous brown** - Back striated, not splashed as 269) - **Split rump - Eyebrow not conspicuous - Breast cinnamon slighty striated** & barely contrasted with rest of underparts... URUGUAY ... Wetlands & seacoasts   III

271) WHITE-RUMPED SANDPIPER

(Playerito Rabadilla Blanca) *Calidris fuscicollis* 15 cm - Tame - Very active - Greyer than 270) - White rump - Striated breast, not cinnamon as 270) & less contrasted than in 269) - [Striated flanks] ... URUGUAY ... Wetlands & seacoasts   V

272) SEMIPALMATED SANDPIPER

(Playerito Enano)   *Calidris pusilla (.)* **12 cm** - The smallest - Tame - Very active - Harsh *chek* - Straight bill, somewhat short - Back brownish grey barely striated, prolonged in **half collar** - Split rump - Conspicuous **forehead & eyebrow white** - **Underparts uniform white** - Legs blackish - Semipalmated footprint... URUGUAY ... Seacoasts [& lake shores]   II

116   (.) *C. minutilla* has recently been observed in Uruguay

273) WHIMBREL
(Playero Trinador)
               Numenius phaeopus (.)

36 cm - Shy - Passive - When disturbed prefers to walk away - Turns head to feed- Sometimes retracts neck - Series of 6 or 7 rapid *teeh*. - Head with blackish & white bands - Striated on back & breast- Rest of underparts whitish - Tail slightly barred- **Bill** (9 cm) **very long & curved** - Migrant A ... [URUGUAY] ... Seacoasts - (Punta Rasa, B. Aires)   II

274) HUDSONIAN GODWIT
(Becasa de Mar)   *Limosa haemastica*
33 cm - Passive - Groups - Wades in fairly deep water - In flight *twitwit* - Brownish grey - Eyebrow, underparts from breast, **wingband & rump white- Tail & underwing coverts black - Long bill** (8 cm) **curved upwards - NP:** Blackish back striated & splashed - **Underparts rufous** with black undulating pattern ... URUGUAY ... Migrant A - Seacoasts & wetlands - (Punta Rasa, B. Aires)   IV

275) WILLLET
(Playero Ala Blanca)
          Catoptrophorus semipalmatus
33 cm - Passive - Loud *keep.*. - Perches on posts - Robust - Resembles 274) - **Bill** (6.5 cm) **straight & thicker** - Lores, **rump & undertail white - Remiges black with white band** very conspicuous in flight - Bluish legs - [NP: Striated]- Migrant A along Pacific to **Tierra del Fuego**   I

276) UPLAND SANDPIPER
(Batitú)   *Bartramia longicauda*
25 cm -Loose groups in **pastures** - Shy- Melodious **trisyllabic whistle** even at night - Glides with arched wings - Perches on posts - Long neck - **Bill rather short** - Cinnamon - Striated - **White long tail & underwing barred** - Yellowish legs ... URUGUAY ... Migrant A - Pastures, marshes & rural areas - (Villa Maria, Cordoba)   III

(.) *N. borealis*, smaller & almost extinct, was also Migrant A   **117**

277) LONG-BILLED DOWITCHER
(Becasina Boreal)
Limnodromus scolopaceus (•)

24 cm - Tame - Dips swiftly & constantly **long & straight bill** (6.5 cm) in mud - Weak *peep* - Neck & legs longer than in 279) - Striated brownish grey - Back splashed black - Long white eyebrow - **Tail finely barred** - Slight wingband, **lower back & rump white** - Legs greenish yellow - Migrant A... Seacoasts in **B. Aires**   II

GALLINAGO: Passive - Mimetic - Sudden high display flight, diving with loud buzz - Short necks & legs (look crouching) - Small foreheads - Bills very long & straight - Big eyes placed high - Heads with black & ochraceous bands - (3 species) (..)

278) CORDILLERAN SNIPE
(Becasina Grande)
Gallinago stricklandii
28 cm - More chestnut than 279) - Tail barred black & chestnut - **Underparts ochraceous** with conspicuous **striations** on breast **& bars** in flanks - Bill 8.5 cm ... From Venezuela along the W ... Andean steppes with vegetation   II

279) COMMON SNIPE
(Becasina Común)
Gallinago gallinago -2R
23 cm - Sometimes on posts - **Dorsal V whitish** or ochraceous - Black tail with cinnamon band - Striated breast - Barred flanks - Rest of underparts white - Bill 7 cm - **Olivaceous yellow legs** - J: Shorter bill - Bluish legs ... From N. America - URUGUAY ... Wetlands   IV

280) PUNA SNIPE
(Becasina Andina)   *Gallinago andina*
20 cm - Very similar to 279) - Perhaps conspecific - Different call - Axillars finely barred black - Bill 6 cm - **Yellow legs ...** Peru, Bolivia & Chile ... Lakes & meadows in NW mountains - Winters at lower heights   II

PN

---

118   (.) *L. griseus*, very similar, might also appear on Buenos Aires' coasts
(..) *G. undulata* has been cited many times for Argentina

Fam. Scolopacidae, see page 32

281) STILT SANDPIPER
(Playero Zancudo)
Micropalama himantopus
18 cm - Passive - Often in shallow water- Low *keep* - Looks like 262) - Does not nod - Shorter neck - **Bill long but slightly curved - Back** more **ashy grey & uniform** - Underparts, conspicuous **eyebrow & rump white** - Breast striated - **Long yellowish legs**- NP: Rufous in face - Underparts barred- Migrant A ... URUGUAY ... Wetlands III

Fam. Phalaropodidae, see page 32

PHALAROPES: Gregarious - Often whirl while swimming - Straight bills - Eyebrows & underparts white - Q: More colored in NP - (3 species)

282) WILSON'S PHALAROPE
(Falaropo Común) *Steganopus tricolor*
18 cm - Flocks in synchronized flight - Wades in shallow water - Elegant -**Bill long & thin** - Appears **white** - **Back pale grey** - No wingband - Wide white rump -**Yellow legs - NP: Rufous in neck & in** plumbeous **back - Black in ocular band descending along neck** - Intermediate plumages ... URUGUAY ... Migrant A - Wetlands IV

283) RED PHALAROPE (Falaropo Pico Grueso) *Phalaropus fulicarius*
16 cm - **Pelagic** - Looks like 282) - **Bill slightly short & thick** - Resembles 284) - Grey back slightly striated - Black ocular patch - **White wingband** - Rump split - **NP**: Unmistakable - Back without rufous ... **White face - Underparts rufous** ... Migrant A - Captured in B. Aires & Neuquen I

284) NORTHERN PHALAROPE
(Falaropo Pico Fino) *Lobipes lobatus*
14 cm - **Pelagic - Bill slightly thinner & more curved** than in 283) - **Back plumbeous with white lines** - Ocular patch more conspicuous - **NP: Plumbeous head** with small white supraocular spot - **Rufous band** from nape to breast - **White throat** ... Migrant A - Captured in Chaco, Corrientes & Patagonia I

● *Fam. Thinocoridae, see page 33*

SEEDSNIPES: Gregarious - Terrestrial - Seem to lay flat on ground - Mimetic - Passive - Look slightly like pigeons - On flight resemble plovers - Strong bill s- Short yellow legs - Back quail-like - (4 species)

285) LEAST SEEDSNIPE
(Agachona Chica)
Thinocorus rumicivorus-2R
18 cm - Size of Picui Ground-Dove (323)- **White throat bordered by black line,** linked with **transversal band** by **tie through** the center of grey **breast**-Rest white - **White wingband** contrasting with black underwing coverts - ♀: Lacks black lines - Breast quail-like, not grey ... Ecuador, Peru, Bolivia & Chile-URUGUAY ... Steppes, meadows & lakes in NW & Patagonia (S Santa Cruz)... Southern population is Migrant
C   V

286) GRAY-BREASTED SEEDSNIPE (Agachona de Collar) *Thinocorus orbignyianus-2R* 20 cm - Low & flutelike *pókoi..*, even at night - Size of Eared Dove (322) - **White throat bordered by black line & grey breast** separated from rest of underparts by **black band - Without tie** - Underwing white patch less conspicuous - Bill yellowish with black culmen - ♀: Like ♀ 285) - Larger ... Peru, Bolivia & Chile ... Steppes & meadows in High Andes & Patagonia - In winter reaches high elevations in central provinces   IV

287) WHITE-BELLIED SEEDSNIPE (Agachona Patagónica) *Attagis malouinus* **25 cm** - Resembles ♀ 286) - Larger - Throat & breast scaled - Rest of **underparts white - White wingband** as in 285) - **Blackish bill** ... Chile ... High Andean & Patagonian steppes   II

288) RUFOUS-BELLIED SEEDSNIPE
(Agachona Grande) *Attagis gayi-2R* 28 cm - Back more cinnamon grey & less quail-like than 287) - Breast less contrasting with rest of **cinnamon underparts** - Underwing whitish with cinnamon coverts ... Ecuador, Peru, Bolivia & Chile ... Puna, & High Andean & Patagonian steppes   II

Fam. Chionididae, see page 33

289) SNOWY SHEATHBILL
(Paloma-Antártica)   *Chionis alba*

35 cm - Groups - Very tame & even audacious - **Coastal** - Frequently in mammal colonies - Passive - Walks slowly - Trots instead of running -Flies reluctantly with much flapping - **Resembles a robust white pigeon** - **Thick** yellowish rosy **bill with black tip** ... Chile & Brazil - URUGUAY ... Breeds in Antarctica & South Atlantic Islands - In winter further N   IV

Fam. Stercorariidae, see page 33

SKUAS & JAEGERS: Oceanic - Pursue birds in acrobatic flight - When on land often keep wings raised - Look like dark gulls with bills more hooked - White patches at base of primaries conspicuous in flight - (292 & 293 have dark phases) - (5 species)

290) GREAT SKUA
(Escúa Común)   *Catharacta skua-4R*

55 cm - Audacious - Robust - **Dark brown** - [Underparts chestnut] ... Peru, Chile & Brazil - URUGUAY ... In continental shelf & coasts - Breeds in Antarctica, South Atlantic Islands & Patagonia-In Winter further N   IV

291) SOUTH POLAR SKUA
(Escúa Polar)
                    Catharacta maccormicki (.)

52 cm - **Similar to 290)** - **Paler** - Hood & underparts ochraceous brown to whitish - Hindneck ochraceous - Seacoasts... Breeds in Antarctica & Shetlands   III

(.) Sometimes considered race of 290)   **121**

292) POMARINE JAEGER
(Salteador Grande)
Stercorarius pomarinus
48 cm - **Pelagic** - Larger & more robust than 293) & 294) - Wings wider - **Protruding central rectrices** (7 cm) blunt & **twisted** - Wide blackish crown - White band on nape - **Sides of neck ochraceous** - Pectoral band & flanks with brown undulating pattern - Rest of underparts white (or brown) - White on primaries less conspicuous than in 290)- J: Central rectrices short - Underparts barred ... Brazil - URUGUAY ... Irregular Migrant A   I

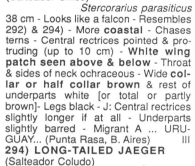

293) PARASITIC JAEGER
(Salteador Chico)
Stercorarius parasiticus
38 cm - Looks like a falcon - Resembles 292) & 294) - More **coastal** - Chases terns - Central rectrices pointed & protruding (up to 10 cm) - **White wing patch seen above & below** - Throat & sides of neck ochraceous - Wide **collar or half collar brown** & rest of underparts white [or total or partly brown]- Legs black - J: Central rectrices slightly longer if at all - Underparts slightly barred - Migrant A ... URUGUAY... (Punta Rasa, B. Aires)   III

294) LONG-TAILED JAEGER
(Salteador Coludo)
Stercorarius longicaudus
34 cm - Difficult to distinguish from 293)- More pelagic, slender & greyish - Chases less - **Protruding central rectrices** (up to 25 cm) - **Inconspicuous white on upperwings** - Without dark phase or collar - Plumbeous legs - J: Conspicuous white on wing - Less barred than J 293) - [With collar] - Migrant A ... URUGUAY   II

Fam. Laridae, see page 33

295) DOLPHIN GULL
(Gaviota Gris)*Leucophaeus scoresbii (.)*
38 cm - Coastal - Tame - Audacious - Sharp *keek* in flight - **Grey** - Plumbeous hood - Wings & mantle blackish - Tail & tip of remiges white - Thick **bill & legs red**- Iris ivory - NP: Without dark hood - J: Head & back brown - White tail with broad black subterminal band - Underparts whitish - Bill rosy with dark tip - Brownish legs ... Chile ... Seacoasts (Seabird colonies)   IV

(.) *L. modestus*, of the Pacific, has been cited for Argentina

Memorize the symbols

296) KELP GULL
(Gaviota Cocinera)
Larus dominicanus-2R

55 cm - Audacious - Follows ships - Often in ports & garbage dumps - White including tail - **Wings & mantle black** - Rectrices with white tip - **Yellow bill with red spot** - Olivaceous legs - J: Often seen - Several brownish plumages - Bill, legs & tailband blackish ... From Ecuador & Brazil - URUGUAY ... Seacoasts & lake shores - Also Antarctica & South Atlantic Islands   VI

297) BAND-TAILED GULL
(Gaviota Cangrejera)   *Larus belcheri (.)*

48 cm - Tame - Looks like 295) - **Hood blackish brown** - **Dorsal collar white** - White tip only on inner remiges - Plumbeous back - **Black tailband** - **Bill yellow with black & red tip** - Yellow legs - NP: Resembles 296) in white head & yellow legs - Bill & tail as in RP - J: Ochraceous brown - More conspicuous pattern tahn in J 296) - Dorsal collar pale - **Bill ivory with black tip** ... Brazil - URUGUAY ... Breeds in S B. Aires province - Seacoasts   III

298) ANDEAN GULL
(Gaviota Andina)   *Larus serranus*

41 cm - Allopatric with 299) & 300) - **Wings & mantle paler** grey - Primaries black with subterminal white patch - Slight brown spots on head - Bill & legs dark red - **NP: Blackish hood** ... Ecuador, Peru, Bolivia & Chile ... **High Andean lakes**   III

299) GRAY-HOODED GULL
(Gaviota Capucho Gris)
Larus cirrocephalus

38 cm - Follows ploughs - Larger than Brown-hooded Gull (300) - Wings & **mantle dark**er - Black & white pattern on primaries more conspicuous - Nape area grey - **Ivory iris** - NP: **Grey hood**... From Ecuador & Brazil, except Chile - [URUGUAY] ... Wetlands   IV

(.) The Argentine form *atlanticus* is usually considered a species apart.

300) BROWN-HOODED GULL
(Gaviota Capucho Café)
Larus maculipennis
35 cm - Resembles Gray-hooded Gull (299) - Also follows ploughs - White head with **brown auricular spot - Back** paler **grey** - Larger & less contrasted white patch on blackish primaries - Brown iris - **NP: Dark brown hood** - White periocular - J: Upperparts splashed brown & cinnamon - Tailband blackish ... Brazil & Chile - URUGUAY ... Wetlands & seacoasts   V

301) FRANKLIN'S GULL
(Gaviota Chica)   *Larus pipixcan*
33 cm - Smaller than 300) - **Back** darker & **plumbeous** - **Head blackish with wide forehead & hindneck white** - Primaries black with white base - White tip on all remiges - Bill & legs black - NP: Black hood - Bill & legs reddish ... Migrant A to Chile - Lakes, rivers & seacoasts II

302) GULL-BILLED TERN
(Gaviotín Pico Grueso)
Gelochelidon nilotica
32 cm - Looks like *Larus* - Resembles 303) - Does not dive - Skims & hunts insects in flight - **Tail slightly forked** - Grey nape striated - **Black ocular band - Short & robust black bill - Legs blackish** red - **NP: Black crown** ... From N. America, except Paraguay, Bolivia & Chile - URUGUAY ... Dunes, coastal beaches, lakes & rivers
III

303) SNOWY-CROWNED TERN
(Gaviotín Lagunero)   *Sterna trudeaui*
30 cm - Dives much - Noisy - More elegant than 302) - **Deeply forked tail - White head** - Conspicuous **black ocular band** - Thin & long black bill with yellow tip - Reddish legs - **NP: Underparts grey - Bill orange with black band** ... Brazil & Chile - URUGUAY ... Lakes, rivers & seacoasts   IV

(.) Sometimes included in Fam. Laridae

TERNS 304) to 307):Flocks of mixed species -Very alike - Backs grey - Underparts white - NP: Black crowns - Bills & legs red, in some individuals not changing to black in RP - (4 species)

PN

304) COMMON TERN
(Gaviotín Golondrina) *Sterna hirundo*

30 cm - Dives little - Medium bill - **Black band on shoulders** - More black on primaries than 306) - Deeply forked **tail** greyish **with outer webs blackish**, does not extend past folded wings - [NP: Underparts grey - Bill red with black tip]"... URUGUAY ... Migrant A - Seacoasts [& lakes] - (Punta Rasa, B. Aires)   III

305) SOUTH AMERICAN TERN
(Gaviotín Sudamericano)
                    Sterna hirundinacea

38 cm - **Long**est **bill** - Back paler than other terns - **Without blackish shoulders** - Long deeply forked white tail, in adults extended past folded wings - **NP: White patch between wide black crown & grey underparts** ... Brazil, Peru & Chile ... URUGUAY ... Coasts of Patagonia & Malvinas - In Winter further N   V

306) ARCTIC TERN
(Gaviotín Artico) *Sterna paradisaea*

33 cm - **Pelagic** - In RP when 305) & 307) in NP - **Bill & legs shorter than in 304) & 305)** - Pale grey even under-. parts - Tail somewhat longer than in 307) scarcely extending past folded wings ... URUGUAY ... Migrant A to Antarctica   I

307) ANTARCTIC TERN
(Gaviotín Antártico) *Sterna vittata-2R*

34 cm - In RP indistinguishable from 306) - **Dark**er **grey** - Bill also short, except in Orkneys - Rump & tail white - **NP: Plumbeous** - White patch between crown & underparts more conspicuous than in 305) ... URUGUAY ... Breeds in Antarctica & South Atlantic Islands - In Winter to Brazil - Seacoasts   III

Reread characters of group with each species

TERNS 308) to 310): Little gregarious - Inland waters - Tails barely forked - (3 species)

308) LARGE-BILLED TERN
(Atí)   *Phaetusa simplex*

36 cm - Dives to fish & hunts insects in flight - Black crown with **white lores** in NP or whitish forehead in RP - Upperparts ashy grey - **Tricolor wing**: primaries black, upper coverts ashy grey & rest white - **Robust yellow bill** - Yellowish legs ... From Panama, except Chile - URUGUAY ... Rivers, lakes & marshes
III

309) YELLOW-BILLED TERN
(Gaviotín Chico Común)
                    Sterna superciliaris (.)

22 cm - Much **smaller** than 308) - Sometimes together - Crown spotted with white - **Primaries**, periocular patch & nape **black** - **Long yellow bill** - Yellowish legs - **NP: Forehead & half eyebrow white** ... S. America, except Chile - URUGUAY ... Rivers, lakes & marshes
III

310) BLACK TERN
(Gaviotín Negro)   *Chlidonias niger*

23 cm - Low flight over water like plovers- Does not dive - Shorter black bill & plumage **dark**er than 309) - Wide forehead, **hindneck** and all underparts **white** - Nape & ocular patch, **back** & inconspicuous half collar **plumbeous** - [**NP**: Head & underparts **black**] ... URUGUAY... Migrant A - Lakes & estuaries
II

126 (.) *S. albifrons*, with black tipped smaller bill & less black on primaries, has been cited for seaco& observed lately in Costanera Sur, Buenos Aires.

311) CAYENNE TERN
(Gaviotín Pico Amarillo) (.)
Sterna eurygnatha
40 cm - Looks like 308) - Different habitat - Tail deeply forked - Wings uniform grey - Forehead & crown white - **Crest on nape,** outer primaries & legs black - **Thin, long, slightly curved yellow bill - NP: Forehead, crown & crest black** - J: Shorter black bill - Back splashed with brown ... From Venezuela, except Chile - URUGUAY ... Coasts of Patagonia - In Winter further N   III

312) SANDWICH TERN
(Gaviotín Pico Negro)
Sterna sandvicensis
38 cm - Very similar to 311) - Perhaps conspecific - **Black bill only with yellow tip** ... [URUGUAY] ... Migrant A - Seacoasts   II

313) ROYAL TERN
(Gaviotín Real)   *Sterna maxima*
44 cm - Noisy - Loud *írree* - Size of gull - Dives often - Somewhat slow flight, often carrying fish in **robust & long vermilion bill** - Resembles a 311) - Similar **crest on nape** - NP: Black hood - Sometimes forehead white or spotted - J: Splashed - Shorter yellowish bill ... Brazil- URUGUAY ... Breeds in Chubut - Seacoasts   III

Fam. Rynchopidae (.), see page 33

314) BLACK SKIMMER
(Rayador)   *Rynchops nigra-3R*
40 cm - Enormous flocks taking short flights - Rests with bill under shoulder - **Slow & short flapping over water, skimming with mandible** - Looks like a tern - Upperparts black - Underparts white - Long wings with tip of inner remiges white - Strange, **long red & black bill - Short red legs** - J: Back edged with white ... Brazil & Paraguay - URUGUAY ... One race Migrant A with dark underwing coverts - Rivers, lakes & seacoasts - (Punta Rasa, B. Aires)   III

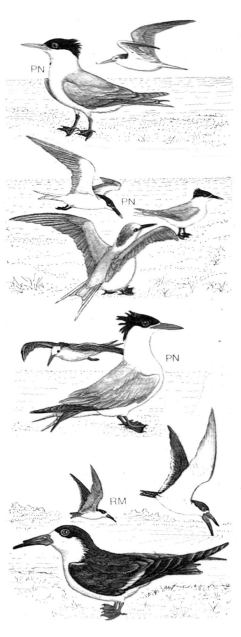

(.) Sometimes included in Fam. Laridae

COLUMBA: Gregarious - Large - Long & pointed wings - (7 species)

315) CHILEAN PIGEON
(Paloma Araucana) *Columba araucana*

34 cm - Resembles 316) - Allopatric - **Violaceous chestnut - White band on nape** - Bronzed hindneck scaled - Tail with black band & pale tip - Black bill- Reddish legs - J: Lacks marks on neck & nape ... Chile ... **Araucano Forest** - (Isla Victoria, Nahuel Huapi NP) II

316) BAND-TAILED PIGEON
(Paloma Nuca Blanca)*Columba fasciata*

34 cm - Perches high on trees - Repeated *kru..ou* - Violaceous grey - **White band on nape** - Bronze green hindneck scaled - Tail like 315) - **Bill & legs golden yellow** ... From N. America along the W, except Chile ... Montane forests in NW II

317) PALE-VENTED PIGEON
(Paloma Colorada)
                    Columba cayennensis

30 cm - Shy - Perches & flies high - Call *ko..ko..ko..oú* more rapidly than Picazuro Pigeon (319) - Plumbeous - **Forehead, coverts, upper back & breast violaceous chestnut** - Throat, tip of tail & lower belly whitish - ♀: More opaque ... From C. America, except Chile - URUGUAY ... Often not far from water in forests of NW & NE III

318) SCALED PIGEON
(Paloma Trocal)   *Columba speciosa*

29 cm - High flight - Call with 5 phrases *kau..koko..koko..koko..kokoú* - Striking - Head & back rufous - **All neck scaled violaceous black**, white & cinnamon - Rest of underparts scaled vinous - Undertail coverts white - Tail blackish - **Bill, periocular & legs red** - ♀ : Back dark brown... From Mexico, except Chile ... Savannas & forests I

319) PICAZURO PIGEON
(Paloma Picazuró)   *Columba picazuro*

34 cm - Somewhat shy - Call *ko..ko..koúu* - Silhouette with longer neck than 320) - Head & breast vinous - **Tight metallic sky blue margins on hindneck - White halfmoon on coverts** more conspicuous in flight - Rest plumbeous - Chestnut iris ... Brazil, Paraguay & Bolivia - URUGUAY ... Various habitats, rural & inhabited areas - Expanding   V

320) SPOT-WINGED PIGEON
(Paloma Manchada)
                Columba maculosa-2R

32 cm - Sometimes with 319) - Tamer & more plumbeous - Call similar but hoarser - Neck without margins - Conspicuous **wing with many white dots** - Grey iris ... Brazil, Paraguay, Bolivia & Peru - URUGUAY ... Forests, wooded steppes, rural & inhabited areas   V

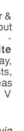

321) ROCK DOVE
(Paloma Doméstica)   *Columba livia*

32 cm - Very well known - Domesticated- **In squares & parks of large cities** - Bluish grey - Green & violet sheen on neck -**Two black bands on folded wing** - Great variety of races & colors - Introduced from Eurasia ... From N. America - URUGUAY ... Inhabited & rural areas - Sometimes gone feral in cliffs   VI

322 EARED DOVE
(Torcaza)   *Zenaida auriculata-2R*

22 cm - Flocks, sometimes enormous - Call *kou..koúkoú..kou* - Rosy - Gold sheen on sides of neck - **Black spots on wings** & face - **Tail** plumbeous **with** black subapical band & **white outertip**... From Antilles - URUGUAY ... Various habitats, rural & inhabited areas   VI

129

323) PICUI GROUND-DOVE
(Torcacita Común)   *Columbina picui (.)*

15 cm - Tame - Semiterrestrial - Near houses - Repeated *koú.*. - Head & neck ashy grey - Coverts with black lines - **Longitudinal white wingband** contrasting with **black remiges** - **Tail** longish **white with central rectrices black** - Underparts whitish rosy - ♀ : More brownish ... Bordering countries - URUGUAY ... Forests, rural & **inhabited areas**   V

324) RUDDY GROUND-DOVE
(Torcacita Colorada) *Columbina talpacoti*

15 cm - Darker & shier than 323) - Not so terrestrial - Monotonous series of *ko..ohó* - **Chestnut**, more rufous on upperparts - **Head ashy grey** - **Black dots on coverts** - **Underwing coverts & outer rectrices black** - ♀ : Rather different ... Brown, almost without chestnut or ashy grey ... From C. America - URUGUAY ... Capueras, forests & savannas   III

325) SCALED DOVE
(Torcacita Escamada)
              Scardafella squammata

18 cm - Tame - Rather terrestrial - Continual & flutelike *kou..kahou* - Unmistakable - **All scaled** with black - **Long black tail with outer rectrices white-** White wingband - Rufous patch on remiges visible in flight ... S. America, except Ecuador, Peru & Chile ...: Capueras in **Misiones**   II

(.) *C. minuta* has been cited for Misiones.

Reread characters of genus with each species

 METRIOPELIA: Terrestrial - Mimetic - Groups - Tame - Sudden flight, low & very noisy showing black remiges & tails - Periocular orange except 327) - Ashy grey - Andean - (4 species)

 ### 326) BLUE-WINGED GROUND-DOVE
(Palomita Cordillerana) *Metriopelia melanoptera*

21 cm - White shoulders conspicuous in flight - Lacks gold on wings of 327) - Underparts rosy - Dark legs ... From Colombia along the W ... Puna, High Andean & Patagonian steppes   IV

 ### 327) GOLDEN-SPOTTED GROUND-DOVE
(Palomita Dorada) *Metriopelia aymara*

19 cm - Resembles 326) - **Short tail** - Long uppertail coverts - **Shoulder with golden spots** not always visible - Without periocular - Underparts lilac - Rosy legs ... From Peru along the W ... Puna & Andean steppes   IV

 ### 328) BARE-EYED GROUND-DOVE
(Palomita Ojo Desnudo) *Metriopelia morenoi*

17 cm - ♂ - Lacking white on wing of 326) & golden of 327) - **Outer rectrices with white tip** - Underparts grey not rosy - **Conspicuous periocular** - Yellowish legs ... Puna & High Andean steppes in NW   III

 ### 329) BARE-FACED GROUND-DOVE
(Palomita Moteada) *Metriopelia ceciliae*

16 cm - Resembles 328) - Conspicuous **brown back edged whitish** - Slight white tip on outer rectrices - Cinnamon breast ... From Peru along the W ... Puna in NW   I

131

LEPTOTILA: Rather hidden - Shy - Terrestrial & low strata - Deep melancholic calls-Somewhat larger than Eared Dove (322) - Without spots on wings - Very alike (even more so in flight) - Tips of tails white-Underparts rosy turning white on lower bellies - **Underwings rufous** *conspicuous in flight - (3 species)*

330) WHITE-TIPPED DOVE
(Yerutí Común)   *Leptotila verreauxi-2R*
26 cm - Bisyllabic *hu..uúuu* - Wide rosy forehead - **Nape & hindneck [glossy] sky blue - Back brown** - Tail blackish-Underparts whiter than 331) & 332) ... From N. America, except Chile - URUGUAY ... Forests, plantations & nearby areas   IV

331) LARGE-TAILED DOVE
(Yerutí Yungueña)   *Leptotila megalura*
27 cm - More gregarious - Trisyllabic *huuu..hu..hu* - Allopatric with 332) - Nape & hindneck [glossy] violaceous - **Lower back & tail chestnut** more conspicuous in flight ... Bolivia ... Yungas
                                                IV

332) GRAY-FRONTED DOVE
(Yerutí Colorada)   *Leptotila rufaxilla*
25 cm - Monosyllabic *uuUuu* - Wide **whitish forehead**, crown sky blue - Nape & neck like 331) - **Chestnut back-** Blackish tail ... From Venezuela, except Chile ... URUGUAY ... Humid forests in NE - (Iguazu NP)   III

 GEOTRYGON: (Quail-doves): Tame - Hidden - Terrestrial - Scratch ground - Forests - Look like Crypturellus - Chubby - Iridescent- Short tails without white tips- Bills, eyelids & legs reddish - (3 species)

333) RUDDY QUAIL-DOVE
(Paloma Montera Castaña)
                    Geotrygon montana
22 cm - Call longer & deeper than 332), like a ship horn - **Chestnut** - Upperparts rufous - **Malar bands white & rufous** Throat & lower belly whitish - ♀ : Upperparts & breast olivaceous brown -Lacking malar bands ... From C. America, except Chile ... Humid forests in **Misiones**   II

334) WHITE-THROATED QUAIL-DOVE
(Paloma Montera Grande)
Geotrygon frenata
28 cm - Call *uú..uú* - Rosy head darker on crown - **Upper back violet** - Rest of upperparts chestnut - **Ocular & malar lines black** linked around cheeks - White throat - Imbricated **black & white pattern on throat** - Rest of underparts ashy grey - Violaceous legs ... Colombia, Ecuador, Peru & Bolivia ... **Yungas** - (Calilegua NP)   II

335) VIOLACEOUS QUAIL-DOVE
(Paloma Montera Violácea)
Geotrygon violacea

23 cm - Resembles a small *Leptotila* - Without any special pattern on face - Tail not short - **Wide forehead** (like 332) throat **& lower belly whitish - Crown & upper back glossy violaceous** - Rest of upperparts chestnut - Breast rosy- ♀: Brown back - Breast brownish - Rest white ... From C. America, except Chile - Humid forests in **Misiones**   II

336) BLUE GROUND-DOVE
(Palomita Azulada)   *Claravis pretiosa*

18 cm - Terrestrial - Striking - Repeated *cau* - **Sky blue** - Forehead & underparts almost whitish - **Black dots on coverts** - Tail without white of 337) - Outer remiges & outer rectrices black - ● : Different - Looks like 324) - Underwing coverts white not black - **Tail & dots on wings rufous** - Underparts ochraceous becoming greyish ... From Mexico, except Chile ... Edges of forests, capueras & yungas in NW (II) & NE   III

337) PURPLE-WINGED GROUND-DOVE   (Palomita Morada)   *Claravis godefrida*

21 cm - Hidden - Resembles sympatric 336) - Call *u..ú* - **Three** wide **wing-bands** (not little spots), one blue & two purple - **Outer rectrices white** - ♀ : Brown - Underparts, wingbands & outer rectrices ochraceous ... Brazil & Paraguay ... Associated with flowering of tacuaras (bamboo) - Humid forests in **Misiones**   II

*ARA (Macaws): Gregarious - Often on trees -Powerful voices- Some **very large** - Blue remiges - Long graded tails -Naked faces- Almost extinct due to commercial hunting - (4 species)*

338) RED-AND-GREEN MACAW
(Guacamayo Rojo)   *Ara chloroptera*

85 cm - Very striking **scarlet red** - Yellowish green spot on wing - Rump, tip of tail & undertail coverts sky blue - White face with red lines ... From Panama, except Chile ... Forests in **Formosa**   I

339) MILITARY MACAW
(Guacamayo Verde)   *Ara militaris*

65 cm - Green - Conspicuous **red forehead - Rump** & undertail coverts **sky blue** - Uppertail red with sky blue tip - **Underwings** & undertail **bronzed** - Face rosy with black lines ... From Mexico along W, except Chile ... Humid forests in NW   I

340) BLUE-WINGED MACAW
(Maracaná Lomo Rojo)   *Ara maracana*

40 cm - Allopatric with 339) - Green - **Red on** forehead, **lower back & belly-** Base of tail chestnut, rest blue - Underwing & undertail bronzed - Yellowish face - Rosy legs ... Brazil & Paraguay ... Forests in NE   I

341) GOLDEN-COLLARED MACAW
(Maracaná Cuello Dorado)
                    Ara auricollis

35 cm - Like *Aratinga* in size - Green - Blackish crown - **Yellow band on nape** - Uppertail blue with rufous base - Undertail bronzed - Whitish face - Rosy legs ... Brazil, Paraguay & Bolivia ... Humid forests in NW   III

ARATINGA: Gregarious - Noisy - Often on treetops - Smaller than Ara - Feathered faces- **Green** *- Underparts paler -* **Perioculars white** *or pale - Long tails, pointed & graded-Under rectrices & remiges bronzed - Pale bills - (4 species - A. aurea in following page)*

342) MITRED PARAKEET
(Calancate Cara Roja) *Aratinga mitrata* 35 cm - Shy - [Hindneck & some body feathers], **forehead & parts of face red** - Orange iris - J: Few red spots - Brown iris ... Peru & Bolivia ... Forests in NW   III

343) BLUE-CROWNED PARAKEET
(Calancate Común)
Aratinga acuticaudata
35 cm - Tamer than 342) - **Bluish hood-Red base on undertail,** visible when opened & in flight - Orange iris ... From Venezuela, except Ecuador, Peru & Chile - [URUGUAY] ... Forests, savannas & plantations   IV

344) WHITE-EYED PARAKEET
(Calancate Ala Roja)
Aratinga leucophthalma
33 cm - Call *tsheerrr* - Paler green than 342) - Without red or blue on forehead - Some red feathers on head - **Red** shoulders & **underwing coverts** becoming yellow, **conspicuous in flight** - J: [Without red] ... From Nicaragua, except Peru & Chile - URUGUAY ... Forests & savannas   IV

345) BURROWING PARROT
(Loro Barranquero)
Cyanoliseus patagonus-3R
42 cm - Noisy flocks - Crowd together on high posts & wires - **Olivaceous - Lower back & rump greenish or yellow** - Blue remiges - Long tail bluish olive - Breast dark brown & rest of **underparts yellow** (or brown) **with red spot** - White periocular ... Chile - URUGUAY ... Savannas, wooded steppes, cliffs & Andean & Patagonian rural areas   IV

346) PEACH-FRONTED PARAKEET
(Calancate Frente Dorada) *Aratinga aurea-2R*

24 cm - Much smaller than other *Aratinga*- **Wide forehead** & periocular **orange yellow** - Bluish crown - Inner remiges blue - Olive breast becoming greenish yellow in rest of underparts - Black bill ... Brazil, Paraguay & Bolivia ... High in trees of forests & savannas in NW & NE   I

347) BLACK-HOODED PARAKEET
(Ñanday) *Nandayus nenday*

30 cm - Looks like *Aratinga* - Loud *kra* - Green - **Black hood** - Rosy periocular - Blue remiges - Tip of tail & breast bluish- **Red thighs** ... Brazil, Paraguay & Bolivia ... Forests, savannas & palm groves in the Eastern Chaqueño District (E Formosa)   III

348) AUSTRAL PARAKEET
(Cachaña)
    Enicognathus ferrugineus-2R

31 cm - Looks like smaller & allopatric 350) - Green undulated black, more conspicuous on crown - Underparts paler & olivaceous - Slight forehead, **spot on belly** & long graded **tail rufous** ... Chile ... **Araucano Forest**
      III

349) MONK PARAKEET
(Cotorra) *Myiopsitta monachus-3R*

27 cm -Very well known - Often in cages or loose as pet - Noisy flocks - Lives & breeds in **large** communal **twig nests** - Green - Wide forehead & throat grey - **Breast ashy grey undulated** with whitish - Blue remiges - Bill orange ... Brazil, Paraguay & Bolivia - URUGUAY ... Forests, plantations, savannas, **rural** & populated **areas**   VI

350) GREEN-CHEEKED PARAKEET (Chiripepé Cabeza Parda) *Pyrrhura molinae*

24 cm - Very much like 351) even in voice & behavior - Allopatric - **Brown head - Ventral spot & all tail reddish - Breast scaled brown** ... Brazil & Bolivia ... Yungas   IV

351) REDDISH-BELLIED PARAKEET (Chripepé Cabeza Verde) *Pyrrhura frontalis*

24 cm - Gregarious - Noisy - Sharp & complex *chiripepé* in flocks - Silent while perched - Green, including head - White periocular - Blue remiges - **Breast scaled olivaceous - Reddish spot on belly** - Long **bronzed tail, reddish only on underparts** ... Brazil & Paraguay - URUGUAY ... Forests in NE   V

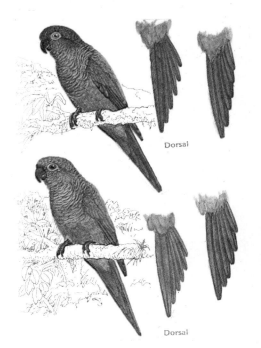

Dorsal

Dorsal

352) GRAY-HOODED PARAKEET (Catita Serrana Grande) *Bolborhynchus aymara*

19 cm - Gregarious - Warbles like a passerine - Elegant - Long tail - Green - **Brownish head** - White throat - **Underparts greyish** with flanks, underwing coverts & lower belly greenish yellow ... Bolivia ... Ravines, High Andean steppes, prepuna & hills   IV

353) MOUNTAIN PARAKEET (Catita Serrana Chica) *Bolborhynchus aurifrons-2R*

17 cm - Resembles 352) - Tail shorter - **Blue on remiges** - Throat & flanks yellowish - Bill & legs orange - ♀ : Dark bill... Peru, Bolivia & Chile ... High Andean steppes, prepuna, mountain ravines & central high hills   III

354) BLUE-WINGED PARROTLET
(Catita Enana)
Forpus xanthopterygius (.)

11 cm - Groups - Continuous flapping in flight - Voice of passerine *piuit.. piuiuit* - **Minute - Short** wedgeshaped **tail** - Green - Underparts paler - **Wing patch & rump blue,** visible in flight - Rosy bill- ♀ : Lacking blue ... Colombia, Brazil, Paraguay, Bolivia & Peru ... Edges of humid forests, capueras & forests in NE
III

355) CANARY-WINGED PARAKEET
(Catita Chirirí)
Brotogeris versicolurus-2R

20 cm - Looks like *Bolborhynchus* - Call *chiri..chiri..ri* - Long graded tail - Green - Primaries a little bluish - Conspicuous **golden yellow band on coverts** ... From Colombia, except Chile ... Capueras, forests, rural & inhabited areas in NW & NE
II

356) RED-CAPPED PARROT
(Catita Cabeza Roja) *Pionopsitta pileata*

20 cm - Very tame - In flight: rapid & sharp *ch..ch..chee,* more musical than 351) - **Short tail** - Green - Conspicuous **wide red crown** - Shoulders, alula, primaries & outer rectrices blue - Thick greyish bill - ♀ : Lacks red - **Cheeks rufous** ... Brazil & Paraguay ... Medium strata in humid forests & rural areas of NE
III

357) SCALLY-HEADED PARROT
(Loro Maitaca)   *Pionus maximiliani-3R*

27 cm - Gregarious - Noisy - Hoarse call- **Short tail** - Smaller than *Amazona* - Deep flapping from body line downwards, with wings nearly touching - Opaque green somewhat scaled - Blackish crown - Outer rectrices blue - Upper breast violaceous - **Undertail coverts red** - Greyish periocular - Bill black & yellow ... Brazil, Paraguay & Bolivia ... Forests, rural areas & savannas in N IV

(.) Sometimes considered a race of *F. passerinus*

*AMAZONA: Gregarious - Short flapping from body line downwards - Robust - **Short tails** - Strong bills - Green [black undulations]-Conspicuous **red wing spot** - Blue in remiges - Greenish yellow tail tips - Slight red spots on undertails, except 361) - (4 species)*

358) VINACEOUS-BREASTED PARROT
(Loro Vinoso)   *Amazona vinacea*
30 cm - **Forehead,** shoulders, iris **& base of bill red** - **Erectile sky blue hindneck,** with black undulations - **Breast violaceous rufous** - Remiges sky blue & black ... Brazil & Paraguay ... Mainly in *Araucaria* forests in **Misiones**
I

359) TURQUOISE-FRONTED PARROT
(Loro Hablador)   *Amazona aestiva*
35 cm - Often in captivity where it learns to speak - A clear *krreo* & other calls - Wide **sky blue forehead - Yellowish crown** - Face, **shoulders** & throat **golden yellow** - J: [Green head] ... Brazil, Paraguay & Bolivia ... Forests & savannas of Chaqueño type & populated areas   IV

360) RED-SPECTACLED PARROT
(Charao)   *Amazona pretrei*
30 cm - **Wide forehead** including ocular patch, **shoulders, front of wing & thighs red** - Base of maxilla orange ... Brazil & Paraguay ... Mainly in *Araucaria* forests in **Misiones**   I

361) ALDER PARROT
(Loro Alisero)   *Amazona tucumana (.)*
30 cm - Resembles 360) - Allopatric - More black undulations - **Only forehead red** - Red wing spot of genus but lacks the one on tail ... Bolivia ... Montane forests in NW   IV

(.) Sometimes considered a race of 360)

Fam. Cuculidae, see page 34

*COCCYZUS: Shy - Hidden among foliage-Clucklike calls - Slender - Curved bills - Bulky throat - **Same sizes** (except 366) - Upperparts brown - **Long graded tails with white tip on each rectrix** - (5 species)*

362) YELLOW-BILLED CUCKOO
(Cuclillo Pico Amarillo)
Coccyzus americanus

26 cm - **Rufous in remiges** conspicuous in flight - **Underparts white** - Big white spots on black undertail - Longish bill with **yellow mandible** ... URUGUAY ... Migrant A - Savannas, forests & plantations   III

363) BLACK-BILLED CUCKOO
(Cuclillo Ojo Colorado)
Coccyzus erythropthalmus

26 cm - Resembles 362) - **Underparts white** - Wings without or little rufous - Undertail grey with black & white tip - Black bill - **Red periocular** ... Migrant A ... Humid forests in NW & NE   I

364) PEARLY-BREASTED CUCKOO
(Cuclillo Ceniciento)   *Coccyzus euleri*

26 cm - Resembles 362) in **yellow mandible** - Lacks rufous on wings - Yellow periocular - **Grey breast** continued white - Colombia, Venezuela, Guianas & Brazil... Humid forest in Misiones   II

365) DARK-BILLED CUCKOO
(Cuclillo Canela)
Coccyzus melacoryphus

26 cm - Ashy grey crown - **Black mask-Yellowish ochre underparts** unique - Pale eyelids - J: Underparts whitish ... From Venezuela, except Chile- URUGUAY ... Migrant B - Forests, savannas & plantations   IV

366) ASH-COLORED CUCKOO
(Cuclillo Chico)   *Coccyzus cinereus*

21 cm - Tamer than others - **Tail** with slight white tip, **neither long nor graded** - Bill short & curved - Dull plumage - Slightly resembles *Myiarchus* - Breast rosy brown turning whitish on belly - **Red eyes** - J: Brown eye ... Brazil, Paraguay & Bolivia - URUGUAY... Migrant B in S - Savannas, forests & plantations   IV

367) SMOOTH-BILLED ANI
(Anó Chico)   *Crotophaga ani (.)*

32 cm - Tame - In visible sites - Noisy groups with unsynchronized flight alternating quick flapping with long glides - Arboreal & terrestrial - Sad bisyllabic melodious call among others - Curved **high & compressed bill** - Looks like Guira Cuckoo (369) - **Black** - Violaceous sheen - Tail bluish, long, wide & pendant - Iridescent little arrows on neck & breast ... From C. America, except Chile - URUGUAY ... Forests, savannas, rural & inhabited areas   V

368) GREATER ANI
(Anó Grande)   *Crotophaga major*

41 cm - Shy - Hidden - Varied chatty calls in chorus - Flight like 367) - Sympatric - Larger - **Bluer** - Greenish sheen on back & breast - **Very long violet tail - Iris olivaceous white** - J: Brown iris ... From Panama, except Chile - URUGUAY ... Migrant B - Forests & savannas near water in N   II

(.) *C. sulcirostris*, very similar, has been cited for arid zones in N Salta

369) GUIRA CUCKOO
(Pirincho)   *Guira guira*
36 cm - Noisy groups - Flight like Ani
(367) - Often with back to the sun - Flute-
like *péeo..péeo..péeo..pr..prrr..prrrrr* -
Ruffled crest - Striated blackish back -
**Lower back & rump whitish - Tri-
color** pendant **tail** - Underparts
ochraceous striated on breast - Orange
bill ... Brazil, Paraguay & Bolivia -
URUGUAY ... Various habitats even
inhabited   V

370) PHEASANT CUCKOO
(Yasiyateré Grande)
                Dromococcyx phasianellus
35 cm - Heard at dusk & night - Difficult
to see - Call similar to 372) *se..see..rrru-*
Excited: ascendant series - Semiterrestrial - **Broad & long graded tail
black** with white tip on each rectrix -
Brown head with **ruffled chestnut
crest** lacks striations - Back dark
brown- Edges on coverts - Throat &
breast with spots (lacking in J) - Rest of
underparts white ... From Mexico, except Chile ... Humid forests in **Misiones**
                                        I

371) PAVONINE CUCKOO
(Yasiyateré Chico)
                Dromococcyx pavoninus
26 cm - Resembles 370) including
voice *se..see..se..se* - Answer *se..see*
or *se..see..see* - **Cinnamon breast
without spots** ... S. America, except
Bolivia & Chile ... Low strata of humid
forests in NE   II

372) STRIPED CUCKOO
(Crespín)   *Tapera naevia*
28 cm - Looks like 369) - Hidden -
Passive - Much more heard than seen -
Melancholic whistle *se..see* even at
night, difficult to localize - Also
se:.se..se..seese - Ochraceous -
Ruffled erectile **rufous crest striated
like back** - Long brown tail - **White
eyebrow** - Black malar band - Yellowish bill, black culmen ... From Mexico, except Chile - URUGUAY ... Migrant
B in S - Savannas & forests   IV

373) SQUIRREL CUCKOO
(Tingazú)   *Piaya cayana-2R*

45 cm - Tame - Shy - Short & gliding flight- Loud & melodious whistle *ju..ee* - Long & rapid series of *tuip* - Mewing & other calls - **Chestnut upperparts - Very long tail** (30 cm) graded, black below **with white tip on each rectrix**- Breast rosy brown contrasting with grey belly - Curved greenish bill ... From Mexico - URUGUAY ... Middle strata in forests & plantations   IV

Fam. Tytonidae, see page 34

374) BARN OWL
(Lechuza-de-Campanario)   *Tyto alba*

36 cm - Nocturnal - In flight looks like a white shadow - **Loud hiss** & long rattle- Without ear tufts - Very pale - **Heart shaped white facial disk bordered by dark line** - Back grey mottled ochre & white - Underparts ochre with slight dots-Long feathered legs white ... Western Hemisphere - URUGUAY ... Different habitats, rural & **inhabited areas** -Often in abandoned buildings   IV

Fam. Strigidae, see page 34

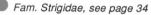

375) GREAST HORNED OWL
(Ñacurutú)   *Bubo virginianus-2R*

50 cm - Not very hidden - Profound *ñacurutú* - **Largest owl** - Conspicuous blackish **triangular ear tufts not joined** - Throat & **collar white** - Underparts whitish finely barred - Tail barred brown ... From N. America - URUGUAY... Forests, savannas, ravines, high altitude grasslands & steppes   III

376) STRIPED OWL
(Lechuzón Orejudo)   *Asio clamator*
36 cm - Sad *jeeeee* - Series of barks *auh..* - Looks like Short-eared Owl (390)- **Ear tufts long**er & **closer together** than in 375) - Facial disk whitish bordered black - **Underparts with conspicuous, thick & uniform black striations** ... From C. America - URUGUAY ... Savannas & plantations   III

143

377) BLACK-BANDED OWL
(Lechuza Negra)   *Ciccaba huhula -2R*
35 cm - Loud & flute-like call
at..at..at..kua - Rounded head without
ear tufts - **Blackish** - Looks **dappled** -
Slight white barring on upperparts - Tail
with 3 bands & tip white-**Underparts,
even tarsi, with conspicuous white
bars** - Bill & toes yellow - Brown iris ... S.
America, except Chile... High strata in
humid forests & capueras of NW & NE II

378) MOTTLED OWL
(Lechuza Estriada)   *Ciccaba virgata*
32 cm - Rounded head without ear tufts-
**Upperparts brown vermiculated
cinnamon** - Facial disk circled brown -
Eyebrows & half circle near bill
ochraceous - White throat - **Cinnamon
underparts** conspicuously **striated** -
Cinnamon thighs - Bluish toes - Brown
iris ... From Mexico, except Chile...High
strata in humid forests of **Misiones** II

379) BUFF-FRONTED OWL
(Lechucita Canela)
　　　　　　　　　Aegolius harrisii -2R
20 cm - Series of rapid *oú* - Big head
without ear tufts - Easily identified -
Chestnut back - Crown, nape, eyebrow &
facial ring blackish - **Wings & tail
spotted white** -Two conspicuous dorsal Vs, one incomplete,one **facial disk
& all underparts** cinnamon ... S.
America, except Peru & Chile - [URU-
GUAY] ... Forests in NW & NE　　　II

380) BURROWING OWL
(Lechucita Vizcachera)
　　　　　　　Athene cunicularia-3R
25 cm - **Terrestrial** - Erect - On posts,
next to its burrow or near vizcacha's - **Diurnal** - At nightfall *cu..curú* - Salutes
with head - Hovers - Very distinct from &
smaller than 390); share habitat - Without ear tufts - Long legs - **Whitish** - Upperparts brown with white dots - Barred
tail - Eyebrow & throat white - Underparts
a little splashed ... From N. America -
URUGUAY ... Prairies, steppes, savannas & **rural areas** - Decreasing　IV

381) TROPICAL SCREECH-OWL
(Alilicucu Común)   *Otus choliba*

22 cm - Hidden - Passive - Flute-like *krrr..cu..cu* - **Small** erectile **ear tufts** - Back brownish grey (or chestnut) splashed black - Whitish half circle near bill - White dots on coverts - **Underparts with fine** black pattern like **little crosses** ... From C. Rica, except Chile - URUGUAY ... Forests, savannas, plantations & even inhabited areas   IV

382) LONG-TUFTED SCREECH-OWL
(Alilicucu Grande)   *Otus atricapillus*

25 cm - Like a **chestnut** 381) - Different call *rrrrru* - Longer ear tufts - **Blacker nape**- **Thicker pectoral striations**... Brazil & Paraguay - [URUGUAY] ... Humid forests in **Misiones**   I

GLAUCIDIUM: Rather diurnal -In visible sites - Harassed by birds - Flick & waggle tails -Without ear tufts-Small-Face-like pattern on nape - White dots on coverts White eyebrows - White chins & throats separated by ·brown collars - Thick chestnut striations on underparts - (2 species)

383) AUSTRAL PYGMY-OWL
(Caburé Grande)   *Glaucidium nanum*

19 cm - Crown & nape more rufous than back, striated ochre - **Blackish brown tail very much barred cinnamon** - Migrant C ... Chile ... **Araucano Forest**   II

384) FERRUGINOUS PYGMY-OWL
(Caburé Chico)*Glaucidium brasilianum*

16 cm - Long series of clucks - Also *wit*- Brownish grey - Crown & nape more uniform than in 383) (or striated) - **Black tail with few white bars** - (Or: all rufous, with uniform or lightly barred brown tail) ... From N. America - URUGUAY ... Forests, savannas, plantations & even inhabited areas   IV

385) SPECTACLED OWL
(Lechuzón Mocho Grande)
Pulsatrix perspicillata

45 cm - Active at dusk - Descending & low rattle *cuu..cuu..* - Robust - Resembles allopatric 386) - Upperparts & **breast** uniform **dark brown** - Conspicuous eyebrow, linked to half circle near bill (**spectacles**), & throat **white** - Wings & tail barred grey - Rest of **underparts cinnamon** - Yellow iris - **J: White - Black mask** ... From C. America, except Chile ... Yungas   II

386) TAWNY-BROWED OWL
(Lechuzón Mocho Chico)
Pulsatrix koeniswaldiana

38 cm - Low call, with same timbre as in similar 385) *brr..brrr..brrr..brrr* or *ut.. ut..út..ut..ut-* Conspicuous **cinnamon** not white **spectacles** - Almost cinnamon collar - **Underparts cinnamon** - Chestnut iris ... Brazil & Paraguay ... Humid forests in NE   II

387) RUSTY-BARRED OWL
(Lechuza Listada)   *Strix hylophila*

35 cm - Descendant series *gu..gu..u..u..* like croaking frogs - Sometimes duets - Looks like 378) (&more so like 388) - Tail & **underparts much barred chestnut** -Short eyebrow linked to half circle near bill, & throat whitish - Dorsal bars, **facial disk** & thighs **cinnamon** - Dark ocular patch ... Brazil & Paraguay ... Forests in NE   I

388) RUFOUS-LEGGED OWL
(Lechuza Bataraz)   *Strix rufipes -2R*

38 cm - Loud growl *kru..kru..* - Facial disk whitish or cinnamon, with concentric dark rings - Slight **whitish** (or black & white) **dorsal bars** - Conspicuous **blackish bars on underparts** - Thighs cinnamon as in 387) ... Paraguay & Chile ... Forests & savannas of **Chaqueño** type & **Araucano Forests**   III

389) STYGIAN OWL
(Lechuzón Negruzco)　　*Asio stygius*

43 cm - Low *hu...* - Different habitat &
behavior than 390) - Nocturnal - Hunts
bats - Conspicuous **black ear tufts** -
Resembles 376) - Dark - **Back & facial
disk blackish** - Tail barred - Underparts
heavy striated - Yellow iris ... From Mexico, except Guianas & Chile ... Forests &
savannas of N　　　　　　　　II

390) SHORT-EARED OWL
(Lechuzón de Campo)
　　　　　　　　Asio flammeus-2R

38 cm - Almost **diurnal & terrestrial** -
Slow flapping of long rounded wings -
Perches on posts & other visible sites -
Glides low over fields - Barks like Stilt
(247) - Often found dead on main roads-
Inconspicuous **small ear tufts fairly
close** - Ochraceous - Back splashed &
barred - Less striated on underparts than
376) - Dark ocular patch on pale facial
disk - Yellow iris ... Western Hemisphere-
URUGUAY ... Prairies, savannas, grasslands & rural areas　　　　　　IV

Fam. Nyctibiidae, see page 35

391) COMMON POTOO
(Urutaú Común)　　*Nyctibius griseus*

34 cm - Heard but rarely seen - By day
erect & motionless at end of medium height **dead trunks** - Mimetic -
Looks like tree bark - At dusk a **long
mournful human-like cry** followed by
5 descending notes - Bill short & wide -
Long barred tail - At night red eyes like
nightjars ... From Mexico, except Chile -
URUGUAY ... Savannas, capueras &
forests　　　　　　　　　III

Fam. Caprimulgidae, see page 35

CAPRIMULGUS (Nightjars): Alike - Low, sudden & erratic flight - Red eyes shine at night - Blackish crowns - Backs brownish, striated & splashed black & ochraceous - **White or ochraceous collars-** *Dots on coverts - Central rectrices like backs, pale tips in outer ones -* ♀♀ *: Different spots - (5 species)*

392) RUFOUS NIGHTJAR
(Atajacaminos Colorado)
Caprimulgus rufus

26 cm - Perches on branches - Rapid & strong *chak..uiuiuiuiu* - Not in open fields or .roads - Resembles 398) - **Upperparts dark** without pale inner remiges - Wide **ochraceous half collar - Cinnamon underparts** more uniformly barred - Outer rectrices with one white & one cinnamon conspicuous spots visible in flight - ♀: Without white on tail ... From C. Rica, except Ecuador, Peru & Chile ... Forests   III

393) SALTA NIGHTJAR
(Atajacaminos de la Yunga)
Caprimulgus saltarius (.)

28 cm - Perched almost erect looks like Potoo (391) - Appears larger than 394) due to **longer tail** - Mottled back chestnut blackish without band on nape - Underparts less blackish - **Cinnamon collar** - Wide conspicuous cinnamon tip of outer rectrices ... Bolivia ... Forests in **Salta** (Aguas Blancas)   III

394) SILKY-TAILED NIGHTJAR
(Atajacaminos Oscuro)
Caprimulgus sericocaudatus

25 cm - Dorsal mottling & barred on tail chestnut - **Chestnut band on nape** unlike 392) and allopatric 393) - **Outer rectrices with whitish tip** not cinnamon - Throat & breast blackish with pale dots - Rest of underparts barred ... Brazil & Paraguay ... Humid forests in **Misiones**   II

395) BAND-WINGED NIGHTJAR
(Atajacaminos Ñañarca)
Caprimulgus longirostris-3R

22 cm - Resembles 396) - Separate whistles *chuít..* - White spot on primaries- **Large white tip on upper outer rectrices - White bands on tip & central undertail - Cinnamon band on nape linked to white collar** - ♀: Wing patch & collar cinnamon - Tail without white tip ... S. America - URUGUAY... Steppes, savannas, hills, rural areas & plantations   III

396) LITTLE NIGHTJAR
(Atajacaminos Chico)
Caprimulgus parvulus

18 cm - Often perched on low branches unlike 395) - Call *pcchrruí..cuícuícuícuí* - **Cinnamon band on nape linked with white triangle on throat** - Only slight white tip on tail - ●: Without white on wings - **Primaries & tail barred cinnamon** - Throat & band on nape like ♂... S. America, except Chile - URUGUAY ... Forests, savannas, plantations (often *Eucalyptus*) & rural areas   III

397)SICKLE-WINGED NIGHTJAR
(Atajacaminos Ala Negra)
Eleothreptus anomalus

17 cm - Peculiar wing shape - Without collar or band on nape - Inner remiges barred cinnamon - **Black primaries** & uppertail with white tip - Dorsal edges white - Underparts splashed blackish - Lower belly & undertail barred - ♀: Normal wing without white ... Paraguay & Brazil [URUGUAY] ... Savannas, palm groves & humid pastures   II

149

Try to remember the abbreviations

398) SEMICOLLARED NIGHTHAWK (Añapero Castaño)
Lurocalis semitorquatus (.)
24 cm - Perches on branches - Nests in trees - Flutelike & sonorous whistle *tweet,* while flying at medium height - Long wings extend beyond **short tail** - Upperparts blackish ocellated & dotted with cinnamon - Primaries lack white - Inner remiges whitish - Conspicuous **white throat** - Blackish breast - Rest of **underparts & underwing coverts rufous barred black** -Migrant B ... Brazil & Paraguay ... Savannas & grasslands in N   II

399) PAURAQUE
(Curiango)   *Nyctidromus albicollis*
28 cm - Terrestrial - Short vertical flights- Frequent *juip* & audible *cuiau* - Long rounded tail with **outer rectrices black & white - Dorsal edges black-** Rufous cheeks - **White triangle on throat - White band on black primaries** - ♀: Ochraceous spot on primaries - Tail & throat less white ... From N. America, except Chile ... Forests & savannas in NW & Mesopotamia   III

400) OCELLATED POORWILL
(Atajacaminos Ocelado)
Nyctiphrynus ocellatus
20 cm - Perches on high branches - Hoarse *brow* - **Rufous,** finely barred black - Ocellated black on scapulars - **White dots on** coverts, **breast & belly - White triangle on throat** - Barred tail with white tip ... From Colombia & Brazil, except Chile ... **Humid forests** in **Misiones**   I

401) COMMON NIGHTHAWK
(Añapero Boreal)
Chordeiles minor-2R
22 cm - **Flocks** - High & sustained flight- Can be seen at dusk - Perches on high branches - **Silhouette falcon-like** - Dark - **White triangle on throat - White spot on** black **primaries - Forked tail** with white band - Underparts barred - ♀ : Ochraceous throat -Without white on tail - Migrant A ... URUGUAY ... Savannas, plantations, rural & **inhabited areas**   III

(.) *L. s. nattereri* often considered separate species

402) NACUNDA NIGHTHAWK
(Ñacundá) *Podager nacunda*
28 cm - **Flocks on ground** or fly at medium height - Fly around street lights- Often seen at dusk - Long series of *cooorrr..coo..* like toads - **Robust** - Shortish **tail with wide white tip** - Variegated back & breast - Large **white patch on blackish primaries - Collar, underwing coverts, belly & lower belly white** - ♀: Tail without white - Slight ventral barring ... S. America, except Chile - URUGUAY ... Forests, savannas, humid, rural & inhabited areas   III

403) SCISSOR-TAILED NIGHTJAR
(Atajacaminos Tijera Común)
Hydropsalis brasiliana
50 cm - On ground & branches - Very sharp chirp *tzig* in flight - Pale plumage - **Without white spots** - Rufous band on nape - White edges on scapulars - **Underparts ochraceous** finely barred - **Tail** (40 cm) **very long, deeply forked,** whitish & brown - ♀ : 30 cm - Tail shorter, forked, without white ... Brazil, Bolivia & Paraguay - URUGUAY... Forests, savannas, plantations & inhabited areas   IV

404) LONG-TRAINED NIGHTJAR
(Atajacaminos Coludo)
Macropsalis creagra
76 cm - Long low flight - Perches on branches - Cinnamon band on nape - **Extremely long** (60 cm) outer **rectrices** hang fluttering in flight - ♀: 30 cm- Forked tail - Lacks long rectrices ... Brazil...Humid forest clearings in **Misiones** (Mocona)   II

405) LYRE-TAILED NIGHTJAR
(Atajacaminos Lira) *Uropsalis lyra*
85 cm - Perches on low branches - Call *tre..cue..* - Resembles allopatric 404) - **Rufous band on nape - Tail lyreshaped - Outer rectrices** (75 cm) **extremely long** with grey tip - ♀ : 25 cm-Forked black tail - Lacks long rectrices ... From Venezuela along the W, except Chile ... Montane forests in **Jujuy**

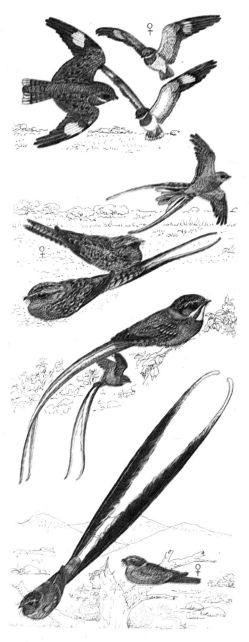

151

406) WHITE-COLLARED SWIFT
(Vencejo de Collar)
Streptoprocne zonaris (.)

20 cm - Gregarious - Rests in caves or behind cascades - In flocks emits loud *cheerreeo* - **Black - Complete white collar** - J: More brownish - Collar inconspicuous ... From Mexico, except Chile-[URUGUAY] ... Hills - (Cueva de los Pajaritos, Tanti, Cordoba) & falls (Iguazu) - In Winter on the plains   III

CYPSELOIDES: Gregarious - Very alike - Medium size - Wings not so narrow - Longer tails than the small similar Chaetura -Dark - Lack pale rumps - (3 species)

407) GREAT DUSKY SWIFT
(Vencejo de Cascada)
Cypseloides senex

18 cm - Flocks like bee swarms - Constant flapping as if trembling - Call *tee...tee...tee..* - Brown - Head slightly striated - **Face** ashy grey, **whitish** towards forehead ... Brazil & Paraguay ... Humid forests in Misiones (always in **Iguazu Falls**)   IV

408) SOOTY SWIFT   (Vencejo Negruzco)   *Cypseloides fumigatus*

15 cm - Smaller & darker than sympatric 407) - In small groups - Without pale face - Indistinguishable from allopatric 409) - **Blackish** brown - Slight pale edge in remiges - J: Belly scaled white ... Brazil ... Humid forests in **Misiones**   II

(.) *S. biscutata,* very similar, with collar interrupted on sides of neck, has been cited for Misiones

409) DARK BROWN SWIFT
(Vencejo Pardusco)
Cypseloides rothschildi

15 cm - Glides with arched wings - In its
distribution similar only to smaller 410) -
Uniform brown ... Bolivia ... Yungas &
forests in **NW**   III

410) ASHY-TAILED SWIFT
(Vencejo de Tormenta)*Chaetura andrei*

11 cm - Call *teep..teep..* - Dark brown -
Visible brownish grey rump & tail -
Pale throat ... S. America, except Bolivia
& Chile ... Migrant B - Forests, savannas
& ravines in N   III

411) GRAY-RUMPED SWIFT
(Vencejo Chico)
Chaetura cinereiventris

11 cm - Rests in hollows - Usually flies
in flocks over rivers & streams in
forests-Resembles 410) - Hoarse
tchree - **Upperparts bluish black** -
Conspicuous **pale grey rump** -
Underparts ashy grey, paler on throat ...
From C. America, except Chile ...
Migrant B - Humid forests & ravines in
Misiones   IV

412) ANDEAN SWIFT
(Vencejo Blanco)
Aeronautes andecolus

13 cm - Unmistakable - Slender - Glides
with long arched wings - Long very
forked tail - Brown back - **Rump**, nape
& underparts white ... Peru, Bolivia &
Chile ... Ravines, steppes, savannas &
high altitude grasslands   IV

413) SCALE-THROATED HERMIT (Ermitaño Escamado) *Phaethornis eurynome*

12 cm - **Crown & throat scaled black** - Back bronzed olive undulated brown - **Two long central rectrices & tip of tail white** - Black ocular band between cinnamon eyebrow & malar - Underparts ochraceous grey - **Long bill** (3.8 cm) **curved** with yellow mandible ... Brazil & Paraguay - Low & medium strata in humid forests of **Misiones**   III

414) PLANALTO HERMIT
(Ermitaño Canela) *Phaethornis pretrei*

12 cm - Resembles 413) - Bill (3.3 cm) & tail slightly smaller - Allopatric - **Brown crown** - Back bronzed green - **Cinnamon rump & underparts** ... Brazil & Bolivia ... **Yungas**   III

415) RED-TAILED COMET
(Picaflor Cometa) *Sappho sparganura*

15 cm - Striking - Unmistakable - Glossy- Short bill (1.5 cm) - Green - **Crimson lower back - Long tail** (9 cm) **red** with few black bars - [Black throat] - ♀: 10 cm - Shorter tail - Throat with dots ... Bolivia ... Forests, ravines, inhabited Andean areas & hills   V

416) BLACK-THROATED MANGO
(Picaflor Vientre Negro) *Anthracothorax nigricollis*

9 cm - Glossy - Long bill (3 cm) slightly curved - Upperparts bronzed green - **Purple tail - Underparts black** flanked blue - ●: Unlike - **Underparts white with longitudinal black band**- Tail less purple with small white tip ... From Panama, except Chile - URUGUAY... Forests & inhabited areas in NE   III

154

Memorize the Topography of a Bird

417) WHITE-SIDED HILLSTAR
(Picaflor Andino)
        Oreotrochilus leucopleurus

10 cm - Sympatric with 418) in NW - Feeds supported on tail like a wood-pecker - Bill (2 cm) slightly curved - Upperparts olivaceous brown - Long & wide **white tail with dark central & outer rectrices** - Black line between **glossy green throat** & **white underparts with bluish black longitudinal band- ●: Throat dotted** - Tail with central rectrices & subterminal band dark - Underparts uniform ochraceous ... Bolivia & Chile ... Prepuna, puna, High Andean & even Patagonian steppes III

418) ANDEAN HILLSTAR
(Picaflor Puneño) *Oreotrochilus estella*

11 cm - Very much like 417) - Green on throat more extended - **White underparts with chestnut longitudinal band** - ●: Throat less dotted - **Tail whiter** ... Ecuador, Peru, Bolivia & Chile... Prepuna & puna in NW   III

419)BLUE-TUFTED
STARTHROAT   (Picaflor de Barbijo)
        Heliomaster furcifer (.)

10 cm - **Forked tail** - Sky blue crown - **Ruby red throat** - Throat tufts & **underparts violaceous blue** - Small white postocular spot - **Long black bill** (3.3 cm) **barely curved** - ♀ & RP: Dull plumage - Underparts whitish - Outer rectrices with white tip ... Colombia, Brazil, Bolivia & Paraguay - URUGUAY... Forests, savannas & inhabited areas IV

(.) Another hummingbird of genus *Heliomaster*, almost surely *H. longirostris,* has been observed nesting in Santa Fe province   **155**

Reread characters of genus with each species

COLIBRI: Similar among themselves - Differ in size - Tails greenish sky blue with blue subterminal band - Auricular tufts - Black bills (as long as heads) almost straight - ♀♀: Slightly smaller & paler - (3 species)

420) SPARKLING VIOLETEAR
(Colibrí Grande)   *Colibri coruscans*

12 cm - Insistant *tzip*... while waggling head - **Throat, tuft & ventral patch blue** -Bill 2.8 cm ... Venezuela, Colombia, Ecuador, Peru & Bolivia ... Ravines, forests & prepuna in NW   IV

421)WHITE-VENTED VIOLETEAR
(Colibrí Mediano)   *Colibri serrirostris*

10.5 cm - Violaceous blue **tuft** turning **purple** - Lacks blue throat & conspicuous ventral patch - **Undertail coverts white** - Bill 2.5 cm ... Brazil & Bolivia ... Edges of forests & savannas in NW   II

422) GREEN VIOLETEAR
(Colibrí Chico)   *Colibri thalassinus*

9 cm - **Like a small 421)** without white undertail coverts - Bill 1.8 cm ... From Mexico along the W, except Chile ... Forests - Captured in **Tucuman**   I

423) BLACK JACOBIN
(Picaflor Negro)*Melanotrochilus fuscus*

9 cm - Unmistakable - **Black** - Lower back & rump green - Abdominal flanks white - **White tail** with dark tip & central rectrices look like traffic lights when open & shut rapidly - Bill (2 cm) slightly curved & thick - **J: Sides of throat & edges of dorsal feathers cinnamon** - Only outer rectrices white ... Brazil - URUGUAY ... Forests, savannas & inhabited areas in NE   II

156

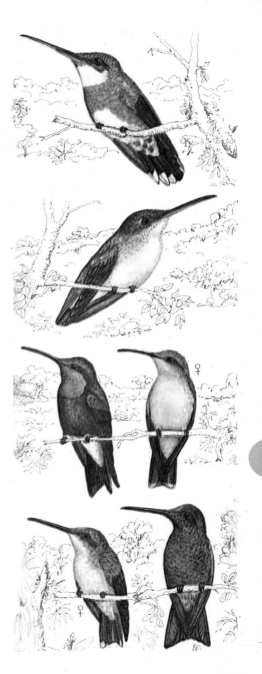

424) WHITE-THROATED HUMMINGBIRD
(Picaflor Garganta Blanca)
Leucochloris albicollis
8 cm - Long succession of rapid, shrill & separate *tsip* - Glossy - Back & **pectoral band green** - Tip of outer rectrices, **throat & belly white** - Black straight bill (2 cm) with red mandible ... Brazil & Paraguay - URUGUAY ... Capueras, forests & plantations, & in Winter in *Eucalyptus* groves, in E - In slow expansion
III

425) WHITE-BELLIED HUMMINGBIRD
(Picaflor Vientre Blanco)
Amazilia chionogaster
8 cm - Tame - Perches in open, repeating a short, shrill & metallic *pic* - Upperparts opaque bronzed green - Tail greenish brown with slight white tip - **Underparts** uniform **white** - Bill (2.2 cm) almost straight, black with red mandible ... Peru & Bolivia ... Yungas & forests in NW   V

426) FORK-TAILED WOODNYMPH
(Picaflor Zafiro) *Thalurania furcata [2R]*
8 cm - Glossy - Green - Lacks sky blue crown of 427) - Blue tail somewhat forked - **Breast & belly violaceous blue** - Lower belly white - Black bill (2 cm) almost straight - ♀: Resembles ♀ 427) - Tail with outer tip white - Underparts whitish ... From Mexico, except Chile ... Forests & inhabited areas in NW & [NE]   I

427) VIOLET-CAPPED WOODNYMPH
(Picaflor Corona Violácea)
Thalurania glaucopis
9 cm - Glossy green - **Crown violaceous sky blue - Forked blue tail - Straight** black **bill** (2 cm) - ♀: Different & smaller (8 cm) - Looks like allopatric 425) - Crown green like back - Tail like ♂ with outer tip white - Underparts whitish - J: Outer tip of tail cinnamon ... Brazil & Paraguay - [URUGUAY]-Humid forests in **Misiones**   IV

Memorize the symbols

428) GREEN-BACKED FIRECROWN
(Picaflor Rubí) *Sephanoides galeritus*

9 cm - Sharp & continuous shrill - Holds on to flowers while sucks - **Glossy red crown** - Back bronzed green - Underparts greyish with **greenish dots**, more conspicuous **on throat** - Short bill (1.6 cm) straight & black - ♀: 8 cm - Without red on crown - Postocular white dot like ♂ ... Chile ... Araucano Forest & nearby areas, plantations & inhabited areas in W Patagonia   III

429) BLUE-CAPPED PUFFLEG
(Picaflor Frente Azul)
Eriocnemis glaucopoides
9 cm - Glossy - **Blue forehead** - Back bronzed green - Underparts green - Blue tail slightly forked - **White tufts on legs** - Black bill (2.3 cm) almost straight- ♀: 8 cm - Without blue forehead - **Large cinnamon bib** - Leg tufts like ♂ ... Bolivia ... Yungas   II

430) SPECKLED HUMMINGBIRD
(Picaflor Yungueño)
Adelomyia melanogenys
7.5 cm - Reclusive - Upperparts bronzed green - Head browner - Conspicuous **postocular white - Cinnamon underparts - Violaceous blue dots on throat** & green on breast- Tail tip cinnamon - Short black bill (1.6 cm) ... From Venezuela along the W, except Chile ... Low strata in yungas   II

431) BLACK-BREASTED PLOVERCREST
(Picaflor Copetón) *Stephanoxis lalandi*
8 cm - Unmistakable - Call cricket-like - Glossy - Green back - **Very long & thin violaceous blue crest** (sometimes worn out or broken) - **Ventral greyish with blue central band** - Straight short black bill (1.7 cm) - ♀: Dull plumage - Resembles ♀ of Emerald (432) & of 427) - Lacks crest & blue ventral - Postocular dot & tip of outer rectrices white also in ♂ ... Brazil & Paraguay ... Humid forests & capueras in **Misiones**   III

158

432) GLITTERING-BELLIED EMERALD (Picaflor Común) *Chlorostilbon aureoventris -2R*

7 cm - Tireless *tzr* - Glossy green - **Blue tail** - [Lower belly golden] - Bill (2 cm) red with black tip - ♀: Dull plumage - Postocular line & tip of tail whitish - Underparts greyish ... Brazil, Paraguay & Bolivia ... Savannas, forests & inhabited areas
V

433) GILDED SAPPHIRE (Picaflor Bronceado) *Hylocharis chrysura (.)*

8 cm - Very loud, shrill & rapid *ii..ii..ii..ii..-* Resembles sympatric 432) - Same bill - Green with **golden sheen - Bronzed tail** - Cinnamon chin - ♀: Similar - Dull green - Lower belly greyish ... Brazil, Paraguay & Bolivia - URUGUAY ... Forests, savannas & inhabited areas IV

434) RUFOUS-THROATED SAPPHIRE (Picaflor Cola Castaña) *Hylocharis sapphirina*

7 cm - Glossy dark green - **Undertail coverts & tail chestnut** (against the light) or bronze or blue (with direct light)- **Violaceous bib** - Bill & chin like 433) - ●: More bronzed - Outer tip of tail & underparts whitish - **Cinnamon chin** Slight green on breast ... Brazil, Paraguay, Bolivia & Peru ... Forests in NE II

435) WHITE-TAILED GOLDENTHROAT (Picaflor de Antifaz) *Polytmus guainumbi*
8 cm - Continuous & clear *tzip..* - Back bronzed green - Crown brown - **Tail green with conspicuous white tip - Black postocular band between white eyebrow & malar line - Bill** (2.4 cm) slightly **curved** with rosy mandible - ●: **Underparts ochraceous** - Green dots on throat & breast ... S. America, except Ecuador, Peru & Chile... Savannas & forests of **Corrientes** II
(.) *H. cyanus* has been cited for Argentina

159

436) VERSICOLORED EMERALD
(Picaflor Esmeralda) *Amazilia versicolor*

7 cm - Glossy bronzed green - **Olive tail** with blue band - **White underparts - Sides of throat & breast with green dots** - Short bill (1.5 cm) straight with red mandible ... Colombia, Venezuela, Brazil, Paraguay & Bolivia... Humid forests in **Misiones**   II

437) FESTIVE COQUETTE
(Coqueta Verde)*Lophornis chalybea (.)*

6 cm - **Minute** - Glossy green - Small crest - Conspicuous **tuft with white dots - White rump** - Breast violaceous grey - Bill (1.5 cm) straight & black - ♀: Lacks small crest or tuft - White throat - Rest of underparts speckled ... S. America, except Paraguay & Chile ... Captured in Villa Gesell, B. Aires   I

438) AMETHYST WOODSTAR
(Picaflor Amatista)
                    Calliphlox amethystina

6 cm - Wing noise like bumblebee - **Minute** - Similar to 439) - Lacks white rump of 437) - **Long deeply forked tail** - Back bronzed green - **Abdominal white spot** conspicuous on flight - Wide glossy **purple on throat** - White collar - Bill (1.2 cm) straight - ●: Dots on throat - White collar - Rest of **underparts** & tip of square tail **cinnamon** ... S. America, except Chile ... Migrant B- Humid forests in **Misiones**   II

439) SLENDER-TAILED WOODSTAR   (Picaflor Enano)   *Microstilbon burmeisteri*

6 cm - Looks like bumblebee - Hunts in flight - Allopatric with 438) - Also forked tail & **white belly** - **Throat** & gular tuft **purple** - Underparts & thighs whitish - Upperparts, flanks & lower belly green - ●: 5 cm - Tail tip, **postocular band & underparts cinnamon** ... Bolivia ... **Yungas**   III

(.) An individual of genus *Lophornis* was seen in Iguazu, Misiones. It might have been this species or, more probably, *L. magnifica*

440) GIANT HUMMINGBIRD
(Picaflor Gigante)   *Patagona gigas -2R*

16 cm - **Enormous** for the family - Flight different, slower - Dull plumage - Upperparts dull green -**Underparts cinnamon - Rump** & lower belly **whitish** - Bill (4 cm) almost straight ... Ecuador, Peru, Bolivia & Chile ... Prepuna, High Andean steppes & villages   III

TROGON: Striking colors - Relatives of Quetzal - Tame but not easy to see because passive - Erect posture - Continued series of clucks - Bills short & robust - Conspicuous eyelids - Pendant, square & graded tails - ♂♂: Coverts finely vermiculated with black & white - Faces & chins black - (3 species)

441) BLACK-THROATED TROGON
(Surucuá Amarillo)   *Trogon rufus*

24 cm - Upperparts & breast metallic green (brown in ♀) - Rest of **underparts yellow** - Undertail barred black & white... From Honduras, except Chile ... Medium & low strata in humid forests of **Misiones**   II

442) SURUCUA TROGON
(Surucuá Común)   *Trogon surrucura*

24 cm - Accelerated repetition of flute-like calls - **Hood & breast metallic blue** - Dark green back - Rest of **underparts red** - Outer rectrices & **undertail white**, not barred - ●: **Dark grey** - **Underparts rosy** ... Brazil & Paraguay... High & medium strata in humid forests of NE   IV

443) BLUE-CROWNED TROGON
(Surucuá Aurora)   *Trogon curucui*

24 cm - Resembles allopatric 442) - Conspicuous **black & white barring in outer rectrices & undertail** - ♀: Resembles ♀ 442) - Tail grey barred like ♂ ... Colombia, Ecuador, Brazil, Peru, Bolivia & Paraguay ... **Yungas**   III

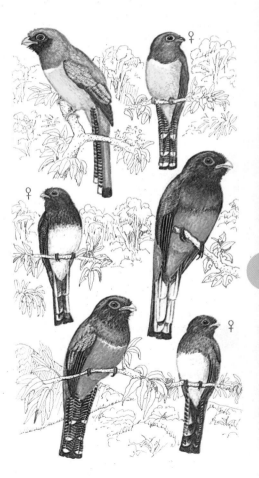

Fam. Alcedinidae, see page 36

KINGFISHERS: *Perch high near water - Passive - Fish by diving - Large heads with small crest s- Bills straight & pointed - Complete white collars - Rounded wings - Undertail barred - (3 species)*

444) RINGED KINGFISHER
(Martín Pescador Grande)
Ceryle torquata -2R

36 cm - Loud rattle in flight - Hovers - **Head & back sky blue grey** - Underwing & undertail coverts white - Rest of underparts - ♀: Breast like back separated from rest of ´rufous underparts by white line - Underwing coverts rufous ... From Mexico - URUGUAY ... Wetlands   IV

445)AMAZON KINGFISHER
(Martín Pescador Mediano)
Chloroceryle amazona

26 cm - Bill rather long - Head & back glossy dark green - **Coverts without white dots** - Rufous breast - **Flanks striated** - Rest of underparts white - ♀: Green half collar... From Mexico, except Chile - URUGUAY ... Wetlands   III

446) GREEN KINGFISHER
(Martín Pescador Chico)
Chloroceryle americana

17 cm - Like a small 445) - **White dots in all coverts** - Barring in underparts of tail more conspicuous - **Flanks spotted** - ♀: Throat cinnamon - Pectoral collar [& vental half collar] green ... From N. America - URUGUAY ... Wetlands IV

Fam. Momotidae, see page 36

447) RUFOUS MOTMOT
(Yeruvá)   *Baryphthengus ruficapillus*

38 cm - Solitary - Crepuscular - Passive-
More heard than seen - Loud & deep
buuu & other calls - Long graded tail,
pendant, which waggles - **Green -
Rufous crown - Black mask** - Ventral cinnamon patch - Often a pair of
black spots on breast ... S. America,
except Venezuela, Guianas & Chile ...
Low & medium strata in humid forests of
Misiones   III

448) BLUE-CROWNED MOTMOT
(Burgo)   *Momotus momota*

40 cm - Semiterrestrial - Allopatric with
447) - Guttural *burg..*, profound *hú..
dudú* & other calls - **Black crown** -
Lacks rufous - Black mask circled with
sky blue - Also pectoral spots - **Tail
ends in two rectrices**, with shaft
partially bare, **like rackets** - Belly &
lower belly greenish ochre ... From
Mexico, except Chile ... Low strata in
humid forests of NW   II

Fam. Ramphastidae, see page 36

449) SPOT-BILLED TOUCANET
(Arasarí Chico)*Selenidera maculirostris*

30 cm - Hidden, unlike other toucans -
Deep low & flute-like call like a toad -
Large hood, including upper back &
breast **black** - Rest of **upperparts olive** - Green ocular patch - Auriculars &
lower belly yellow - Undertail coverts
red- Greenish **bill with black lines -
♀: Different - Chestnut hood** ...
Brazil & Paraguay ... Low & medium
strata, often in "palmito" groves in humid
forests of **Misiones**   II

163

450) SAFFRON TOUCANET
(Arasarí Banana) *Baillonius bailloni*

33 cm - Passive - Acrobatic - Groups -
Upperparts olive - Rump & periocular red - **Underparts** & iris **yellow** - Bill greenish with red base ... Brazil & Paraguay ... Humid forests of **Misiones**   II

451) CHESTNUT-EARED ARACARI
Fajado) (Arasarí *Pteroglossus castanotis*

37 cm - Sharp & metallic call - Large **hood,** even breast, **black** with chestnut patches - Rest of **underparts yellow with red band** - Back & tail blackish green - Red rump - Black bill with yellow marks ... S. America, except Venezuela, Guianas & Chile ... Humid forests & capueras of **Misiones**   III

452) RED-BREASTED TOUCAN
(Tucán Pico Verde)
Ramphastos dicolorus

45 cm - Noisy groups - Nasal *aa* - Tame - Upperparts & thighs black - Periocular reddish - From throat to **breast yellow with diffuse orange zone** - Rump & **rest of underparts red** - Bill & iris yellowish olivaceous ... Brazil & Paraguay ... Forests   IV

453) TOCO TOUCAN
(Tucán Grande) *Ramphastos toco* -2R

53 cm - Noisy groups - Conspicuous - Loud & nasal *krroc* similar to the Caracara's (192) - **Black - Rump & bib white** - Orange periocular patch - Undertail coverts red - **Large orange & yellow bill with black tip** - J: Bill without black tip ... Guianas, Brazil, Paraguay & Bolivia ... Forests & capueras in NW & NE   IV

*PUFFBIRDS & NUNLET: Very tame & passive - Crepuscular - Fine whistles - **Large heads** - Narrow pendant tails - **Thick hooked bills** - Look like kingfishers -(4 species)*

454) RUSTY-BREASTED NUNLET

(Chacurú Chico)   *Nonnula rubecula*
13 cm - Amongst vegetation - Dull plumage - Upperparts olivaceous brown - **Two white spots**, one loral & one malar - **Throat & breast cinnamon**, turned whitish on lower belly -Eyelid white - Black bill not too thick ... Venezuela, Brazil, Peru & Paraguay ... Humid forests & capueras in **Misiones**   II

455) SPOT-BACKED PUFFBIRD

(Durmilí)   *Nystalus maculatus*
18 cm - In the open - Melancholic *pree.pree..pree..* - Upperparts brown undulated ochre - **Complete orange ochre collar** - Tail barred ochre & black- Pale eyebrow - **Underparts white with black striations** - Yellow iris ... Brazil, Paraguay & Bolivia ... Forests & Chaqueño type savannas   III

456) WHITE-EARED PUFFBIRD

(Chacurú Cara Negra) *Nystalus chacuru*
18 cm - In the open - Complex & musical morning duet - Trisyllabic call - Upperparts chestnut undulated black - Black tail barred ochre - Eyebrow & **nape band white - Auricular patch white surrounded with black** - Underparts ochraceous - **Bill deep rose** ... Brazil, Paraguay, Bolivia & Peru ... Humid forests & capueras in NE   III

457) WHITE-NECKED PUFFBIRD

(Chacurú Grande)
        Notharchus macrorhynchus
23 cm - On high branches - Short & heavy flight - **Upperparts black** - Eyebrow & **complete collar** (even cheeks) **white** - Black **pectoral band** - Rest of **underparts cinnamon** - Red iris ... From Mexico, except Chile... Humid forests & capueras in **Misiones**   II

*COLAPTES: In open places, **terrestrial** or **in rocky** habitats, except 462) - Do not drum - Loud calls- Wide **pale rumps** - Shafts of remiges yellow - Red malar in ♂♂ - black in ♀♀ , except 460) - (5 species)*

458) FIELD FLICKER
(Carpintero Campestre)
Colaptes campestris (.)

28 cm - Slightly arboreal - Strident & rapid *kuik..* - Also *wit..wit* - Barred dorsally black & whitish - **Face & breast golden yellow** - Crown & nape black - Throat whitish - Rest of underparts barred black - Bill 3.5 cm ... Brazil, Paraguay & Bolivia - URUGUAY ... Savannas, grasslands & rural areas   V

459) ANDEAN FLICKER
(Carpintero Andino) *Colaptes rupicola*

31 cm - Tame - **Flocks** -Rock dweller - Not arboreal - Noisy -Loud & repeated *yek* - Also loud trill - Dull plumage - Looks like 460) - Allopatric - **Bill** (4.5 cm) **long** - **Grey crown** - Barring on upperparts like 458) - **Underparts ochraceous, dotted on breast** - Yellowish iris ... Peru & Bolivia ... Prepuna, puna & **High Andean steppes** in NW
IV

460) CHILEAN FLICKER
(Carpintero Pitío)   *Colaptes pitius*

29 cm - Tame - Groups - Arboreal - Perches - Loud *peet..eo* - Also *wit..wit* in duet - Dull plumage - **Grey crown** - Barring on upperparts somewhat dark - Ochraceous face - **WIthout malar mark** - **Underparts barred** black & white - Ivory iris - Bill 3.5 cm ... Chile ... **Araucano Forest** & nearby areas in SW   III

(.) The southern form *C. campestroides* is no longer considered a separate species

461) GOLDEN-BREASTED WOODPECKER
(Carpintero-Real Común)
Colaptes melanolaimus (.) -3R
23 cm - More arboreal than 458) - Loud & spaced *keep..* - Also *ki..errr* - Black crown - **Red small crest on nape** - Back black barred yellowish - **White face** - Red malar continued black - Throat striated black - Yellow breast with black dots - Rest of underparts whitish dotted & barred - Bill longer than in 462)- ♀: Black malar ... Bolivia & Paraguay - URUGUAY ... Forests, savannas, plantations & rural areas   V

462) GREEN-BARRED WOODPECKER
(Carpintero-Real Verde)
Colaptes melanochloros-2R
23 cm - Resembles 461) - Similar call - Very arboreal - **Greenish** - Back & lower belly barred - Red **malar without black** - Breast (not yellow) with dots - Shorter bill ... Brazil & Paraguay ... Edges of forests in NW (I) & NE   III

463) BLOND-CRESTED WOODPECKER
(Carpintero Cabeza Amarilla)
Celeus flavescens
23 cm - Resembles 464) - Allopatric - Weak drumming - Rump, **hood & erectile crest yellow** - **Back** & wings **black** barred whitish - Red malar - **Underparts** uniform **black** - ♀: Malar striated... Brazil & Paraguay ... Humid forests & capueras in **Misiones**   III

464) PALE-CRESTED WOODPECKER
(Carpintero Cabeza Pajiza)
Celeus lugubris
23 cm - Rump, **hood & ruffled crest straw colored** - **Back** dark **brown** (not black as in 463) barred ochraceous- Rufous bars on remiges & uppertail coverts - Black face - Red malar - **Underparts** uniform dark **brown** - ♀: **Malar & face dark brown** ... Brazil, Paraguay & Bolivia ... Forests, savannas & palm groves in NE   III

(.) Often considered conspecific with 462)

167

*PICULUS: Drum - Smaller than Colaptes - Apparently all allopatric - **Backs golden olive** - **Underparts barred** - Red malar - (3 species)*

465) GOLDEN-GREEN WOODPECKER
(Carpintero Dorado Común)
Picuius chrysochloros

21 cm - **Crown & small crest on nape red** - Olive ocular band - Throat & long malar line (continued along neck) yellow - Underparts barred yellow & olive- Underwing cinnamon - **Ivory iris -** ♀: Without red - **Olive crown** ... From Panama, except Chile ... Forests & savannas of **Chaqueño** type   IV

466) WHITE-BROWED WOODPECKER
(Carpintero Dorado Verdoso)
Piculus aurulentus

21 cm - Resembles 465) - Similar pattern, but also **yellow eyebrow** - Underparts olive barred whitish (seems darker) - Underwing blackish barred cinnamon - Chestnut iris - ♀: Olive crown, but nape & malar spot red ... Brazil & Paraguay ... Medium & high strata in humid forests of NE   II

467) GOLDEN-OLIVE WOODPECKER   (Carpintero Dorado Gris)   *Piculus rubiginosus*

20 cm - **Wide plumbeous forehead- Hindcrown & nape red - White face** - Throat very much striated black- Underparts barred whitish & black - Underwing yellowish - ♀: Lacks red malar ... From Mexico along W to Bolivia... Yungas   III

468) YELLOW-FRONTED WOODPECKER
(Carpintero Arcoiris)

Melanerpes flavifrons

17 cm - Striking plumage - Often hunts in flight - Somewhat frugivorous - **Forehead,** eyelid **& throat golden yellow-**Ocular band & back bluish black - Crown, nape & **ventral patch red** - Lower back & rump white - Olivaceous breast - Flanks barred - ♀: Crown & nape black ... Brazil & Paraguay ... High strata in humid forests of **Misiones**   III

469) WHITE-FRONTED WOODPECKER
(Carpintero del Cardón)

Trichopicus cactorum

16 cm - Sometimes in groups - Hunts in the air & eats fruit - Loud *wip* - **Black back - Wide forehead** & nape **white-** Red in crown - **Wings,** flanks, rump **& tail barred** - Yellow throat - Breast ochraceous grey - ♀: Without red ... Brazil, Paraguay, Bolivia & Peru - [URUGUAY] ... Cacti fields, forests & savannas of **Chaqueño** type   IV

470) CHECKERED WOODPECKER
(Carpintero Bataraz Chico)

Picoides mixtus -3R

15 cm - Tame - Audible & rapid drumming- Climbs branches, not trunks - **Dappled - Crown striated** - Red nape- Eyebrow & malar whitish - Brown auricular - **Back & wings spotted** (almost without bars) **- Tail very much V-barred** - Underparts striated - ♀: Lacks red ... Brazil, Paraguay & Bolivia - URUGUAY ... Medium height in forests, savannas & plantations   III

471) STRIPED WOODPECKER
(Carpintero Bataraz Grande)

Picoides lignarius

16 cm - Very similar to 470) - Different habitat - **Crown** almost **without striations - Back barred** - Wings spotted & barred **- Tail with few white bars** - Ventral striations thicker & conspicuous... Bolivia & Chile ... **Araucano Forest**   II

Memorize the symbols

VENILIORNIS: Small - Olivaceous - Underparts barred (except 472) - More red on crowns than Picoides - ♀♀ Lack red.

472) SMOKY-BROWN WOODPECKER
(Carpintero Oliva Oscuro)
Veniliornis fumigatus
15 cm - **Olivaceous brown,** not barred - **Red crown striated black** - [Slight red edges on upperparts] - ♀: Brown crown ... From Mexico, along W, except Chile ... Humid forests in **Jujuy** (Calilegua NP)   II

473) WHITE-SPOTTED WOODPECKER
(Carpintero Oliva Manchado)
Veniliornis spilogaster
14 cm - Harsh *cheek..* & *cherr..* - Insectivorous & frugivorous - Black crown striated red - **Olive back barred** ochraceous - Conspicuous **whitish eyebrow & malar** - Throat striated - **Underparts dappled** - ♀: Blackish crown with white dots ... Brazil & Paraguay - URUGUAY ... Damp forests in NE   IV

474) DOT-FRONTED WOODPECKER
(Carpintero Oliva Yungueño)
Veniliornis frontalis (.)
15 cm - Very much like 475) - Allopatric- Forehead brown dotted white - Red crown & nape - **Back golden olive** lightly barred white - **Coverts dotted white** - Underparts blackish barred white - ♀: All crown brown with white dots... Bolivia ... Yungas   III

475) LITTLE WOODPECKER
(Carpintero Oliva Chico)
Veniliornis passerinus
14 cm - Slightly different to 474) - Wider forehead - **Only nape red - Uniform back** - ♀: Brown crown without red or dots ... S. America, except Chile ... Forests in NE   III

170   (.) Sometimes considered conspecific with 475)

PICUMNUS: Tame - Active - Little or non climbers - Often perch on horizontal branches - Audible & fast drumming - Low & medium strata - **Minute** *- Short bills-* Black caps dotted white - Wing bars pale - **Black tails with three white bands,** not *used as support -* ♂♂: *Wide red foreheads-(4 species)*

476) MOTTLED PICULET
(Carpinterito Ocráceo)
Picumnus nebulosus

9 cm - Slight small crest - Brown back - **Underparts ochraceous striated** black (not barred) ... Brazil - URUGUAY... Bamboo thickets on borders of forests & capueras of NE   I

477) OCELLATED PICULET
(Carpinterito Manchado)
Picumnus dorbignyanus

8 cm - Allopatric with 476) & 478) - **Back** brownish grey **spotted white - Underparts white scaled black** ... Peru & Bolivia ... Yungas in **Salta**   II

478) OCHRE-COLLARED PICULET
(Carpinterito Cuello Canela)
Picumnus temminckii

8 cm - *Wirrr* like cricket - Slight small crest - Brown back - **Face & neck cinnamon - Underparts white barred black** ... Paraguay & Brazil ... Humid forests & capueras in NE   III

479) WHITE-BARRED PICULET
(Carpinterito Común)
Picumnus cirratus -3R (.)

8 cm - Descending *wirrr* - **Not in humid forests** - Resembles 478) even in **underparts barring** - Lacks cinnamon neck - [Slight & pale dorsal barring] ... Paraguay & Bolivia ... Forests & savannas, especially of **Chaqueño** type   III

(.) 477) & 478) could also be races of 479)

171

480) WHITE WOODPECKER
(Carpintero Blanco)
Leuconerpes candidus
24 cm - Groups - Rather high flight in open spaces - Often hunt on wing - Frugivorous - Loud & repeated *trrrr* - Unmistakable - **White** - Upper back, wings & tail black - Periocular, nape & belly yellow - ♀: White nape ... Suriname, Brazil, Paraguay & Bolivia - URUGUAY ... Forests, savannas, palm groves & plantations   III

DROYCOPUS: Look like Campephilus - Fast drumming - Climb high - Black - Conspicuous crests (not hoods) & malar red - Whitish line from bill to shoulder - ♀♀ : Lack red malar - Front of crest (except forehead) red not black as Campephilus ♀♀ - (3 species)

481) HELMETED WOODPECKER
(Carpintero Cara Canela)
Dryocopus galeatus
27 cm - Smaller than 482) - **Cinnamon forehead & throat - Face with fine black & cinnamon lines** - Cinnamon wingband & underwing coverts - Wide **ochraceous rump** - Underparts barred black & ochraceous - Brown iris - Ivory bill .... Brazil & Paraguay ... Humid forests in **Misiones** - Perhaps in danger of extinction   II

482) LINEATED WOODPECKER
(Carpintero Garganta Estriada)
Dryocopus lineatus [2R] (.)
30 cm - Probably allopatric with 483) - [Two white dorsal lines not joined, commoner & more conspicuous in NW]- Plumbeous face & **throat somewhat striated**, which 485) lacks - White wing-band - Black breast - Rest of **underparts** whitish **barred** black - Yellow iris - Dark horn colored bill - Pale mandible - ♀: Forehead & malar black... From Mexico, except Chile ... Forests & capueras in NW & NE   IV

483) BLACK-BODIED WOODPECKER
(Carpintero Negro) *Dryocopus schulzi*
28 cm - Resembles 482) - White lines on neck [& upper back] - **Underparts black lack bars** - Face & throat greyish - Chestnut iris - Bill horn colored ... Paraguay & Bolivia ... Forests & savannas of **Chaqueño** type   II

(.) The form *erythrops,* without dorsal lines, has been considered a separate species

Reread characters of genus with each species

*CAMPEPHILUS: Look like Dryocopus -
Slower noisy drumming - Climb high -
Black - Red hoods that includes necks,
except 485) - ♂♂: Black & cream oval spot
on cheeks & ivory bills, except 487) - Yellow
iris - (4 species)*

484) CREAM-BACKED WOODPECKER
(Carpintero Lomo Blanco)
Campephilus leucopogon -2R
28 cm - **Creamy dorsal triangle** (V-shaped when present in 483) - **Underparts uniform black** - Cinnamon underwing coverts - ♀: Front of crest black - Cream & black malar ... Brazil, Paraguay & Bolivia - URUGUAY ... Savannas & forests IV

485) CRIMSON-CRESTED WOODPECKER
(Carpintero Garganta Negra)
Campephilus melanoleucus
28 cm - Resembles 482) - **Red head** without plumbeous face - **White line on sides of neck joined in V shape on upper back** - Black breast and throat lacking striations -Rest of underparts barred ochraceous -**Underwing coverts white** - ♀: Front of crest black - **White line starting like moustache**... From Panama, except Chile ... Forests in NW & NE II

486) ROBUST WOODPECKER
(Carpintero Grande)
Campephilus robustus
31 cm - Looks like 485) - **Large red hood until breast - Cream triangle** (not V) **on upper back** continued on cinnamon rump - Underparts from breast barred black & ochraceous - Underwing barred cinnamon - ♀: **Black forehead** - Cream malar surrounded by black ... Brazil & Paraguay ... Humid forests & capueras in **Misiones** III

487) MAGELLANIC WOODPECKER
(Carpintero Gigante)
Campephilus magellanicus
36 cm - **Allopatric with other black woodpeckers - Red hood** - White patch on remiges - Black bill - ♀: **Black hood** with curled crest - Red face ... Chile ... **Araucano Forest** III

173

488) GREAT RUFOUS WOODCREEPER
(Trepador Gigante)
Xiphocolaptes major -2R

30 cm - Somewhat terrestrial - Series of descending notes - **Chestnut** - Dark tail- Underparts paler - Lores & periocular black - **Thick** slightly curved ivory **bill** ... Brazil, Paraguay & Bolivia... **Chaqueño** type forests   IV

489) WHITE-THROATED WOODCREEPER
(Trepador Garganta Blanca)
Xiphocolaptes albicollis

27 cm - Call somewhat similar to that of 488) - Resembles 490) - Almost without forehead - Black **bill** (4 cm) **long**er & higher - Brown - Crown & nape striated-Uniform wings - **White throat** lacks striations - Striated breast & barred belly inconspicuous - Chestnut iris ... Brazil & Paraguay ... Forests in NE   III

490) PLANALTO WOODCREEPER
(Trepador Oscuro)
Dendrocolaptes platyrostris

25 cm - Descending series of *week..* - More conspicuous forehead than 489) - **Bill** (3.5 cm) **shor**ter & straighter - Wings with slight striations - **Throat slightly scaled** - Brown iris ... Brazil & Paraguay ... Forests in NE   III

491) BLACK-BANDED WOODCREEPER
(Trepador Colorado)
Dendrocolaptes picumnus

25 cm - Smaller than sympatric 488) - Crown & upperback striated - Upperparts chestnut - **Throat scaled ochraceous**, not white- Underparts cinnamon inconspicuously striated & barred - Bill (3.8 cm) as long as head ... From Guatemala, except Chile ... Forests in NW   II

NE   NO

492) SCIMITAR-BILLED WOODCREEPER
(Chinchero Grande)*Drymornis bridgesii*

26 cm - Rather terrestrial - Repeated & strident *wruis..*, accelerating - Small crest - Conspicuous **white eyebrow & malar band** - Scaled underparts - **Bill** (8 cm) **very long** & curved... Brazil - URUGUAY ... Chaqueño type forests & plantations   IV

LEPIDOCOLAPTES: Medium size climbers - Alike - Not very long thin curved bills - Backs brown to chestnut - Crowns & napes blackish dotted with ochre - (3 species)

493) NARROW-BILLED WOODCREEPER
(Chinchero Chico)
Lepidocolaptes angustirostris-4R

18 cm - Series of descending *peah* & bisyllabic *peah huy* - **Wide eyebrow** & throat **white** - Lightly scaled on pale underparts ... Brazil, Paraguay & Bolivia - URUGUAY ... Forests in gallery & plantations   IV

494) SCALED WOODCREEPER
(Chinchero Escamado)
Lepidocolaptes squamatus

17 cm - Call drier and sharper than in 493) - Probably allopatric - **Underparts** more **contrasted, dark & scaled** - Less conspicuous white eyebrow - **White throat** more conspicuous ... Brazil & Paraguay...Humid forests in NE   III

495) LESSER WOODCREEPER
(Chinchero Enano)
Lepidocolaptes fuscus

15 cm - Series of rapid *teek..* like laughter, louder than in 499) - Dots on crown become **striations on upper back** - **Eyebrow & throat ochraceous** - **Scaled pale underparts** less conspicuous than in 494) ... Brazil & Paraguay ... Humid forests in **Misiones**   II

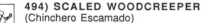

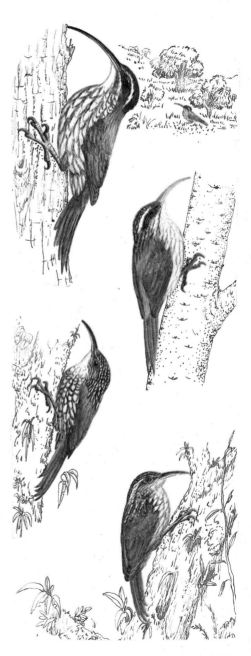

Fam. Dendrocolaptidae, see page 37

496) BLACK-BILLED SCYTHEBILL
(Picapalo Oscuro)
Campylorhamphus falcularius

19 cm - Brown - Unmistakable - **Extremely long & thin very curved black bill** (6.5 cm) used by turning head side ways - Striations on black crown continue although not so conspicuous on upper back & breast - Chestnut wings & tail ... Brazil & Paraguay ... Capueras in **Misiones** II

497) RED-BILLED SCYTHEBILL
(Picapalo Colorado)
Campylorhamphus trochilirostris

21 cm - Resembles 496) - Allopatric - More **rufous** - Similar **bill** even **long**er (8 cm) **reddish** ... From Panama, except Chile ... Forests & savannas of **Chaqueño** type III

498) PLAIN-BROWN WOODCREEPER
(Arapasú) *Dendrocincla fuliginosa*

19 cm - More heard than seen - Descending series of some 20 similar notes which lengthen - **Dull uniform** brown **coloration** - Looks like a thrush-Crown slightly striated - Rufous tail - Underparts a little paler - **Bill** (2.8 cm) **short** for this family ... From Honduras, except Chile ... Low strata in humid forests of **Misiones** II

499) OLIVACEOUS WOODCREEPER
(Tarefero) *Sittasomus griseicapillus -2R*

14 cm - Moves swiftly along vertical trunks - Separate & accelerating sharp whistles resembling those of 498) - Short & straight bill (1.5 cm) - Elegant - Seems **divided in two colors: anterior half olivaceous & rear** (including somewhat long tail) **rufous** - Ochre wingband ... From Mexico, except Chile ... Forests in NW & NE IV

176

GEOSITTA: *Terrestrial - Tame - Prefer walking or running - Alike - Dull plumage - Pale eyebrows- **Colored short tails & rufous on wings** conspicuous in flight - (6 species)*

500) RUFOUS-BANDED MINER
(Caminera Colorada)
Geositta rufipennis -5R

15 cm - **Short bill** - Back brownish, gre-yish, cinnamon or blackish, according to race - **Rufous tail** with subterminal black band - Underparts whitish or cinna-mon ... Bolivia & Chile ... High Andean steppes & high elevations   IV

501) CREAMY-RUMPED MINER
(Caminera Grande) *Geositta isabellina*

16 cm - Groups - *Feet.. feet..* in flight - **Long bill & wings** - Back brownish to cinnamon brown - **Black tail with wide base & outer rectrices ochraceous-** Underparts whitish ... Chile ... High Andean steppes, even snowed - (Laguna Horcones, Mendoza)   – II

502) COMMON MINER
(Caminera Común)
Geositta cunicularia -4R

14 cm - Trill - Flicks rear third of body - **Bill rather long, thin & somewhat curved** - Light striations on crown - Back brownish (ochraceous in NW) - **Black-ish tail with cinnamon base** - [Ochraceous auricular ending in dark line] - Conspicuous white eyebrow - Underparts whitish with **breast scaled...** Brazil, Bolivia, Peru & Chile - URUGUAY ... Open areas in Andes, Pat-agonia & pampas   IV

503) PUNA MINER
(Caminera Puneña) *Geositta punensis*

13 cm - Resembles Andean race of 502) - Even paler - **Does not flick rear third of body** -Call *twit* - **Bill short & strong- Underparts** uniform **whitish...** Peru, Bolivia & Chile ... High Andean steppes in NW   II

177

504) SHORT-BILLED MINER
(Caminera Patagónica)
Geositta antarctica

16 cm - Similar to the Common (502) - Larger - **Bill shorter & stronger** (as in 500) - **Wings** with cinnamon areas **lack rufous** - Tail like 502) but with outer rectrices (not only webs) ochraceous - **Underparts** ochraceous **with inconspicuous scales** ... Chile ... Patagonian steppes   III

505) SLENDER-BILLED MINER
(Caminera Picuda) *Geositta tenuirostris*

17 cm - **Resembles 507) with short** rufous **tail** & blackish tip - **Bill (3.5 cm) long,** thin **& curved** - Ochraceous underparts with slight pectoral striations... Peru & Bolivia ... High Andean & high elevations in NW - (El Infiernillo, Tucuman)   III

UPUCERTHIA: Similar to Geositta in coloring, behavior, habitat & distribution (except 508) - Long bills & tails - Lack distinctive base of tails - (5 species)

506) BUFF-BREASTED EARTHCREEPER
(Bandurrita Andina)
Upucerthia validirostris-2R

19 cm - Similar to 507) - Erect tail - **Bill (4 cm) very curved** - Chestnut tail with central rectrices brown - **Underparts** ochraceous **without scaling** ... Bolivia... High Andean steppes & high elevations   III

507) SCALE-THROATED EARTHCREEPER
(Bandurrita Común)
Upucerthia dumetaria -3R

20 cm - Sings on bushes - Repeated *feet* while walking - Does not raise tail - Curved bill (3 cm) - Underparts whitish with conspicuous **scaled breast** ... Peru, Bolivia & Chile - [URUGUAY]... Southern population is Migrant C - High Andean shrubby & Patagonian steppes, & high elevations   IV

508) CHACO EARTHCREEPER
(Bandurrita Chaqueña)
Upucerthia certhioides -2R

16 cm - More heard than seen - Often hidden in thickets - Repeated & loud *cheep.., teeo* & *twit* - **Wings & tail** (which does not raise) **chestnut** - Conspicuous **white throat** contrasted with rest of underparts - Bill (2.5 cm) not very long, almost straight ... Paraguay ... Forests, savannas & hilly areas of **Chaqueño** type   IV

509) ROCK EARTHCREEPER
(Bandurrita Cola Castaña)
Upucerthia andaecola

18 cm - Very similar to 510) - Bill (3 cm) somewhat curved - **Rufous tail without black** - Ochraceous eyebrow - **Underparts** more **scaled** ... Bolivia ... High Andean steppes in NW   II

510) STRAIGHT-BILLED EARTHCREEPER
(Bandurrita Pico Recto)
Upucerthia ruficauda

18 cm - Climbs & quickly moves about rocks - Cricket-like *trrr* - Similar to 509) & 511) - Back brownish cinnamon - **Tail** (less conspicuous than in 511) **blackish with** outer webs of outer rectrices **rufous** - White eyebrow - White on throat turning cinnamon with slight striation in rest of underparts - **Bill** (3 cm) **straight** ... Peru, Bolivia & Chile ... High Andean & Patagonian steppes   III

511) BAND-TAILED EARTHCREEPER   (Bandurrita
Patagónica)   *Eremobius phoenicurus*
16 cm - ♀ - Terrestrial - While walking flicks erect tail - Often in bushes - Call & appearance of 510) - Shorter **bill** (2.5 cm) also **straight** - Back brownish - **Tail rufous & black** (all outer rectrices with rufous base) - Conspicuous **white behind eye** - Ochraceous auricular - Underparts like 510) ... Patagonian & shrubby steppes   II

179

CINCLODES: Tame - *Look like Geositta
Longer tails without colorful base -* **Near
water** *- Terrestrial - Low trill - Most raise
tail - Alike - (7 species)*

512) BLACKISH CINCLODES
(Remolinera Negra)
Cinclodes antarcticus -2R
18 cm - Almost uniform **blackish** - Only
one **without eyebrow or wingband**
(very slight in Malvinas race) -
Ochraceous spots on throat ... Chile ...
Southern **seacoasts**   III

513) DARK-BELLIED CINCLODES
(Remolinera Araucana)
Cinclodes patagonicus-2R
18 cm - Flicks non erect tail - Strong bill
(2 cm) - **Upperparts blackish** brown -
Cinnamon wingband - Conspicuous
eyebrow & malar white - Throat
somewhat spotted - **Dark underparts**
striated white on breast & belly ...
Chile... Lakes & streams in W Patagonia
& seashores in Tierra del Fuego   V

514) WHITE-WINGED CINCLODES
(Remolinera Castaña)
Cinclodes atacamensis -2R
20 cm - Long bill - Rufous back - **Wingband** (always visible), eyebrow, throat
& tip of outer rectrices white -
Underparts grey turned chestnut on
lower belly ... Peru & Chile ... Andean &
high elevations streams   IV

515) OLROG'S CINCLODES
(Remolinera Chocolate)
Cinclodes olrogi
16 cm - ♀ - Smaller than 514) - Cinnamon
outer rectrices - Resembles 518) (perhaps conspecific) & northern races of
517) - Allopatric - Chestnut back -
Wingband whitish ochre - White
eyebrow conspicuous behind eye -
Underparts cinnamon brown slightly
striated on breast turned whitish on
lower belly ... Streams in high
elevations- **(Pampa de Achala,** Cordoba)   IV

516) CHESTNUT-WINGED CINCLODES
(Remolinera Serrana) *Cinclodes comechingonus* 16 cm - ♂ - Resembles 517) (perhaps conspecific) - Sympatric in Winter - Raises tail - Brown back - **Wingband** & tip of outer rectrices **rufous** - Ochraceous eyebrow - Base of mandible yellow more conspicuous in J... Streams in high elevations & nearby areas - (**Pampa de Achala**, Cordoba)
IV

517) BAR-WINGED CINCLODES
(Remolinera Común)
Cinclodes fuscus -3R
16 cm - Does not raise but flicks tail - Bill somewhat short - Brown upperparts - Ochraceous eyebrow - Whitish malar - **Cinnamon wingband** - Spotted throat- Breast ashy grey, paler in lower belly - Tip of outer rectrices ochraceous- **Northern races:** raise tail - **Upperparts chestnut** - Underparts paler - Flanks cinnamon brown - **Whitish ochre wingband** - Tip of outer rectrices cinnamon ... From Venezuela along W - URUGUAY ... Southern race Migrant C- Andean & Patagonian streams & lakes
V

518) GRAY-FLANKED CINCLODES
(Remolinera Chica) *Cinclodes oustaleti-2R* 16 cm - Upperparts like 513) - Smaller - Thin bill (1.5 cm) - Whitish eyebrow & malar less conspicuous - **Cinnamon wingband** - Tip of outer rectrices brown, not ochraceous as in 517) - Underparts with lower belly whitish like 515) (not dark as in 513) ... Chile ... Andean streams & southern coasts
III

519) SHARP-TAILED STREAMCREEPER
(Macuquito) *Lochmias nematura-2R* 13 cm - In marshes - Tame, hidden or exposed - Behavior of *Cinclodes* - Loud *see..seek* & short trill *trrrt* - Curved bill - **Blackish brown - Short tail** black - Dotted postocular eyebrow - **Underparts spotted with white** (less so in NW) ... From Panama, except Chile - URUGUAY ... Thickets & rocky rivers of humid forests in NW & NE
II

181

520) RUFOUS HORNERO
(Hornero)　　　*Furnarius rufus-3R*

18 cm - Argentina's National Bird - **Sings in duet with different notes- Nest of mud** like little oven, placed in a variety of places - Fairly terrestrial - Walks elegantly - Back brown or chestnut - Inconspicuous cinnamon wingband - **Rufous tail** - Whitish throat- Rest of underparts ochraceous or cinnamon grey ... Brazil, Paraguay & Bolivia - URUGUAY ... Various habitats & inhabited areas　　　　　　VI

521) CRESTED HORNERO
(Hornerito Copetón) *Furnarius cristatus*

15 cm - Resembles 520) - Similar behavior & calls - Also repeated *prrr* - When alarmed: *fuit* - Conspicuous **crest** - Underparts more cinnamon ... Paraguay ... Forests of **Chaqueño** type　　　　　　III

522) BROWN CACHOLOTE
(Cacholote Castaño)
　　　　　　　Pseudoseisura lophotes

23 cm - Tame - Acrobatic - Rather terrestrial - **Noisy** - Sings duets - Flight slow & undulating - Enormous nest - Strong bill - Conspicuous **dark crest** - **Chestnut back -** Rump & tail rufous - Mandible & iris ivory ... Brazil, Paraguay & Bolivia ... URUGUAY ... Savannas, plantations & inhabited areas　　　IV

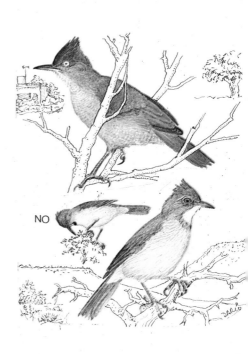

523) WHITE-THROATED CACHOLOTE
(Cacholote Pardo)
　　　　　　Pseudoseisura gutturalis-2R

21 cm - ξ - Voice less strident than 522)- Looks & behavior similar - Less tame - Smaller **crest brownish grey,** not chestnut - Incomplete white eyelid - Blackish tail - **White throat** separated from ochraceous grey underparts by **black collar** ... Andean & Patagonian shrubby areas　　　　　　III

NO

182

524) CANEBRAKE GROUNDCREEPER
(Tacuarero)
Clibanornis dendrocolaptoides
20 cm - Loud & harsh *chk.. chk..* - Looks like 560) - Chestnut back - Crown & long tail rufous - Pale eyebrow wider behind eye - **White throat surrounded by black dots** - Underparts grey - Flanks & undertail coverts brown ... Brazil & Paraguay... Low & medium heights in bamboo thickets near water in **Misiones** II

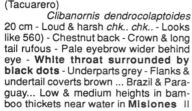

525) WHITE-EYED FOLIAGE-GLEANER
(Ticotico Ojo Blanco)
Automolus leucophthalmus
18 cm - Resembles 524) - Tame - Noisy *teeli.. teeli* even in flight & loud *cheek..cheereek* - Scraps leaves on ground - Chestnut small crest & back - Underwing coverts orange - **White on throat** turning brownish in undertail coverts & flanks - **White Iris** ... Brazil & Paraguay ... Low strata in humid forests & capueras of **Misiones** III

526) CURVE-BILLED REEDHAUNTER
(Pajonalera Pico Curvo)
Limnornis curvirostris
16 cm - In marshes - Reclusive - Curious- Loud & repeated *chek* - Chubby - Strong & long **curved bill** - Chestnut back - **Tail short rounded & rufous - Wide** postocular **eyebrow** & throat **white** - Underparts whitish ... Brazil - URUGUAY... **Reed beds** - (Magdalena, B. Aires) III

527) STRAIGHT-BILLED REEDHAUNTER
(Pajonalera Pico Recto)
Limnoctites rectirostris
15 cm - In marshes - Often hidden - Series of *tee..* accelerated to a trill - Climbs stems of marsh plants - **Straight very long bill** (2.8 cm) - Back olivaceous brown - Coverts rufous - **Pointed rufous tail** - Thin postocular line & underparts white - [Reddish iris] - J: More ochraceous ... Brazil - URUGUAY ... *Eryngium* beds - (Benavidez, B. Aires) I

528) SULPHUR-BEARDED SPINETAIL
(Curutié Ocráceo)
Cranioleuca sulphurifera
15 cm - In marshes - Tame - Reclusive - Noisy - Call *cheek.. cheek.. cheereek.. cheek* ended in a trill - **Dull** & pale **plumage** - Rufous on coverts - Pointed cinnamon tail (not as 526) - Thin white eyebrow - **Yellow throat spot** - Greyish underparts slightly striated on breast - Base of mandible & iris yellowish ... Brazil - URUGUAY ... Reed beds   III

529) YELLOW-THROATED SPINETAIL
(Curutié Colorado)   *Certhiaxis cinnamomea*
13 cm - In marshes - Tame - Restless - Repeated & loud *tee..* & gurgle similar to that of 548) - **Chestnut back** - Rufous wings with black tip of remiges - Short rounded **rufous tail** - Central rectrices dark - Yellow chin - Eyebrow & **underparts whitish** ... From Venezuela along the E - URUGUAY ... Reed beds   IV

530) WREN-LIKE RUSHBIRD
(Junquero) *Phleocryptes melanops -2R*
13 cm - In marshes - Restless - Tame - **Loud tapping & harsh chirp frog-like** - Chubby - **Short tail - Back striated** black, grey, chestnut & whitish- Patch on coverts & wingband cinnamon - Conspicuous **whitish eyebrow-** Underparts ochraceous ...   Bordering countries & Peru - URUGUAY ... **Reed beds**   V

531) BAY-CAPPED WREN-SPINETAIL
(Espartillero Enano)
Spartonoica maluroides
13 cm - In marshes - Reclusive - Low flight, after hovering for an instant dives into rush bed - Repeated shriek - Slender - Slightly long tail graded in points - **Wide rufous forehead - Upperparts striated black** - Eyebrow & underparts whitish - J: Lacks rufous forehead ... Brazil - URUGUAY ... Reed beds & nearby vegetation   III

532) DES MURS' WIRETAIL
(Colilarga)
Sylviorthorhynchus desmursii
22 cm - Tame - Reclusive - Continuous
call - Small body (7 cm) - **Two very long
& thin rectrices** (15 cm) & two shorter
ones - Somewhat long thin bill - Chestnut
forehead - Cinnamon brown back ...
Chile ... Bamboo thickets & thick under-
growth in Araucano Forest & steppes in
Santa Cruz   III

533) THORN-TAILED RAYADITO
(Rayadito)   *Aphrastura spinicauda*
14 cm - Very active - Tame - Pecks leaves
& bark - Acrobatic - Hops up trunks -
Sometimes terrestrial - Shrill & continu-
ous *teeteetee..* & other calls - **Pointed
tail** - Colorful plumage - Black head-
Long & wide cinnamon eyebrow -
Rufous rump - Whitish throat ... Chile ...
Araucano Forest   VI

**534) STRIPE-CROWNED
SPINETAIL**
(Curutié Blanco)*Cranioleuca pyrrhophia*
14 cm - Restless - Tame - Acrobatic -
Hangs from and climbs thin twigs without
tail support - Various sharp trills - Con-
structs double entrance roosting cham-
bers - **Crown striated** black - Brown
back - Conspicuous **rufous on coverts** - **Wide eyebrow & underparts
white** - Brown tail in points - Outer
rectrices rufous ... Brazil, Paraguay &
Bolivia - URUGUAY ... Chaqueño type
forests   IV

535) OLIVE SPINETAIL
(Curutié Oliváceo)*Cranioleuca obsoleta*
13 cm - Resembles 534) - Behavior & call
similar (perhaps conspecific) - **Darker &
olivaceous** - Lacks striations on crown-
Thin white **eyebrow** - Rufous in coverts less conspicuous - **Rufous tail** ...
Brazil & Paraguay ... Humid forests,
capueras & plantations in NE   III

185

536) FIREWOOD-GATHERER

(Leñatero)　　*Anumbius annumbi*
18 cm - Exposed **voluminous nest of twigs** & the ringing *tee.. tee.. ree.. tee..* better known than the bird itself - Chestnut forehead - Upperparts striated - **Black tail with white terminal band- Black dots surround white throat** ... Brazil　& Paraguay - URUGUAY ... Savannas, rural & inhabited areas　　　　　　　　　V

537) LARK-LIKE BRUSHRUNNER

(Crestudo)　　*Coryphistera alaudina*
15 cm - Rather terrestrial - Small groups- Sharp trill - Conspicuous & fine **erect blackish crest** - Upperparts **striated** black & underparts with cinnamon-White face with cinnamon spot - Orange legs ... Brazil, Paraguay & Bolivia - URUGUAY ... Forests, rural & inhabited areas　　　　　　　V

CANASTEROS (538-543): Alike - Restless - Nest of twigs - Dull plumage - Backs brownish grey - Underparts ochraceous white - Inconspicuous wingbands - (6 species) (.)

538) SHORT-BILLED CANASTERO

(Canastero Chaqueño)
　　　　　　Asthenes baeri -2R
14 cm - Tame - Terrestrial & on bushes- Monotone long trill - Bill & **erect tail** not as long as in 539) - Central rectrices black, outer ones rufous - **Throat spot chestnut** ... Brazil & Paraguay - URUGUAY ... Forests & shrubby steppes - IV

539) LESSER CANASTERO

(Canastero Coludo)
　　　　　　Asthenes pyrrholeuca -2R
15 cm - Shy - Hidden - Non terrestrial, unlike 538), 542) & others - Flight short & low, diving into vegetation - Soft *wit* - Non erect long **tail flutters in flight** - Orange throat spot - Bill rather fine ... Chile, Bolivia & Paraguay - URUGUAY... Southern population　　Migrant　C - Shrubby & Patagonian steppes & marsh vegetation　　　　　　　　　IV

　　(.) *A. humicola* has been cited for Mendoza

540) CHESTNUT CANASTERO
(Canastero Castaño)
Asthenes steinbachi

15 cm - ♂ - Little known - Similar to 541)-
A little darker - Cinnamon rump - **Two
pairs of outer rectrices uniform
rufous - Striations surround white
throat -** No spot on throat ... High Andean & shrubby steppes in W   II

**541) CREAMY-BREASTED
CANASTERO**
(Canastero Rojizo) *Asthenes dorbignyi*

15 cm - Tame - Rather terrestrial - Trill
tee.. tee.. tee.. tee.. trrrr - Erect tail - **More
rufous** than 538) **including** coverts,
**wide rump, flanks & underwing
coverts - Black tail** with less rufous in
outer rectrices than 540) - Throat spot
rufous ... Peru, Bolivia & Chile ... Puna &
shrubby steppes in W   IV

**542) CORDILLERAN
CANASTERO**
(Canastero Pálido)
Asthenes modesta -3R

15 cm - **Resembles 539)** - Different
behavior - **In arid habitats - Tail
erect -** Continuous *peet. & rapid rattle
trrrrr-* **Throat spot** orange **[flanked by
little black dots]** - Rufous tail with all
inner webs blackish ... Peru, Bolivia &
Chile ... High Andean, Patagonian & high
elevation steppes   IV

543) PATAGONIAN CANASTERO
(Canastero Patagónico)
Asthenes patagonica

15 cm - ♂ - Tame - Bill shorter than other
canasteros' - **Black tail** (with outer
webs chestnut) - **Throat spot black
with white dots** - Cinnamon belly...
Shrubby & Patagonian steppes   III

*CANASTEROS (544-547): Nests made out of grass on ground except 546) - **Backs striated** - Long wide tails ending in points - Chestnut wingbands - Orange throats spot - Pale eyebrows - (4 species)*

544) HUDSON'S CANASTERO
(Espartillero Pampeano)

Asthenes hudsoni

17 cm - Tame but reclusive - Terrestrial - Low flight, after hovering for an instant dives into rush bed - Sharp *rtttttrr* ringing accelerated at the end - **Two whitish lines on** well contrasted **back** - Underparts cinnamon ochre - Flanks striated... [Brazil & Paraguay] - URUGUAY... Marsh **vegetation,** often **salty**   III

545) CORDOBA CANASTERO
(Espartillero Serrano)

Asthenes sclateri - 2R

16 cm - Terrestrial - Resembles 544) - Allopatric - Loud & continuous *trrr* & ascending trill - Back more uniform - Plenty of rufous on coverts - Longer **erect tail** ... Bolivia ... High Andean & high elevation grasslands - (Pampa de Achala, Cordoba)   IV

546) AUSTRAL CANASTERO
(Espartillero Austral)

Asthenes anthoides

15 cm - **In** hill **shrubs** rather often - Loud trill *prrrrrt* - Back resembles more that of 545) than of 544) - Tail smaller than either one - Breast & flanks spotted... Chile... Thickets in W Patagonia   III

547) SCRIBBLE-TAILED CANASTERO
(Espartillero Estriado)

Asthenes maculicauda

16 cm - Terrestrial - **Tail striated** - Sympatric only with 545) - **Wide rufous forehead** - White **throat without spot** -Slight striations on underparts ... Peru & Bolivia .... High Andean steppes in NW - (Aconquija, Tucuman)   II

548) CHOTOY SPINETAIL
(Chotoy)*Schoeniophylax phryganophila*

18 cm - Voluminous nest - Loud clucking-Colorful - **Very long tail with two spines** -Crown & shoulders rufous - **Back striated** black - Yellow chin - **Throat black** flanked white - Cinnamon pectoral area - J: Pale - Shorter tail - Lacks yellow chin ... Brazil, Paraguay & Bolivia - URUGUAY ... Savannas & isolated shrubs in rural areas   IV

SYNALLAXIS: In low strata - More heard than seen - Tame - Long tails - Brown backs - Rufous coverts - Throat spot black -JJ: Lack rufous crowns- (7 species)

549) BUFF-BROWED SPINETAIL
(Pijuí Ceja Canela)
                    Synallaxis superciliosa

16 cm - Call [*trr*]..*pee.. hoo.. ee* - Brown forehead - Crown & very long tail rufous-**Ochraceous eyebrow** - Underparts brownish with white center ... Bolivia ... Yungas   IV

550) SOOTY-FRONTED SPINETAIL
(Pijuí Frente Gris)
                    Synallaxis frontalis-2R

15 cm - Sharp *pee.. huee* - Resembles 549) - Shorter tail - **Rectrices with rufous** edges - Lacks conspicuous eyebrow - Underparts greyish ... Brazil, Paraguay & Bolivia - URUGUAY ... Southern population migrates N - Forests   IV

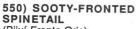

551) PALE-BREASTED SPINETAIL
(Pijuí Cola Parda)
                    Synallaxis albescens-2R

14 cm - Harsh *prr...huee* - Resembles 550) - **Brown tail** - Faint throat spot - Underparts more whitish ... From C. Rica, except Chile ... Southern population migrates N ... Savannas, forests & **rural areas**   IV

189

552) RUFOUS-CAPPED SPINETAIL
(Pijuí Corona Rojiza)
Synallaxis ruficapilla

15 cm - Resembles 549) - Allopatric - Repeated *trrrr* & harsher & shorter bars than 554) - **Crown orange rufous** - **Rufous tail** - Conspicuous **ochraceous postocular eyebrow** - Upperparts like 549) ... Brazil & Paraguay ... Humid forests & capueras in NE   II

553) OCHRE-CHEEKED SPINETAIL
(Pijuí Canela)   *Synallaxis scutata*

13 cm - Tame - **Hops on the ground** or in very low vegetation -Sharp *willy ... bini* similar to 555) - Rather short rufous tail - Crown olivaceous brown - **Long thin eyebrow & underparts cinnamon - White throat with wide black spot** ... Brazil, Paraguay & Bolivia ... Forests in NW   III

554) CHICLI SPINETAIL
(Pijuí Plomizo)   *Synallaxis spixi*

15 cm - Unmistakable *whit.. tee ree ree ree* - Dark like 555) - **Plumbeous-Forehead & crown rufous - Brown tail** ... Brazil & Paraguay - URUGUAY ... Forests & shrubs in E - (Magdalena, B. Aires)   III

555) GRAY-BELLIED SPINETAIL
(Pijuí Negruzco) *Synallaxis cinerascens*

13 cm - Call like 553)) - **Crown olivaceous brown**, not rufous, unlike 554) -**Rufous tail** -Almost inconspicuous black throat spot striated white - **Underparts plumbeous** ... Brazil & Paraguay - URUGUAY ... Small clearings in humid forests & capueras in NE   II

LEPTASTHENURA: Tame - Acrobatic - Move about a lot - **Two very long rectrices** - Short fine bills - Cinnamon wingbands - Underparts ochraceous - (4 species)

556) TUFTED TIT-SPINETAIL
(Coludito Copetón)
Leptasthenura platensis
16 cm - Sharp & descending *teereeteeteetrrr* - Brownish grey - **Conspicuous crest** slightly striated - Outer rectrices cinnamon - Throat slightly striated ... Brazil - URUGUAY ... Outer branches of trees & bushes in forest & steppes   IV

557) BROWN-CAPPED TIT-SPINETAIL
(Coludito Canela)
Leptasthenura fuliginiceps-2R
16 cm - Call *fweet..fweet* - **Chestnut crest** - Visible **rufous** patch on wings & **tail** ... Bolivia ... Bushy cliffs & ravines in High Andean steppes & high elevation areas - Winters in plains   III

558) PLAIN-MANTLED TIT-SPINETAIL
(Coludito Cola Negra)
Leptasthenura aegithaloides -2R
16 cm - Long sharp cricket-like *prrr* - **Black crown striated cinnamon** - Lacks crest - **Black tail** - Whitish throat flanked with slight striations ... Peru, Bolivia & Chile ... Bushes, cliffs, even on ground, in High Andean & Patagonian steppes   IV

559) ARAUCARIA TIT-SPINETAIL
(Coludito de los Pinos)
Leptasthenura setaria
17 cm - Small groups - Rapid *tee.. tee.. tee.. tee ..teereee..* - **Black crest striated white** - Rufous upperparts - Tail longer than in rest of genus, rufous with blackish center - Striated bib - Cinnamon underparts ... Brazil ... **In *Araucaria* forest canopy in Misiones**   II

PHACELLODOMUS: Large hanging nests (except 564) - Tame - Somewhat reclusive - Noisy - Alike - Strong bodies & bills- Broad rounded tails - Brown backs (except 560) - Underparts whitish - (6 species)

560) GREATER THORNBIRD
(Espinero Grande)
Phacellodomus ruber
18 cm -Similar call to 564) - Sings duets- Chestnut - More **rufous** on crown, wings & tail -**Yellow iris** ... Brazil, Paraguay & Bolivia ... Forests, trees near water & gallery humid forests
IV

561) RUFOUS-FRONTED THORNBIRD
(Espinero Frente Rojiza) *Phacellodomus rufifrons*
16 cm - Sings in duet - Slightly raises **brown tail** - **Wide rufous forehead**- Conspicuous **whitish eyebrow** - Lacks rufous on shoulders & rectrices unlike 562) ... Venezuela, Colombia, Peru, Brazil, Paraguay & Bolivia ... **Transition forests in NW** IV

562) STREAK-FRONTED THORNBIRD
(Espinero Andino) *Phacellodomus striaticeps*
15 cm - Resembles 561) - At greater height & in different habitat in mountains- Slight forehead, base of remiges & **shoulders rufous** - Crown barely spotted - **Rufous tail with central rectrices blackish** - Slight whitish eyebrow - Yellow mandible ... Peru & Bolivia ... **Puna & ravines in high elevations** in NW III

563) LITTLE THORNBIRD
(Espinero Chico)
Phacellodomus sibilatrix
12 cm - Restless - Moves about bushes calling *cheep.. cheep* - Sings in duet - Looks like a small 562) - Crown not dotted ... Paraguay - URUGUAY ... Forests IV

564) FRECKLE-BREASTED THORNBIRD

(Espinero Pecho Manchado)
Phacellodomus striaticollis
16 cm - Strident *teeoh.. tee.. tee.. tee.. tee* - Smaller & much less rufous than 560) - Yellow iris less conspicuous - Non hanging nest - Forehead brown - Crown rufous - **Brown tail** with outer rectrices rufous - Whitish eyebrow - **Cinnamon breast slightly dotted white** - J: Brown iris ... Brazil, Paraguay & Bolivia - URUGUAY ... Forests, grasslands & sometimes reedbeds - (Magdalena, B. Aires) IV

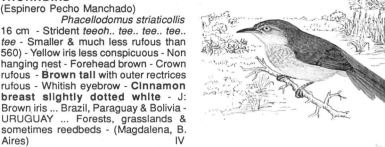

565) SPOTTED-BREASTED THORNBIRD

(Espinero Pecho Moteado)
Phacellodomus maculipectus (.)
16 cm - Resembles 564) - Allopatric - Hanging nest - Very quick *teeteeteetee* in duet - Same tail - Smaller bill - **Forehead** & crown **rufous** - **Whitish eyebrow** - **Spotted breast** more conspicuos- Rest of underparts more chestnut - **Pale olive iris** ... Bolivia ... Transition forests in NW III

566) RUFOUS-BREASTED LEAFSCRAPER

(Raspahojas) *Sclerurus scansor*
16 cm - Reclusive - Terrestrial - Scraps leaves noisily - Loud *seek* & rapid metallic trill - Does not climb but often stands vertically on tree trunks - Walks touching ground with **black tail - Bill long & straight** - Looks **blackish** - Rump & breast rufous - Throat dotted ... Brazil ... Humid forests in **Misiones** II

567) BUFF-BROWED FOLIAGE-GLEANER

(Ticotico Común)
Syndactyla rufosuperciliata -2R
16 cm - Climbs or hops about branches- Scraps leaves noisily - Strident *chek* like a snap - Also a slow rattle - **Straight bill** with mandible slightly upwards - **Upperparts olivaceous** brown -**Rufous tail with points** - Thin eyebrow ochraceous - White throat - **Underparts olive striated white** ... Peru, Bolivia, Paraguay & Brazil - URUGUAY ... Forests IV

(.) In general considered race of *Ph. striaticollis* **193**

568) WHITE-BROWED
FOLIAGE-GLEANER (Ticotico
Ceja Blanca) *Anabacerthia amaurotis*
15 cm - Very sharp *tzip.*. like an insect -
Resembles 567) - **Dark brown crown
slightly dotted - Back** chestnut
not olivaceous - Rufous tail -
Conspicuous **whitish eyebrow** & throat
- Less conspicuous underparts
cinnamon brown with **pectoral striation**
white ... Brazil ... Low strata in humid
forests of Misiones   II

*PHILYDOR: Acrobatic - Alike - Under-
parts cinnamon ochre (more cinnamon in
570) - Scrap leaves in medium & upper
strata of humid forests in* **Misiones** *- (3
species)*

569) BUFF-FRONTED
FOLIAGE-GLEANER
(Ticotico Grande)   *Philydor rufus*
17 cm - Series of sharp & descending
metallic *seenk* - **Wide forehead**, conspicuous eyebrow **& cheeks ochre** -
Crown & ocular band plumbeous - Back
olivaceous brown - Tail & wings rufous ...
From Venezuela, except Chile   III

570) BLACK-CAPPED
FOLIAGE-GLEANER
(Ticotico Cabeza Negra)
                    Philydor atricapillus
15 cm - Long & descending flute-like trill -
The most colorful - **Forehead, crown
& ocular & malar bands black**
separated by two ochre lines - Chestnut
back - Rufous tail - White periocular ...
Brazil & Paraguay   III

571) OCHRE-BREASTED
FOLIAGE-GLEANER
(Ticotico Ocráceo)*Philydor lichtensteini*
15 cm - The least conspicuous - Bill
rather short - **Forehead**, crown & ocular band **plumbeous - Long postocular** ochre **eyebrow** - Back &
central rectrices olivaceous brown -
Wings & outer rectrices rufous ... Brazil
& Paraguay   IV

572) WHITE-THROATED TREERUNNER
(Picolezna Patagónico)
Pygarrhichas albogularis
15 cm - Tame - Resembles a small woodpecker - Climbs & pecks tree trunks - **Bill somewhat curved upwards** - Dark brown back - Rump, coverts & flanks rufous - Rufous tail ending in points - Conspicuos & wide **white bib** - Rest of underparts scaled ... Chile ... **Araucano Forest**   III

XENOPS: Curious - Restless - Acrobatic - Climbers - Small - Short bills - (3 species)

573) SHARP-BILLED TREEHUNTER   (Picolezna Estriado)   *Xenops contaminatus*
12 cm - Slow metallic trill - Resembles 574) - **Bill not curved upwards -** Blackish crown, brown **back &** pale **underparts striated** - Rufous tail - **Long eyebrow & throat ochraceous** ... Brazil & Paraguay ... Medium & high strata in humid forests of **Misiones**   II

574) STREAKED XENOPS
(Picolezna Rojizo) *Xenops rutilans -2R*
12 cm - Slow sharp trill & snap - Crown, nape & **underparts striated - Bill curved upwards** -Chestnut back - Rump & tail rufous - Conspicuous ochraceous eyebrow & throat - White malar ... From C. Rica, except Chile ... Different strata in humid forests of NW & Misiones   III

575) PLAIN XENOPS
(Picolezna Chico)   *Xenops minutus*
11 cm - Resembles 574) - Same bill - **Olivaceous brown back** - Conspicuos cinnamon on wings - **Tail cinnamon & black** (central & outer rectrices cinnamon) - **Uniform underparts** with slight pectoral striation ... From C. America, except Chile ... Medium & high strata in humid forests of **Misiones**   II

576) GIANT ANTSHRIKE
(Batará Gigante)   *Batara cinerea-2R*
33 cm - Tame but hidden - Very loud call
klue..arrr and others - Long tail - Robust bill with hook - Conspicuous
**black crest - Black upperparts
barred white** - Ashy grey underparts-
⬤: Looks like Striped Cuckoo (372) -
Chestnut crest - Upperparts cinnamon barred black - Underparts
ochraceous grey ... Brazil, Paraguay &
Bolivia ... Low strata in clearings of
humid forests in NE (I) & NW (Calilegua
NP)   III

577) LARGE-TAILED ANTSHRIKE
(Batará Pintado) *Mackenziaena leachii*
25 cm - Appearance & behavior like
576) - Smaller - More terrestrial -
Ascending series of 5 clear whistles *tee..*
then descending - Lacks crest - **Black-
Back dotted white** - Tail almost
uniform - ⬤ : **Cinnamon crown** dotted
black - Back dotted white ... Brazil &
Paraguay ... Low strata in humid
for-   ests & capueras of NE   III

578) TUFTED ANTSHRIKE
(Batará Copetón)
                    Mackenziaena severa
22 cm - Tail shorter than 577) - Ascending series of 6   long melancholic
whistles *who..* - Looks **black** - Plumbeous - Black head with **conspicuous
crest** - ⬤: **Orange rufous crest** -
Rest black **barred** ochre & cinnamon... Brazil & Paraguay ... Low strata
& bamboo thickets in humid forests of
Misiones   II

**579) SPOT-BACKED
ANTSHRIKE**   (Batará
Goteado) *Hypoedaleus guttatus*
19 cm - Reclusive - Long & continuous
vibrating whistle which ascends & falls
accelerating - **Upperparts** black **with
conspicuous white spots** (cinnamon in ♀) - Long barred tail - Underparts greyish turning   cinnamon ...
Brazil & Paraguay ... Thick vegetation
in medium & high strata in humid forests of **Misiones**   I

THAMNOPHILUS (.): Very tame - Medium size - Strong bill - Medium & low strata - (3 species)

580) BARRED ANTSHRIKE
(Choca Listada) *Thamnophilus doliatus*

15 cm - Flicks head - Waggles tail - Melodiuos *feeoh* - Also rhythmical series of cluckings - Looks like a small 576) - **Black barred white** - Black erectile small crest - **Ivory iris** - Pale sky blue legs - **♀**: Different - **Small crest** & back **rufous** - **Face & neck grey striated black** - Cinnamon breast - Iris & legs like ♂ ... From Mexico, except Chile ... Forests & savannas in N (E Formosa) III

581) RUFOUS-CAPPED ANTSHRIKE
(Choca Corona Rojiza)
Thamnophilus ruficapillus-2R

16 cm - Powerful song of somewhat spaced repeated notes - Brown - **Rufous crown** - Graded tail barred black & white underneath - Underparts whitish - **Breast barred black** - Red iris - ♀: Dull plumage - Looks like a Furnariidae with strong bill - Crown & tail rufous - Ochraceous underparts - Slightly barred breast ... Brazil, Paraguay, Bolivia & Peru - URUGUAY ... Forests in E (Magdalena, B. Aires) & NW III

582) VARIABLE ANTSHRIKE
(Choca Común)
Thamnophilus caerulescens-4R

13 cm - Nasal kitten-like call - Upperparts plumbeous - **Black coverts with white bars** - Crown & tail black - Rectrices graded with white tip - Underparts cinnamon or with grey breast or all grey, according to race - ♀: Upperparts brown or olivaceous grey - Underparts cinnamon - [Chestnut crown] ... Brazil, Paraguay, Bolivia & Peru - URUGUAY ... Forests IV

(.) *Th. schistaceus* has been cited doubtfully for NW

Fam. Formicariidae, see page 37

583) GREAT ANTSHRIKE
(Chororó) *Taraba major*
20 cm - Terrestrial & in bushes - Loud & melodious *chok..chok..chrrr* like a rattle & other calls - Short black bill - **Red iris - Upperparts black** - Conspicuous white bars on coverts - **Underparts white with tail barred black - ♀: Upperparts chestnut**-Wings without bars - Tail rufous not barred ... From C. America, except Chile ... Forests, savannas & clearings
V

584) WHITE-SHOULDERED FIRE-EYE
(Batará Negro) *Pyriglena leucoptera*
16 cm - Terrestrial - 7 or 8 short equal whistles - **Black** - Conspicuos **white bars on coverts** - [White scapular spot] **Red iris - ♀:** Often away from♂ - Brown - **Black tail** - Pale throat ... Brazil & Paraguay ... Thick & low strata in humid forests of **Misiones**
IV

585) WHITE-BEARDED ANTSHRIKE (Batará Pecho Negro) *Biatas nigropectus*
16 cm - **Black head & breast** - **Ochraceous white nape band** - White throat - Olivaceous brown back - Wings & long tail rufous - ♀: Lacks black-**Rufous crown** - Underparts ochraceous ... Brazil ... Humid forests in **Misiones**
I

586)STRIPE-BACKED ANTBIRD
(Batará Estriado)
Myrmorchilus strigilatus
14 cm - Tame - Rather terrestrial - Flicks tail - Loud *cheea..* & sharp trisyllabic melancholic whistle - **Upperparts striated rufous & black** - Conspicuous white bars & spots on coverts - **Rufous tail,** outer rectrices black with white tip - **Wide black bib** contrasted with whitish underparts - ♀: Lacks bib - **Breast striated blackish** ... Brazil, Paraguay & Bolivia ... Forests & savannas of Chaqueño type - (Copo Reserve, Santiago del Estero)
IV

587) PLAIN ANTVIREO

(Choca Amarilla) *Dysithamnus mentalis* 10 cm - Tame - Series of low & melodious descending whistles accelerated at end - Short bill & tail - **Plumbeous head** - Back olivaceous grey - Pale bars on coverts - Dark auricular spot - Grey throat turning yellowish in rest of underparts - ♀: **Rufous crown -** Whitish eyelid - Looks like 797) ... From Mexico, except Guianas & Chile... Various strata in humid forests of **Misiones**   IV

588) SPOT-BREASTED ANTVIREO
(Choca Estriada) *Dysithamnus stictothorax* 11 cm - Resembles 587) - Sometimes together - Series of not accelerated whistles - Conspicuous **white postocular dots** - Some rufous on remiges - Underparts yellowish **striated on breast** - Red iris - ♀: Rufous crown, more conspicuous than in 587)- Spotted & striated like ♂ ... Brazil... Medium & high strata in humid forests of **Misiones**   I

589) FERRUGINOUS ANTBIRD
(Tiluchi Colorado)
                Drymophila ferruginea 12 cm - Audible & showy *pee.payh* - Short & thin bill - Erect tail with white tip on each rectrix - **Rump & underparts orange rufous - Black crown & ocular band - White eyebrow & malar** - Conspicuous white bars on black coverts - ♀: Paler... Brazil & Paraguay ... Low & medium thick strata, in clearings of humid forests in **Misiones**   III

590) DUSKY-TAILED ANTBIRD
(Tiluchi Estriado) *Drymophila malura* 13 cm - Appearance & behavior of 589) - Tail similar without white - Loud hiss - **Dark ashy grey - Hood & breast striated white** - White bars on coverts - ♀: **Brown** - Head striated with ochre ... Brazil & Paraguay ... Low strata in humid forests of **Misiones**   III

Fam. Formicariidae, see page 37

591) RUFOUS-WINGED ANTWREN
(Tiluchi Ala Rojiza)
Herpsilochmus rufimarginatus
10 cm - Sometimes in mixed flocks - Continuous *huhuhu* - Series of quick chirps ending in trill - Rather colorful - **Black crown - White eyebrow** - Plumbeous back - Coverts black with white bars - Conspicuous **rufous remiges** - Tail like 592) less conspicuous - Underparts yellowish - ♀ : **Chestnut crown** - Olivaceous back ... From Panama, except Guianas and Chile - **High strata** of humid forests in **Misiones** III

592) BLACK-CAPPED ANTWREN
(Tiluchi Plomizo)
Herpsilochmus pileatus
11 cm - Looks like a small 582) - Appearance, behavior & call of 591) - Allopatric - **Black tail with tip & outer rectrices white** - Underparts greyish not yellowish - ♀ : Forehead brownish- Crown striated - Olivaceous back - Underparts ochraceous ... Brazil, Paraguay, Bolivia & Peru ... **High strata** in yungas & forests of NW II

593) STREAK-CAPPED ANTWREN
(Tiluchi Enano) *Terenura maculata*
9 cm - Active - Acrobatic - Minute - Short tail without white - As 591) & 592) resembles a Tyrannidae - Sharp call - **Head striated black & white - Rufous back** - White bars on coverts- **Breast** grey striated **black** - Yellowish belly - ♀: More ochraceous, even striations on crown & breast ... Brazil & Paraguay ... Thick medium strata in humid forests of **Misiones**
III

594) RUFOUS GNATEATER
(Chupadientes)
Conopophaga lineata (.)
11 cm - Passive - Perched on branches or bamboo near ground - Curious - Snap like sucking of teeth - Various chirps *u*... increasing - Chubby - Small crest - Short tail - Short bill with rosy mandible - Dull plumage - **Grey eyebrow- Auricular & throat orange cinnamon** - [White tuft] ... Brazil & Paraguay ... Low strata in humid forests & capueras of **Misiones** III

(.) Previoulsy in Fam. Conopophagidae; no longer valid

200

595) SHORT-TAILED ANTTHRUSH
(Tovaca Común)
Chamaeza campanisona
20 cm - Terrestrial - More heard than seen - Runs like a chicken - Monotonous repetition of a flute-like note (cricket-like) ending with several quick *chup..* - Looks like a thrush - Upperparts olivaceous brown - Conspicuous **white postocular eyebrow** - Waggles short erect rufous tail with subterminal black band & ochre tip - White throat - Rest of **underparts** ochraceous **striated** - Lilac bill - Long rosy legs ... From Venezuela except Chile ... Humid forests in NE   IV

GRALLARIA: Terrestrial - Hop - Shy - More heard than seen - Large heads & eyes -Very short tails - Long lilac legs- Underwing coverts rufous - Low & thick strata in humid forests, (3 species)

596) VARIEGATED ANTPITTA
(Chululú Pintado)   *Grallaria varia*
19 cm - Repeated *boo..* at dusk - Crown & nape plumbeous & back olivaceous brown slightly striated white - Rufous tail - **Blackish throat flanked by ochraceous malar & separated from breast by whitish spot** - Rest of underparts barred... Venezuela, Guianas, Brazil & Paraguay ... In NE   III

597) WHITE-THROATED ANTPITTA   (Chululú Cabeza Rojiza) *Grallaria albigula*
20 cm - Bisyllabic & flute-like *hu..* - **Rufous head** - White periocular - Olivaceous brown back - **White throat** - Rest of underparts grey ... Peru & Bolivia ... In NW (Calilegua NP)   III

598) SPECKLE-BREASTED ANTPITTA   (Chululú Chico) *Grallaria ochroleuca*
12 cm - Looks like a small 595)- Waggles body when excited - Olivaceous upperparts - White periocular - Underparts ochraceous splashed black ... Brazil & Paraguay ... Low strata in humid forests of **Misiones**   II

599) BLACK-THROATED HUET-HUET
(Huet-Huet) *Pteroptochos tarnii*

22 cm - Terrestrial - Scratches ground - Reclusive - More heard than seen - Series of descending notes - Also a low *huet..huet..* - When alarmed quick & loud *too..too..too..too* - Short bill - Blackish back & throat - **Crown, rump & rest of underparts rufous** - Black tail - Yellow iris ... Chile ... Araucano Forest   II

600) OCHRE-FLANKED TAPACULO
(Churrín Grande) *Eugralla paradoxa*

14 cm - Looks like a large 608) with **strong bill** - Harsh & repeated *chek* - **Rump & lower belly cinnamon** - Mandible & legs yellowish - J: Back barred dark - Underparts whitish ... Chile ... Cited for Araucano Forest in **Rio Negro**   I

601) CHUCAO TAPACULO
(Chucao) *Scelorchilus rubecula*

17 cm - Terrestrial - Reclusive - More heard than seen - Runs short distances - Loud frog-like croak or turkey goggle - Dark brown - Much smaller than 599) - **Eyebrow & bib rufous** - Rest of **underparts barred** black & white ... Chile ... Araucano Forest   III

602) CRESTED GALLITO
(Gallito Copetón)
Rhinocrypta lanceolata

21 cm - Runs through clearings - Sometimes on top of bushes jumping to ground - Loud & gentle *chup..* or *cheeo..* & other calls - Somewhat long tail - Conspicuous brown **crest & neck striated white** - Olivaceous grey back - Underparts whitish - **Rufous flanks** ... Paraguay & Bolivia... Forests & shrubby steppes IV

603) SANDY GALLITO
(Gallito Arena)   *Teledromas fuscus*

16 cm - ♀ - Looks like a short billed **pale** Furnariidae - Behavior like 602)- Repeated & loud *peeuk* - Sings on top of bushes - Call like Green-barred Woodpecker (461) - Upperparts brownish cinnamon - Tail brown to blackish - Eyebrow & underparts whitish - Shrubby steppes, **prepuna bare sandy areas & salt flats**-III

604) OLIVE-CROWNED CRESCENTCHEST
(Gallito de Collar)
Melanopareia maximiliani (.) - 2R

14 cm - Rather hidden - Low *tok..tok*-Song with frog-like resonance or slow trill according to race - Does not raise tail - Striking plumage - Upperparts olivaceous brown [with white spot] - Conspicuous **cinnamon long eyebrow & throat** separated by **black mask - Collar black** - Rest of underparts rufous ... Bolivia & Paraguay ... Thickets, grasslands & rocky areas in forests & savannas   III

(.) Sometimes considered Formicariidae. Its exact taxonomic position is undetermined still.

605) SPOTTED BAMBOOWREN
(Gallito Overo)*Psilorhamphus guttatus*
12 cm - Reclusive - Moves about thick vegetation - Sequence of some 40 *hood... resembling* that of Pygmy-owl (384) from afar - Looks like 769) - Elegant - Long tail - Thin bill - **Crown & upperback ashy grey, rest of upperparts chestnut, all with spaced white dots** - White wing bars- **Outer rectrices with** lines of **ochraceous spots** - Underparts dotted white - Cinnamon lower belly with barred flanks - ♀: More cinnamon- Dorsal dots more conspicuos ... Brazil... Medium height in bamboo thickets in humid forests of **Misiones**   II

SCYTALOPUS: Somewhat terrestrial - Small - Look like blackish wrens- Alike - Allopatric - Tend to flee - More heard than seen - Restless- Move about vegetation - Straight & thin bills- Short tails - Long yellowish or rosy legs - (3 species)

606) WHITE-BROWED TAPACULO
(Churrín Plomizo)
                    Scytalopus superciliaris
10 cm - Loud, hoarse & repeated *me..teeo* - Upperparts olivaceous brown - **Postocular line & throat white** - Underparts plumbeous ... Bolivia ... **Yungas**   III

607) MOUSE-COLORED TAPACULO   (Churrín Plomizo)   *Scytalopus speluncae*
10 cm - Series of sharp *tze..* - **Plumbeous** - Ashy grey underparts - **Rump & lower belly cinnamon barred black** - ♀ : Browner ... Brazil & Paraguay ... Bamboo thickets in humid forests of **Misiones**   II

608) ANDEAN TAPACULO
                    (Churrín Andino)
Scytalopus magellanicus -2R
10 cm - Repeated *patrás* - **Blackish - [White forehead]** - J: Even more like 769) - Brown with small spots - Tail barred ... From Venezuela along W ... **Araucano Forest** & humid ravines
                    III

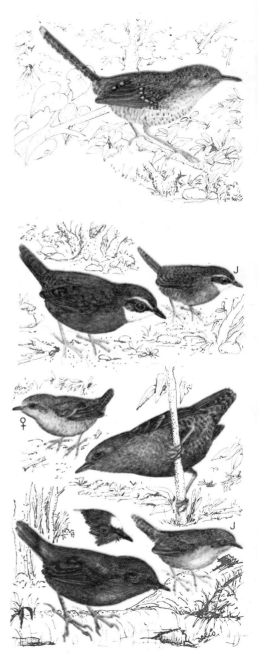

609) RED-RUFFED FRUITCROW
(Yacutoro)   *Pyroderus scutatus*

♂ 42 cm - ♀: 37 - Loud *buup*, like lowing - **Largest passerine** - Strong bill - **Black** with slight sheen - **Large orange red bib** - J: Wing & underparts stained chestnut ... S. America except Chile & Bolivia ... Medium & high strata in humid forests & capueras of NE   III

610) BLACK-TAILED TITYRA
(Tueré Grande)   *Tityra cayana (.)*

19 cm - In high & visible sites - Quiet - Nasal growl *reck.*. - Strong - Resembles 611) - Sympatric - White - Flat **head, remiges & short tail black** - Grey back - **Ocular patch, lores & base of bill red** - Rest of bill black - ❶: **Very striated** ... S. America except Chile ... Forests & capueras in NE   III

611) BLACK-CROWNED TITYRA
(Tueré Chico)   *Tityra inquisitor (.)*

16 cm - Aspect & behavior of 610) - **Lacks red** - Black bill - ❶: **Black crown - Reddish face - Underparts lack striations**... From C. America except Chile ... Forests & capueras in NE   III

612) BARE-THROATED BELLBIRD   (Pájaro Campana)   *Procnias nudicollis*

23 cm - More heard than seen - Loud metallic notes, often at intervals - Unmistakable - **White** - **Greenish blue areas on face & throat** - ❶: Greyish head - **Olive back** - **Underparts** yellowish **striated** - J: Like ♀ - Black hood ... Brazil & Paraguay ... Migrant B - High strata in humid forests of NE   I

(.) Currently included in Fam. Tyrannidae   **205**

BECARDS (.): *Solitary - Quiet - Large heads - Look like tyrants with strong & broad bills - (4 species)*

613) CRESTED BECARD
(Anambé Grande) *Platypsaris rufus-2R*
17 cm - Sharp trill similar to that of 662)- Resembles 614) - Without white wingbars - White spot on scapulars - Underparts ochraceous in NE - ●: **Plumbeous small crest** - Rufous upperparts - Cinnamon underparts ... Brazil, Paraguay, Bolivia & Peru ... Medium & high strata in forests & humid ravines... III

NE

614) WHITE-WINGED BECARD
(Anambé Común)

Pachyramphus polychopterus
15 cm - Both sexes emit various similar notes - Melancholic *peew..peew..peew peew* - Looks like Misiones' race of 582)- Somewhat darker than 613) - Blackish - **Glossy black small crest**- Plumbeous underparts - Conspicuous **white wingbars** - Rectrices with white tips - ●: Upperparts olivaceous brown - **Wingbars & tip of tail cinnamon** - Lores whitish - Underparts yellowish ... From Guatemala except Chile - URUGUAY ... Forests & plantations IV

615) CHESTNUT-CROWNED BECARD
(Anambé Castaño) *Pachyramphus castaneus*
14 cm - Delicate & ascending *twee..ee..ee* - Looks like ♀ 613) - Sexes alike - **Upperparts rufous, including crown** surrounded by **grey headband** -Sides of neck & underparts cinnamon ... S. America, except Chile ... High strata in humid forests of **Misiones** III

616) GREEN-BACKED BECARD
(Anambé Verdoso)

Pachyramphus viridis
14 cm - Sequence of pleasant chirps - Colorful - Looks like 799) - **Black crown** surrounded with grey - Olive upperparts - Whitish underparts - **Yellow breast** - ●: Olivaceous crown - **Rufous spot on coverts** ... S. America, except Chile - URUGUAY ... High strata in forests & savannas III

(.) Currently included in Fam. Tyrannidae

617) SWALLOW-TAILED COTINGA
(Tesorito)　　*Phibalura flavirostris*
21 cm -Tame - Quiet - Pairs on high &
visible sites - **Showy & striking
colors** - Small crest - **Long deeply
forked tail** - Orange spot on nape -
**Yellow back slightly barred
black - Golden throat** - White breast
barred - Rest of underparts yellow
slightly spotted - J: Paler - Lacks small
crest or golden throat - Shorter tail-
Rectrices with white tips ... Brazil,
Paraguay & Bolivia ... High strata in
humid forests & capueras of
Misiones　　　　　　　　　I

**618) WHITE-NAPED
XENOPSARIS**
(Tijerilla)　　*Xenopsaris albinucha (.)*
12 cm - Tame - Slender - **Black
crown** - Upperparts brownish grey -
**Underparts white - ●: Chestnut
crown** - J: Upperparts striated brown
& cinnamon ... S. America except Peru
& Chile ...Forests, savannas & humid
areas　　　　　　　　　　　II

Fam. Pipridae, see page 37

**619) WHITE-BEARDED
MANAKIN**
(Bailarín Blanco) *Manacus manacus*
10 cm -Tame - More heard than seen-
Swollen throat - **White - Crown,
wings & very short tail black** -
Grey rump - Orange legs - ♀: Very
different & dull - Olive back - Oliva-
ceous grey underparts ... S. America...
Humid forests in **Misiones**　　　I

**620) SWALLOW -TAILED
MANAKIN**
(Bailarín Azul)　　*Chiroxiphia caudata*
14 cm - ♂ more abundant than ♀ -
Very loud & melodious *eevo..eevo..
cheeveeoh.. cheeveeoh* - Striking -
**Blue -Black hood with wide red
crown**-Wings & tail (with **elongated
central rectrices**) black - ♀: Olive -
Lacks black or red ... Brazil & Paraguay ... Medium & low strata in humid
forests & capueras of NE　　　III

(.) Currently included in Fam. Tyrannidae

Fam. Pipridae, see page 37

621) BAND-TAILED MANAKIN
(Bailarín Naranja)   *Pipra fasciicauda*

10 cm - Hidden - Striking **reddish orange** plumage - Black back - White wingband - **Very short tail** with yellowish basal band - Underparts yellower - ♀ : Dull plumage - Upperparts olive - Underparts yellow, olivaceous on flanks & breast - Rosy grey iris - Lilac legs ... Brazil, Paraguay, Bolivia & Peru... Low & medium strata of humid forests & capueras in **Misiones**   II

622) WING-BARRED MANAKIN
(Bailarín Verde)   *Piprites chloris*

12 cm - Very loud & sonorous rythmic series of chirps, followed by a higher & more accentuated one - Thick & short bill - Cinnamon forehead - Upperparts olive - Conspicuous **whitish wingbars & inner remiges** - Grey face - Underparts olivaceous yellow ... S. America, except Chile ... Medium & high strata in humid forests of **Misiones**   III

623) BLACK-CAPPED MANAKIN
(Bailarín Castaño)   *Piprites pileatus*

12 cm - Restless - Very different & showier than 622) - **Black crown - Rufous upperparts** - Blackish remiges with greenish edges & white spot visible in flight - Central rectrices black - Underparts cinnamon - Short **yellow bill** - ♀: Olive back ... Brazil ... *Araucaria* forests in **Misiones**   I

624) GREENISH MANAKIN
(Bailarín Oliváceo) *Schiffornis virescens*

14 cm - Hidden - Quiet - Moves about vegetation - Melodious bisyllabic whistle - Dull plumage - Dark **olivaceous - Wings & tail brown** ... Brazil & Paraguay ... Low & medium strata in humid forests of **Misiones**   III

208

AGRIORNIS: Tame - On low & visible sites - Somewhat terrestrial - Silent (except 628) - Chase other birds (except 628 & 629) - Look like thrushes with robust & hooked bills - Dull brownish plumages - Striated white throats - (5 species)

625) GREAT SHRIKE-TYRANT

(Gaucho Grande) *Agriornis livida*
26 cm - Allopatric with 627) - Pale bars on inner remiges - Blackish tail with white outer web - **Cinnamon lower belly** ... Chile ... Arid & shrubby steppes, often near Araucano Forest, in Patagonia   III

626) GRAY-BELLIED SHRIKE-TYRANT

(Gaucho Gris) *Agriornis microptera-2R*
23 cm - Call *pwit* - Resembles 625) - Lacks cinnamon - Long **pale eyebrow** ... Peru, Chile, Bolivia & Paraguay ... Southern population migrates N- Patagonian & High Andean shrubby steppes   IV

627) WHITE-TAILED SHRIKE-TYRANT

(Gaucho Andino) *Agriornis albicauda*
26 cm - Resembles 628) - Much larger - Whitish eyebrow - **Conspicuous throat striation** - Almost without bars on inner remiges - **White tail** with only central pair of rectrices dark - Whitish lower belly - **Yellowish mandible** ... Ecuador, Peru, Bolivia & Chile ... High Andean steppes in **Aconquija**   II

628) BLACK-BELLIED SHRIKE-TYRANT

(Gaucho Serrano)
Agriornis montana-3R
21 cm - Low mewing - Almost human whistle at dawn - **White bars on inner remiges** - **White tail with base & central rectrices dark** - Slight & short eyebrow - Throat striation little conspicuous - Underparts with racial variation ... Colombia, Ecuador, Peru, Bolivia & Chile ... High Andean steppes, prepuna & grasslands on high elevations   IV

629) LEAST SHRIKE-TYRANT
(Gaucho Chico)   *Agriornis murina*

16 cm - Terrestrial & on bushes - Looks like a small 626) - Lighter flight - More ochraceous underparts - **Pale bars on coverts & inner remiges** - Eyebrow & outer webs of tail whitish - **Cinnamon flanks** ... Migrant C to Paraguay & Bolivia ... Arid shrubby steppes   IV

NEOXOLMIS: Terrestrial - Conspicuous - Rufous, white & black - (3 species)

630) CHOCOLATE-VENTED TYRANT   (Monjita Chocolate)   *Neoxolmis rufiventris*

23 cm - Flocks in winter often with Tawny-throated Dotterel (252) - Broken flight- Shy - Opens & shuts tail quickly - **Ashy grey** - Forehead & face black - **Wing pattern black, rufous & white** - Blackish tail with pale outer web - Chestnut lower belly ... Migrant C to Brazil [& Chile] - URUGUAY... Patagonian steppes   III

631) RUSTY-BACKED MONJITA
(Monjita Castaña) *Neoxolmis rubetra*

18 cm - ♂ - Flocks in winter - **Cinnamon upperparts more rufous on crown- Primaries black bordered rufous - Coverts & tertiaries much whiter** - Blackish tail with pale outer web - Conspicuous & **long white eyebrow** - Underparts white with striated breast ... Migrant C ... Shrubby steppes   III

632) SALINAS MONJITA
(Monjita Salinera)
             Neoxolmis salinarum

16 cm - ♂ - Resembles 631), ♀ even more (can be conspecific) - More conspicuous **nape band & larger patch on coverts white - Whitish rump** - Underparts white, almost without striations ... Salt pans - (Ambargasta, Santiago del Estero)   III

XOLMIS & PYROPE: Conspicuous - Perch on visible sites - Passive - Low & lazy flight s- White, black & grey - (5 species)

633) BLACK & WHITE MONJITA
(Monjita Dominica) *Xolmis dominicana*

19 cm - ♂ looks like 636) - **Remiges & tail black** - Rest white, including tip of primaries, conspicuous in flight - ♀: **Crown, neck & upper back brownish** grey with V-shaped white band between them & black wings ... Brazil & Paraguay - URUGUAY ... Wet grasslands in E   II

634) GRAY MONJITA
(Monjita Gris) *Xolmis cinerea*

20 cm - Looks like White-banded Mockingbird (772) even more so in flight - **Greyish - Lores, subocular, spot on primaries conspicuos in flight,** lower belly & throat white - Black malar - Whitish tip on black tail - **Red iris** ... Suriname, Brazil, Bolivia & Paraguay - URUGUAY ... Savannas, palm groves, & forests, often near water - (El Palmar NP)   III

635) BLACK-CROWNED MONJITA
(Monjita Coronada) *Xolmis coronata*

20 cm - Looks like a black & white Kiskadee (672) - **Black crown & ocular band** separated by **white headband** - Upperparts brownish grey - Black remiges & tail - Wingbars & **wingband** white ... Brazil, Paraguay & Bolivia - URUGUAY ... Migrant C - Forests & shrubby steppes   IV

636) WHITE MONJITA
(Monjita Blanca) *Xolmis irupero*

17 cm - Conspicuous white, even at a distance - Hovers -**Primaries & tip of tail black** ... Brazil, Paraguay & Bolivia - URUGUAY ... Savannas, forests & rural areas   V

211

637) FIRE-EYED DIUCON
(Diucón) *Pyrope pyrope*
19 cm - Looks like 634) - Allopatric - Passive - Sometimes terrestrial - Hunts in short flights or runs - Weak whistle - Bulky throat - **Plumbeous upperparts** - Pale rump - Underparts grey with **throat** and lower belly **whitish** - Pale outer web of tail - **Red iris-** J: Brown iris ... Chile ... Clearings in Araucano Forest   IV

MUSCISAXICOLA: Terrestrial - Tame-Open & shut tails - Erect - Dispersed groups even of mixed species - Alike - Long legs - Square black tails with pale outer webs- Backs grey to brownish - Whitish underparts - JJ: Cinnamon bars on coverts & remiges - (9 species)

638) BLACK-FRONTED GROUND-TYRANT
(Dormilona Frente Negra)
Muscisaxicola frontalis
18 cm - Conspicuous **white lores - Black forehead continued on crown** ... Chile, Bolivia & Peru ... Migrant C - High Andean steppes- (Horcones, Mendoza) & high elevations - (Somuncura, Rio Negro)
III

639) PLAIN-CAPPED GROUND-TYRANT
(Dormilona Cenicienta)
Muscisaxicola alpina -2R
15 cm - Dull plumage - **Lacks patch on nape or forehead** - Brown wings contrasted with ashy grey back - Slight pale eyebrow ... Colombia, Ecuador, Peru, Bolivia & Chile ... High Andean steppes, prepuna & near streams   IV

640) DARK-FACED GROUND-TYRANT
(Dormilona Cara Negra)
Muscisaxicola macloviana -2R
15 cm - Sometimes on shrubs - Dull plumage - **Blackish face changing to brown on crown** - J: Lacks blackish face ... Peru & Chile - [URUGUAY]... Migrant C - Andean steppes, often near water, seacoasts & wet grasslands- IV

212

641) CINNAMON-BELLIED GROUND-TYRANT
(Dormilona Canela)
Muscisaxicola capistrata

16 cm - The most cinnamon colored - **Forehead & lores black** - Chestnut on crown & nape - **Belly & undertail coverts cinnamon** - J: Without chestnut on crown ... Peru, Bolivia & Chile ... Migrant C - Humid steppes in Tierra del Fuego - Winters in High Andean & high elevation grasslands IV

642) RUFOUS-NAPED GROUND-TYRANT
(Dormilona Gris)
Muscisaxicola rufivertex-3R

16 cm - **Pale grey back** - Slight white eyebrow - **Underparts white - Clear cinnamon patch on crown** & nape - J: Less cinnamon on crown... Peru, Bolivia & Chile ... High Andean steppes, prepuna & high elevation grasslands - (Pampa de Achala, Cordoba) IV

643) PUNA GROUND-TYRANT
(Dormilona Puneña)
Muscisaxicola juninensis

16 cm - Very similar to 644) - Back paler & more greyish - **Cinnamon patch on crown smaller & more diffuse** - Smaller & inconspicuous eyebrow ... Peru, Bolivia & Chile ... High Andean steppes in NW I

644) WHITE-BROWED GROUND-TYRANT
(Dormilona Ceja Blanca)
Muscisaxicola albilora

16 cm - Allopatric in summer with 643) - Conspicuous, **long white eyebrow** - Wide **cinnamon brown** forehead **turned rufous in** rest of **crown**, not so conspicuous as in 642) ... Ecuador, Peru, Bolivia & Chile ... Migrant C - High Andean & high elevation steppes- (Somuncura, Rio Negro) & near streams III

Characters of genus *Muscisaxicola,* see page 212

645) OCHRE-NAPED GROUND-TYRANT
(Dormilona Fraile)
Muscisaxicola flavinucha-2R

18 cm - Unmistakable - White forehead & lores - **Yellow patch on nape** lacking in J ... Peru, Bolivia & Chile ... Migrant C ... High Andean & high elevation steppes - (Somuncura, Rio Negro)   III

646) SPOT-BILLED GROUND-TYRANT
(Dormilona Chica)
Muscisaxicola maculirostris (.)

13 cm - Less elegant than other *Muscisaxicola* species - Tamer - Walks among grass - Nuptial flight like pipit's- Dull plumage - Back **browner** - **Cinnamon bars on** coverts **& remiges** - Underparts slightly ochraceous - **Mandible with yellow base** ... From Colombia through W - High Andean & high elevation steppes - (Somuncura, Rio Negro), prepuna & Andean valleys- Winters also in elevations   IV

647) RUFOUS-BACKED NEGRITO
(Sobrepuesto Común)
Lessonia rufa-2R (..)

11 cm - Terrestrial - In marshes - Tame- Rarely cn bushes or low posts, in open- Restless - Short runs - **Black - Rufous back** - (NW race paler - White underwing) - ♀ : Brown - **Cinnamon back** (chestnut in NW) - Blackish tail - Pale underparts - Undertail coverts white ... Bordering countries & Peru - URUGUAY ... Southern race Migrant C- Near water, including seacoasts & high Andean lakes in NW   V

214   (.) *M. fluviatilis* is very similar & has been cited for NW

648) WHITE-BROWED CHAT-TYRANT

(Pitajo Gris)   *Ochthoeca leucophrys*
13 cm - Tame - Terrestrial & on bushes- Hunts in flight - Short *kuek* - Short bill - Plumbeous crown turned chestnut on lower back & rump - Two conspicuous **rufous wingbars** - Visible **long white eyebrow** - White outer caudal web - **Underparts ashy grey** ... Peru, Bolivia & Chile - Humid ravines in elevations & near montane forests   III

649) D'ORBIGNY'S CHAT-TYRANT

(Pitajo Canela)   *Ochthoeca oenanthoides*
14 cm - Tame - Terrestrial & on bushes- Short *peet* - Looks like a Warbling-Finch - Short bill & visible **long white eyebrow** like 648) - Brownish grey back - Cinnamon rump - Slight ochraceous wingbars - **Greyish throat - Rest of underparts cinnamon** ... Peru, Bolivia & Chile ... Prepuna & High Andean steppes in NW   III

650) SPECTACLED TYRANT

(Pico de Plata)
                Hymenops perspicillata-2R
13 cm - Exposed on top of shrubs & posts - Often terrestrial - Short runs - Sallying flight - **Black - White primaries** conspicuous in flight - Bill & **periocular yellowish** - ♀: Different & inconspicuous - Rather hidden - Rarely near ♂- **Brown, striated - Rufous wing patch** conspicuous in flight - J: Like ♀ - Lacks periocular ... Bordering countries - URUGUAY ... Wetlands & nearby areas even in high altitudes   V

651) BLACK PHOEBE

(Viudita de Río)   *Sayornis nigricans*
17 cm - Tame - Active - Perches on stones & branches on water - Flicks tail - Sallying flight - Small crest - **Black** - Conspicuous **bars on coverts & remiges,** outer caudal web & **lower belly white** ... From N. America through W to Bolivia & streams in yungas   IV

652) LONG-TAILED TYRANT
(Yetapá Negro) *Colonia colonus*

22 cm - Tame - In open - Sallying flight - Sharp whistle - Unmistakable - **Two long central rectrices** (♂: 9 cm; ♀ : 2 cm) - **Black** - Rump, **crown & nape white** - J: Lacks white - Normal tail ... From Honduras to Bolivia & Paraguay ... Migrant B - Humid forests & capueras in **Misiones**   III

653) STREAMER-TAILED TYRANT
(Yetapá Grande) *Gubernetes yetapa*

40 cm - In open perching low - Strong - Unmistakable - Ashy grey rather striated - Black wings with rufous band - Black **tail** (22 cm) **very long & deeply forked -White throat surrounded by rufous ...** Brazil, Paraguay & Bolivia... Reed beds & savannas near water in NE   II

654) STRANGE-TAILED TYRANT
(Yetapá de Collar) *Yetapa risora*

31 cm - In view on shrubs & fences - Tail (20 cm) with **very long & wide rectrices,** fluttered in flight - Upperparts & **wide collar black** - Underparts white - Orange throat & bill - ●: 20 cm - Different-Upperparts brownish - **Long rectrices** shorter & **thin** - Ochraceous collar - J: Striated ... Brazil & Paraguay URUGUAY ... Wet grasslands of NE (Ibera, Corrientes)   III

655) COCK-TAILED TYRANT
(Yetapá Chico) *Alectrurus tricolor*

18 cm - Looks like 654) - Smaller - **Two strange central rectrices** (6 cm) **very wide & vertical** - Upperparts & half collar black - Forehead, conspicuous **wing patch & underparts white** - Orange bill - ♀: Upperparts brownish - Normal wings & tail darker - Underparts whitish ... Brazil, Paraguay & Bolivia ... Wet grasslands in NE   II

216

KNIPOLEGUS: Tame - Passive - Hunt in flight - White wingbands- ♀♀ *(except 656): Different - More colorful & not near* ♂♂ *-Brownish grey backs -* **Rufous rumps -Conspicuous pale wing bars** *- Brown irises - (6 species)*

656) CRESTED BLACK-TYRANT
(Viudita Copetona) *Knipolegus lophotes* **19 cm** - Allopatric with 657) - Pairs perched well in sight - **Sexes alike-Black** - Bluish sheen - Conspicuous & pointed **erect crest** - Black bill - Brown iris ... Brazil ... Open fields & hills, often near water in **URUGUAY**

657) WHITE-WINGED BLACK-TYRANT
(Viudita Común) *Knipolegus aterrimus* 16 cm - Half crest - **Black** without sheen - Shiny plumbeous bill - Iris chestnut, not red - ♀: Rufous tail with half end black - **Underparts cinnamon, not striated** ... Peru, Bolivia & Paraguay ... Not in wetlands - Various habitats IV

658) BLUE-BILLED BLACK-TYRANT
(Viudita Pico Celeste) *Knipolegus cyanirostris* 14 cm - Resembles 657) - Different habitat - Inconspicuous wing patch - **Sky blue bill - Red Iris -** ♀: **Chestnut crown** - Brown back - Rectrices edged rufous - Conspicuous **black ventral striation** ... Brazil & Paraguay - URUGUAY ... Forests & capueras often near water in NE (El Palmar NP) III

659) HUDSON'S BLACK TYRANT
(Viudita Chica) *Knipolegus hudsoni* 13 cm - Little known - In open - Low flight diving into reed beds - Resembles 657) - Smaller - **White spot on flanks** in flight forms a semicircle with wingband - (Two outer primaries very pointed) - ♀: Looks like ♀ 657) - Smaller - Cinnamon crown - **Underparts** whitish, without striations breast ... Brazil, Paraguay & Bolivia ... Probable Migrant C ... Forests & shrubby steppes, often near water II

217

660) PLUMBEOUS TYRANT

(Viudita Plomiza) *Knipolegus cabanisi*
15 cm - Perched in open - Sallying flight- **Olivaceous plumbeous** - Wings & tail black - Bill shiny grey - **Red iris** - ♀: Olivaceous brown - Plumbeous breast [with slight pale striation] - **Rectrices with rufous** & black **webs** ... Peru & Bolivia ... Medium strata in montane forests & nearby areas in NW   IV

661) CINEREOUS TYRANT

(Viudita Chaqueña)
                    Knipolegus striaticeps
12 cm - Falling display flight, with vertical wings & tail - Low trill - **Plumbeous** - Blackish face & tail - Greyish wing bars - **Red iris** - ♀: **Cinnamon crown** - Rectrices edged rufous - Iris like ♂ ... Brazil, Paraguay & Bolivia ... Forests & savannas of Chaqueño type   III

662) VARIEGATED FLYCATCHER

(Tuquito Rayado) *Empidonomus varius*
17 cm - Tame - Passive - Hunts on wing- Loud *cheek..* & sharp whistle - More slender & smaller than 663) - **Bill not long** - Small crest - Blackish head with **long eyebrow & malar white** - Hidden golden crown - Blackish **back barely scaled** - Rufous rump - Rufous & black rectrices - Whitish **underparts with** wide brown **striations** - J: Lacks striations - Looks like 671) ... S. America through the E to Bolivia & Paraguay- URUGUAY ... Migrant B - Medium & high strata in forests & capueras   IV

663) STREAKED FLYCATCHER

(Benteveo Rayado)
                    Myiodynastes maculatus
19 cm - More heard than seen - **Noisy-** Restless - Load *kwit..i & rek* - Repeated *weero..weero..weet* - Stocky - Kiskadee (672) shaped - **Bill longer & thick**er than in 662) - More conspicuous **dorsal & ventral striations** - Eyebrow shorter ... From C. America, except Chile ... URUGUAY ... Migrant B- High strata in forests   IV

218

664) PIED WATER-TYRANT
(Viudita Blanca) *Fluvicola pica*

12 cm - Quite terrestrial - In marshes - In open - Showy - **Black upper-parts- Wide forehead, face,** thin rump, bars in coverts & remiges & **underparts white** - J: Resembles ♀ 665) - Brown crown & back ... From Panama, except Chile - URUGUAY ... Flooded savannas, marshes & lakes
IV

665) WHITE-HEADED MARSH-TYRANT
(Lavandera)
Arundinicola leucocephala

12 cm - Looks like 664) but showier - Same habitat & behavior - Less terrestrial - **Black - White hood** - Orange in mandible - ♀: Upperparts brown - Forehead & underparts whitish ... S. America except Chile ... Reed beds & marshes in N
II

666) SOOTY TYRANNULET
(Piojito Gris) *Serpophaga nigricans*

11 cm - Tame - In marshes - In open - Even on floating vegetation - Flicks & opens tail - Sallying flight - Short *chik* on perching - **Grey - Black tail** - Brown wings with pale bars - Hidden white crown - [Yellowish undertail coverts] - Chestnut iris ... Brazil, Paraguay & Bolivia - URUGUAY ... Wetlands
IV

667) MANY-COLORED RUSH-TYRANT
(Tachurí Sietecolores)
Tachuris rubrigastra-2R

10 cm - Tame but reclusive - In marshes -Pleasant call - Showy plumage - Black **crown with red center-** Olive back - Wingband & outer rectrices white - **Half collar & tail black-** Underparts golden yellow - **Undertail coverts rosy** - J: Pale ... Bordering countries & Peru - URUGUAY ... Reed beds
IV

668) CATTLE TYRANT
(Picabuey)   *Machetornis rixosus*
17 cm - Tame - Gurgling song, rare in tyrants - Hunts in **short runs** - Around **& on cattle** - Also arboreal - Looks like 676) - **Pale** - Ashy grey head turned brownish on back - **Hidden red** erectile **crown** - Underparts yellow ... S. America except Ecuador, Peru & Chile - URUGUAY ... Savannas, forests, rural & **Inhabited areas**   V

669) YELLOW-BROWED TYRANT
(Suirirí Amarillo)
            Satrapa icterophrys-[2R]
16 cm - Tame - Passive - **Olive upperparts** (plumbeous in NW) - Whitish bars on coverts & inner remiges - Conspicuous **golden yellow eyebrow & underparts** ... Venezuela, Brazil, Bolivia & Paraguay - URUGUAY ... Savannas & montane forests, almost always near water   IV

670) YELLOW TYRANNULET
(Mosqueta Ceja Amarilla)
            Capsiempis flaveola
11 cm - Pairs or flocks in winter - Tame - Repeated *woo..tee..ree..ree..* - Also low *brrr* - Resembles 669) - Different habitat - Thin tail - Conspicuous **eyebrow,** two bars on coverts **& underparts golden yellow** ... From Nicaragua through the E to Bolivia & Paraguay ... Low & medium strata of forest edges in **Misiones**   III

671) PIRATIC FLYCATCHER
(Tuquito Chico)   *Legatus leucophaius*
14 cm - Near caciques' colonies in breeding season - Pirates closed nests - Repeated & sharp whistle *fee..eeoh* - Resembles 662) (even more to J) - Smaller - Short bill - **Upperparts uniform** brown - Hidden yellow crown - Rump & **tail lack rufous** - Dark small crest, ocular band & moustache, separated by white eyebrow, malar & throat - Underparts yellowish striated on breast ... From Mexico except Chile ... Medium strata in capueras & forests of N   III

Reread characters of group with each species

FLYCATCHERS from 672) to 675):
Alike - Differ in sizes, bills & calls - Hunt
on wing - Olivaceous brown backs - Black
heads with conspicuous white eyebrows (headbands in 672 & 673) -
Underparts yellow - JJ: Cinnamon
bars in coverts & remiges - (4 species) (.)

672) GREAT KISKADEE
(Benteveo Común)
        Pitangus sulphuratus -[2R]
22 cm - Very well known - Audacious -
Fishes & hovers - Noisy - Sharp
kiskadee & other calls - Large head -
Strong bill but less than in 673) - Cin-
namon bars on remiges ... From N.
America, except Chile - URUGUAY...
Various habitats, often wet ones - In-
habited places   VI

673) BOAT-BILLED
FLYCATCHER
(Pitanguá)   *Megarhynchus pitangua*
21 cm - In open - Noisy - Rasping
teerrree.. & repeated *chueereebeer-
eebeeree,* unmistakable with calls of
672) - **Enormous & wide bill** with
curved maxilla - Short legs ... From
Mexico, except Chile ... High strata in
forests of NE   III

674) VERMILION-CROWNED
FLYCATCHER   (Benteveo
Mediano)   *Myiozetetes similis*
16 cm - In open on bushes near or in
water - Series of sharp & repeated
whistles *whit...* - Much smaller &
smaller head than 672) - Short bill -
Throat also **white** - Bars on coverts
& remiges - Hidden orange crown
rarely visible ... From C. America to
Bolivia & Paraguay ... Medium height
in humid forests & capueras of NE IV

675) THREE-STRIPED
FLYCATCHER
(Benteveo Chico) *Conopias trivirgata*
14 cm - Resembles 674) - Similar bill-
Harsh *cree..cree* - Back slightly more
olive - Lacks hidden spot on crown and
bars on coverts - **Yellow throat** as
rest of underparts ... Brazil & Paraguay ... High strata in humid forests &
capueras of NE   III

(.) *Pitangus lictor,* small with thin bill, recently captured in B. Aires   **221**

676) TROPICAL KINGBIRD
(Suirirí Real)   *Tyrannus melancholicus*

20 cm - In open & high perches - Sallying flight - Rapid, sharp & almost a trill
seereeree - **Triangular forked tail** -
Grey hood - Hidden orange crown -
Back & breast olivaceous grey - Rest of
underparts golden yellow - Migrant B ...
From N. America, except Chile - URU-
GUAY ... Forests, savannas, clearings,
plantations & rural areas   V

677) FORK-TAILED FLYCATCHER
(Tijereta)   *Muscivora tyrannus*

38 cm - Hunts on wing - Unmistakable-
Head & very long tail (28 cm)
black- Hidden yellow crown - Grey
back - **White underparts** - ♀: Tail 14
cm - J: Tail short - Migrant B (in flocks)
until N. America, except Chile & Peru-
URUGUAY ... Savannas, forests,
shrubby steppes & rural areas   V

678) EASTERN KINGBIRD
(Suirirí Boreal)   *Tyrannus tyrannus*

18 cm - Groups - Slender - Looks like J
677) - **Black head** - Hidden red
crown- Plumbeous back - **Black tail
with white tip - Underparts white**,
greyish on breast - Migrant A - High
strata in forests of N   II

679) SIRYSTES
(Suirirí Silbón)   *Sirystes sibilator*

17 cm - Tame - Flies around - In open -
Continuous whistle *fuí.fuí..fuí..fuio* -
Slender - Looks like *Myiarchus* & 681)
Ashy grey - Conspicuous **crest,
wings & tail black** - Back with inconspicuous brown striations - **Grey bars
on coverts** & inner remiges ... From
Panama, except Chile ... High strata in
humid forests of **Misiones**   IV

680)SHEAR-TAILED GRAY-TYRANT
(Viudita Coluda)   *Muscipipra vetula*

21 cm - In open - Sallying flight - Bisyllabic whistle, low but characteristic - **Grey in contrast with black of wings & of long forked tail** ... Brazil & Paraguay ... High & medium strata in capueras & humid forests of **Misiones** (Mocona)   II

681) CROWNED SLATY-FLYCATCHER
(Tuquito Gris)
Empidonomus aurantioatrocristatus
17 cm - **Very tame** - In open - Sallying flight - Cricket-like *yeet..*- **Slender-Small crest -Almost uniform brownish grey** -Underparts greyish-[Lower belly yellowish] - **Black crown** with hidden golden yellow center - **Grey eyebrow** - J: Whitish eyebrow - Rufous bars on remiges & rectrices - Lacks hidden crown ... Colombia, Ecuador, Brazil & Paraguay - URUGUAY ... Forests & savannas of Chaqueño type   IV

682) RUFOUS-TAILED ATTILA
(Burlisto Cabeza Gris) *Atila phoenicurus (.)*
17 cm - Continuous & rythmic trisyllabic sequence - Resembles various birds, like 683) - **Plumbeous head -Rest rufous**, paler on rump & underparts ... Venezuela, Brazil & Paraguay... Medium & high strata in humid forests of **Misiones**   I

683) RUFOUS CASIORNIS
(Burlisto Castaño)   *Casiornis rufa (.)*
16 cm - Descending series of sharp trisyllabic whistles - Resembles 682), 615), ♀ 613), ♀ 828), ♀829), etc - Upperparts **rufous** more conspicuous in small crest, coverts & tail - **Ochraceous underparts,** cinnamon on breast & undertail coverts - **Bill with cinnamon base & black tip** ... Brazil, Paraguay & Bolivia ... Medium strata in forests & savannas in N   II

(.) Previously included in Fam. Cotingidae

MYIARCHUS: Alike - Tame - Passive - Sing at dawn - Several diurnal calls - Slender - Erect postures - Conspicuous small crests - Long bills & tails - Olivaceous brown upperparts - Grey throats & breasts - Rest of underparts yellowish - JJ: Slight rufous edges on rectrices - (4 species)

684) BROWN-CRESTED FLYCATCHER (Burlisto Cola Castaña) *Myiarchus tyrannulus* 18 cm - Short & repeated whistles *kuit..-* Pale bars on coverts & inner remiges -**Rufous bars on primaries** inconspicuous - **Edges of rectrices rufous,** visible ventrally ... From N. America, except Chile ... Forests & savannas   IV

685) SWAINSON'S FLYCATCHER (Burlisto Pico Canela) *Myiarchus swainsoni-*2R 18 cm - Resembles 686) (Sympatric race of NE even more) - Melancholic guttural *mauu* - Whistle *wío*, not *wirrrr* call - Tail somewhat short in relation to pointed wings - Conspicuous **white bars** (inconspicuous in NE) - **Blackish face & cinnamon rump** (not in NE race) - Bill not black - Base or all **mandible cinnamon** ... S. America, except Chile - URUGUAY ... Migrant B-Forests, even in dry areas & savannas   IV

686) SHORT-CRESTED FLYCATCHER (Burlisto Pico Negro) *Myiarchus ferox* 18 cm - **Low trill** *wirrrr* - Rattle - Does not call *mauu* or *kuit* - Almost indistinguishable from NE race of 685) - Inconspicuous bars in coverts & remiges - Tail somewhat long in relation to rounded wings - **Black bill** without brown or cinnamon mandible ... S. America, except Chile ... Forests & savannas of NE   II

687) DUSKY-CAPPED FLYCATHER (Burlisto Corona Negra) *Myiarchus tuberculifer* 16 cm - Hunts on wing - Melancholic whistle & call *wirr* - **Black crown - Olivaceous back** - Without bars on coverts - Belly yellower ... From N. America, except Chile ... Yungas   III

688) GREATER PEWEE
(Burlisto Copetón)
Contopus fumigatus
17 cm - Tame - Passive - In heights in open - Often on dry trees - Continuous & repeated *peet* - Looks like *Elaenia* with rather long bill - Dull plumage - Slender - Conspicuous **erect small crest** - Brownish grey - Greyish underparts - Whitish lower belly - Slight bars on coverts & remiges ... From Venezuela along W except Chile ... Forests & yungas III

689) TROPICAL PEWEE
(Burlisto Chico)
Contopus cinereus - 2R
13 cm - Resembles 688) - Slight small crest - Whistle *fuit..fuit..fuit* & sonorous *pewee* while **waggles head** - Dark - Whitish lores - **Yellow mandible** ... From Venezuéla, except Chile ... Humid forests & capueras
III

690) EULER'S FLYCATCHER
(Mosqueta Parda)
Empidonax euleri - 2R
12 cm - Tame - Hunts hopping or with sallying flight - Restless - Whistle *fee..feewee* - Resembles 699) without striations - Smaller than 692) & lacks eyebrow - **Brown upperparts**- Blackish wings with conspicuous **cinnamon bars on coverts** & barely some on inner remiges - Ochraceous lores - Greyish breast turning whitish on lower belly - Pale mandible ... From Venezuela, except Chile - URUGUAY... Low & medium strata in capueras & forests III

691) TRAILL'S FLYCATCHER
(Mosqueta Boreal) *Empidonax traillii*
12 cm - Passive - Flicks tail - Dull plumage - Brownish upperparts - **Two white bars on** blackish **wings** - Underparts whitish, more greyish on breast & yellowish on lower belly - Pale mandible ... Migrant A ... Humid forests of NW & NE II

225

Memorize the Topography of a Bird

692) FUSCOUS FLYCATCHER
(Mosqueta Ceja Blanca)
Cnemotriccus fuscatus
14 cm - Passive & inconspicuous - Clear whistle *uuuuui* & other calls - Resembles 690) - Larger - **Whitish eyebrow- Brown back,** more chestnut on rump - **Cinnamon bars** on coverts & inner remiges - Ashy grey breast turned whitish on belly - Black bill ... From Venezuela, except Chile ... Medium & low strata in forests & savannas in NW & NE   II

693) SCRUB FLYCATCHER
(Suirirí Pico Corto) *Sublegatus modestus*
13 cm - In open - Whistle *feeí* - Looks like *Elaenia* - **Small crest** - Lacks periocular or hidden crown - Slight eyebrow, bars on coverts & inner remiges whitish - Grey breast - Rest of underparts yellowish - **Short black bill** ... From Costa Rica, except Chile - URUGUAY ... Savannas, forests & shrruby steppes (not in humid forests) III

694) SUIRIRI FLYCATCHER
(Suirirí Común)   *Suiriri suiriri*
13 cm - Sallying flight - Loud, short & nasal *eu* - Also *teeoh..teeoh..prrr* & other calls - **Upperparts** brownish **grey,** greyer on head & neck - Wings & tail black - Conspicuous **whitish bars on coverts** & inner remiges - Greyish breast - Rest of **underparts white** [slightly yellowish on lower belly] - Black bill ... Brazil, Paraguay & Bolivia- URUGUAY ... Savannas & forests III

695) GREAT SUIRIRI FLYCATCHER
(Suirirí Grande)   *Suiriri affinis (.)*
14 cm - Somewhat resembles 694) (in general considered conspecific) - Bill longer & stronger - Soft call - Sings while lifting both wings - Noisy - Song in duet - **Flicks tail** slightly - **Whitish rump** - **Yellow belly** ... Brazil ... Forests & capueras   I

226   (.) Besides being cited once for Salta, there is one probable nesting record in Pilcomayo NP, Formosa

696) STREAK-THROATED BUSH-TYRANT (Birro Grande) *Myiotheretes striaticollis* 21 cm - Visible on high trees - Hunts on wing returning with slow flaps - Frequent *fíui* - Looks like 697) - Robust & long bill - **Rufous remiges & tail, with black tip**, conspicuous in flight- **White throat striated black - Cinnamon underparts** ... From Venezuela along W, except Chile ... Yungas
III

697) CLIFF FLYCATCHER (Birro Común)
Hirundinea ferruginea - 2R
16 cm - Very tame - Hunts on wing in acrobatic flight, like a swallow - On perching a trill *buirrrr* - Smaller than 696) - Rufous - Brown upperparts - **Remiges & tail with black tip** ... From Venezuela, except Chile - URUGUAY ... Humid ravines, forests & mainly **inhabited areas**
III

698) CINNAMON FLYCATCHER (Birro Chico) *Pyrrhomyias cinnamomea* 12 cm - Tame - Restless - Hunts on wing - Musical trill *chirrrr* - Smaller than 697) - Olivaceous back - Hidden golden crown - Ochre rump - Blackish wings & tail - **Rufous patch on remiges & bars on coverts - Underparts rufous** turned cinnamon on lower belly ... From Venezuela along W, except Chile ... High & medium strata in yungas
III

699) BRAN-COLORED FLYCATCHER (Mosqueta Estriada)
Myiophobus fasciatus
12 cm - Tame - Various monosyllabic calls & melodious trills, strange in a tyrant - **Cinnamon chestnut back** - Hidden yellow or orange crown - Black wings with **cinnamon bars on coverts** - Whitish underparts with conspicuous **dark pectoral striations**, not in 690) ... From Costa Rica, except Chile - URUGUAY ... Migrant B in S... Low & medium height in forests & plantations, often near water
IV

700) LARGE-HEADED FLATBILL
(Picochato Cabezón)

Ramphotrigon megacephala
13 cm - Call *ho..hoo* - Wide & flat bill - **Blackish** brown **crown** - Olivaceous back - Two **cinnamon bars on** blackish brown **coverts** - Thin **yellowish eyebrow** - Olivaceous breast turned yellowish on lower belly - Mandible with rosy base ... From Venezuela, except Ecuador & Chile ... High strata in humid forests of **Misiones** - II

701) YELLOW-OLIVE FLYCATCHER
(Picochato Grande)

Tolmomyias sulphurescens - 3R
13 cm - Reclusive - Three emphatic whistles *feet* - Characteristic **hanging nest** - Resembles 700) & other humid forest tyrants - Lores & cheeks pale - Dark postauricular - Upperparts olive - Two yellow bars on blackish coverts - Yellowish underparts with slight pectoral striations - Wide black maxilla & **white to rosy mandible** - Greyish iris... C. America, except Chile ... Medium & high strata in yungas & forests in N (Guaycolec, Formosa)   III

702) RUSSET-WINGED SPADEBILL
(Picochato Chico)

Platyrinchus leucoryphus
11 cm - Looks like 703) - **Bill** also **very wide** (12 mm) with black maxilla & rosy mandible - **Hidden white crown**- Upperparts olivaceous brown - **Chestnut wings** - Eyebrow, periocular & underparts whitish - Brown pectoral band ... Brazil & Paraguay ... Low & medium strata in humid forests of **Misiones**   I

703) WHITE-THROATED SPADEBILL
(Picochato Enano)

Platyrinchus mystaceus
9 cm - Tame - Reclusive - Short & noisy flight - Minute - Chubby - **Very short tail** - Very wide & flat bill - Hidden yellow crown - **Upperparts cinnamon brown** - Large eye with periocular & eyebrow white - Postocular & malar bands black - **White throat** - Underparts cinnamon white - ♀: Lacks yellow on crown ... From C. America, except Chile ... Low & medium strata in humid forests of NE   II

704) DRAB-BREASTED PYGMY-TYRANT (Mosqueta de Anteojos) *Hemitriccus diops* 10 cm - Difficult to see - Call *bit* or *bitbuit* - Small crest - **Olive upperparts - Loral half eyebrow white-** Without wing bars - Slight white spot on upper breast - Breast cinnamon grey turned whitish in rest of underparts ... Brazil & Paraguay ... Low & medium strata not far from water, in humid forests & capueras of **Misiones**   II

705) OCHRE-FACED TODY-FLYCATCHER (Mosqueta Cabeza Canela) *Todirostrum plumbeiceps-2R* 9 cm - Much more heard than seen - Low *brrrp* - Minute - **Cinnamon hood** with crown (& auricular in NE) plumbeous - Olive back - Whitish underparts - Two cinnamon bars on blackish coverts ... Brazil, Paraguay, Bolivia & Peru ... Low & dense strata in yungas, humid forests & capueras in NE & NW - (El Rey NP)   III

706) PEARLY-VENTED TODY-TYRANT (Mosqueta Ojo Dorado) *Idioptilon margaritaceiventer* 10 cm - Tame - Moves about vegetation - More heard than seen - Loud *chic..chac..chic..chic..* (reminding one of 716) - Also *chic..chic..chierrr* - **Large grey head** - Olivaceous back- Two pale wingbars - **Underparts whitish barely striated grey** on throat & breast - Somewhat long chestnut bill - **Golden iris** ... From Venezuela, except Ecuador & Chile ... Low & medium strata in forests & savannas of Chaqueño type   III

707) EARED PYGMY-TYRANT (Mosqueta Enana) *Myiornis auricularis* **7 cm** - Tame - Restless - Very rapid wing movement - Loud continuous call like sharp taps *pric* - Minute - Tail short & narrow - Upperparts olivaceous - Conspicuous **black auricular halfmoon** patch - Cinnamon face - Yellow bars on coverts, remiges, outer rectrices & underparts - **Throat & breast striated black** ... Brazil, Paraguay, Bolivia & Peru ... Edges of humid forests & capueras in **Misiones**   III

229

Reread characters of genus with each species

PHYLLOSCARTES: *Small - Somewhat erect tails except 708) - Alike & similar to other green tyrants - Olive backs - Tails rather long - (4 species)*

708) SOUTHERN BRISTLE-TYRANT
(Mosqueta Media Luna)
Phylloscartes eximius
10 cm - Active & noisy - Bill thin & short- **Blackish crown** - Long & discontinuous **white eyebrow** - **Yellow cheek** almost enclosed by **black halfmoon**- Wings & tail with green bars - Yellow belly - Rosy mandible ... Brazil & Paraguay ... Low & medium strata in humid forests & capueras in **Misiones** III

709) BAY-RINGED TYRANNULET
(Mosqueta Cara Canela)
Phylloscartes sylviolus
10 cm - Small crest - Bill thin & short - **Cinnamon periocular patch** - Wings & tail with green bars - **Whitish underparts** - Golden iris ... Brazil & Paraguay ... Medium strata in humid forests of **Misiones**   II

710) SAO PAULO TYRANNULET
(Mosqueta Oreja Negra)
Phylloscartes paulistus
10 cm - **Black auricular** ("ear") **spot**- **Green bars on remiges, not on coverts** - Olivaceous breast turned yellow on belly ... Brazil & Paraguay ... High strata in humid forests of **Misiones**   I

711) MOTTLED-CHEEKED
TYRANNULET   (Mosqueta Común)   *Phylloscartes ventralis - 2R*
10 cm - Tame - Active - Moves about vegetation - Continuous *cheeck* - Loud song - Soft trill *trrr* - Two conspicuous **yellowish bars on coverts** & slight ones on **blackish** brown remiges - **Yellow eyebrow** & underparts ... Brazil, Paraguay, Bolivia & Peru - URUGUAY ... Medium & high strata in humid forests & yungas   IV

230

712) TAWNY-CROWNED PYGMY-TYRANT

(Barullero) *Euscarthmus meloryphus*
10 cm - Much more heard than seen - Loud & repeated *prrreekecheekek* - Dull plumage, except for almost concealed **orange crown** - Upperparts uniform brown - Whitish underparts turned yellowish on lower belly ... From Venezuela, except Chile - URUGUAY ... Bushes & low vegetation in savannas & forests of Chaqueño type   IV

713) BEARDED TACHURI

(Tachurí Canela)
                    Polystictus pectoralis
9 cm - Hunts on wing - Small crest - Slight eyebrow - **Blackish hood striated white** - Cinnamon brown back - **Cinnamon** rump, **breast & flanks** - Cinnamon bars on coverts & remiges - Rest of underparts ochraceous white - ♀: Lacks hood ... From Venezuela, except Ecuador, Peru & Chile - URUGUAY ... Marsh vegetation & nearby areas   III

714) SHARP-TAILED TYRANT

(Tachurí Coludo) *Culicivora caudacuta*
10 cm - Looks like Red-capped Wren-Spinetail 531) - Long & narrow tail ending in points - White striations on blackish crown - Conspicuous **white eyebrow** - **Back striated cinnamon & blackish** - Cinnamon rump- Underparts cinnamon white - J: Shorter tail ... Brazil, Paraguay & Bolivia ... Grasslands & marshes in NE   II

715) VERMILION FLYCATCHER

(Churrinche) *Pyrocephalus rubinus*
13 cm - Shows itself - Short sallying flight - Soft *peent,* & *ch..churreen* in display flight - Showy - Conspicuous **red crown, small crest & underparts** - Rest blackish - ●: Dull plumage- Brownish grey back - **Breast striated grey - Undertail coverts rosy** - J: Like ♀ - Yellow lower belly ... From N. America - URUGUAY ... Migrant B (some individuals remain in N) ... Savannas, forests, shrubby steppes, & rural areas   IV

231

PSEUDOCOLOPTERYX: In marshes - Sing on top of stems - Rather reclusive - Small - Slender - Alike - Pale bars on coverts & inner remiges - (4 species)

716) WARBLING DORADITO
(Doradito Común)
Pseudocolopteryx flaviventris

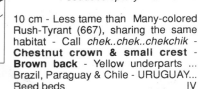

10 cm - Less tame than Many-colored Rush-Tyrant (667), sharing the same habitat - Call *chek..chek..chekchik* - **Chestnut crown & small crest** - **Brown back** - Yellow underparts ... Brazil, Paraguay & Chile - URUGUAY... Reed beds   IV

717) SUBTROPICAL DORADITO
(Doradito Oliváceo)
Pseudocolopteryx acutipennis

10 cm - **Olivaceous** small crest & **back** - Wings & tail brown - **Golden yellow underparts** ... Colombia, Ecuador, Peru & Bolivia ... Marsh vegetation on hills and mountains   II

718) DINELLI'S DORADITO
(Doradito Pardo)
Pseudocolopteryx dinellianus

9 cm - Loud & complex *chek..chek.. churee..churee* - Flight similar to that of 719), with call *chik* - Small crest & **crown brown** (not chestnut nor olive)- Back brown somewhat olivaceous - **Golden yellow throat turned olivaceous yellow on rest of underparts** ... Paraguay & Bolivia ... Marsh vegetation - (NE Cordoba)   III

719) CRESTED DORADITO
(Doradito Copetón)
Pseudocolopteryx sclateri

9 cm - Often flies with body in vertical position - **Erectile crest black streaked yellow** [very conspicuous]- Olivaceous **back striated** dark - Conspicuous yellow bars on blackish coverts - **Whitish eyebrow** - Golden yellow underparts ... Guianas, Brazil & Paraguay ... Reed beds & rural areas II

Fam. Tyrannidae, see page 38

720) GREATER WAGTAIL-TYRANT
(Calandrita)
Stigmatura budytoides-2R
13 cm - Noisy - Rapid & loud trisyllabic call in duet - **Olivaceous grey upperparts** - Conspicuous bars on coverts & inner remiges - **Long tail, somewhat erect, with white tip** - Conspicuous **yellowish eyebrow** & underparts ... Brazil, Paraguay & Bolivia ... Savannas, forests & shrubby steppes   IV

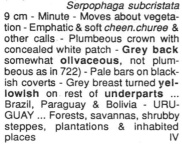

721) WHITE-CRESTED TYRANNULET
(Piojito Común)
Serpophaga subcristata
9 cm - Minute - Moves about vegetation - Emphatic & soft *cheen.churee* & other calls - Plumbeous crown with concealed white patch - **Grey back** somewhat **olivaceous**, not plumbeous as in 722) - Pale bars on blackish coverts - Grey breast turned **yellowish** on rest of **underparts** ... Brazil, Paraguay & Bolivia - URUGUAY ... Forests, savannas, shrubby steppes, plantations & inhabited places   IV

722) WHITE-BELLIED TYRANNULET
(Piojito Vientre Blanco)
Serpophaga munda(.)
9 cm - Prolonged & loud *chee..cheereereeree* - Looks like a small Suiriri Flycatcher (694) - Similar to 721) - Tail slightly longer - **Upperparts plumbeous** - White bars on blackish coverts - Grey breast turned **white** on rest of **underparts** ... Brazil, Paraguay & Bolivia - [URUGUAY] - Forests & savannas of W   II

723) PLAIN TYRANNULET
(Piojito Picudo)   *Inezia inornata*
9 cm - Resembles 721) - **Bill** more **robust** - **Lacks concealed patch on ashy grey crown** ... Brazil, Paraguay, Bolivia & Peru ... Savannas & *Tesaria* riverine forests in NW   II

(.) Sometimes considered conspecific with 721)   **233**

724) YELLOW-BILLED TIT-TYRANT
(Cachudito Pico Amarillo)
Anairetes flavirostris

10 cm - Tame - Restless - Conspicuous & **thin erect crest black** with white basal striation - Two whitish bars on coverts - Thick & conspicuous **black-ish pectoral striation** - Rest of underparts yellowish - Black bill with base of **mandible orange yellow** ... Peru, Bolivia & Chile ... Savannas, forests & shrubby steppes   III

725) TUFTED TIT-TYRANT
(Cachudito Pico Negro)
Anairetes parulus-3R

10 cm - Resembles 724) in coloration & behavior - Rapid *peerebeereebee* - Thin & conspicuous **blackish pectoral striation - Black bill** ... From Colombia through   W ... Forests, shrubby & Patagonian steppes & Andean ravines   III

726) WHITE-THROATED TYRANNULET
(Piojito Gargantilla)
Mecocerculus leucophrys

12 cm - Restless - Noisy - Loud & sharp *breep* & other calls - Upperparts olivaceous brown- Conspicuous ochraceous bars on coverts & inner remiges - Short eyebrow & **bulky throat white** - Breast ashy grey - Rest of underparts yellowish ... From Venezuela & Brazil along W to Bolivia ... Yungas   V

727) BUFF-BANDED TYRANNULET
(Piojito de los Pinos)
Mecocerculus hellmayri

10 cm - **Plumbeous crown - Olive back - Cinnamon rump** - Conspicuous bars more olivaceous than in 726)- White eyebrow - Olivaceous breast - Yellowish belly ... Peru & Bolivia ... Montane forests in **Jujuy** (Calilegua NP)   II

234

ELAENIA: Difficult to tell appart - (Pay attention to details & calls) - Tame - Passive- Short bills - Most follow this pattern: concealed white crowns, olivaceous brown backs, whitish bars on coverts & inner remiges, grey breasts, rest of underparts yellowish, pale eyelids & orange mandibles - [Migrants B] - (8 species)

728) HIGHLAND ELAENIA
(Fiofío Oscuro)　　*Elaenia obscura-2R*
16 cm - Loud low trill similar to that of 578) - **Large - Lacks concealed crown** - Two conspicuous ochraceous or white bars on coverts - Bars on remiges greenish yellow - **Underparts** rather dark & **olivaceous (not grey)**, yellowish on lower belly ... Brazil, Paraguay, Bolivia & Peru ... Medium strata in humid forests of NW & NE III

729) LARGE ELAENIA
(Fiofío Grande)　　*Elaenia spectabilis*
16 cm - Not in humid forests - Explosive whistle *pfeu* or *fuiu* - **Larger** than 730) - Bill higher & darker - More uniform grey breast ... Colombia, Brazil, Paraguay, Bolivia & Peru ... Capueras, forests & savannas　　　　III

730) YELLOW-BELLIED ELAENIA
(Fiofío Copetón)　　*Elaenia flavogaster*
14 cm - Resembles 729) - Harsh *vik..kriup..kriup*; also *riii*, sometimes in duet - **Conspicuous crest** - Bill browner, wider & lower - Conspicuous **bars on coverts** & tertiaries - Yellow on belly becomes slight striations on breast ... From C. America, except Chile ... High & medium strata in forests & savannas of N　　　　III

731) SLATY ELAENIA
(Fiofío Plomizo)　　*Elaenia strepera*
14 cm - Series of trills *t..t..t..trrr* ascending & descending - Different from other elaenias - **Plumbeous** - Inconspicuous wing bars - Lower belly whitish - ● & J: More **olivaceous** - Lower belly yellowish ... Venezuela, Colombia, Brazil, Bolivia & Peru ... Medium strata in yungas　　　　III

Details of genus *Elaenia* on previous page

732) WHITE-CRESTED ELAENIA
(Fiofío Silbón)   *Elaenia albiceps-2R*
13 cm - Often in open - Spaced & sad
feeo - Thin bill - **Small crest** more
conspicuous than in 733), **divided by
white triangle** down to nape -
Olivaceous grey breast ... From
Colombia & Brazil - URUGUAY ...
Southern race Migrant C - Araucano (V)
& Chaqueño Forests, shrubby steppes
& even inhabited areas   IV

733) SMALL-BILLED ELAENIA
(Fiofío Pico Corto)
                    Elaenia parvirostris
13 cm - Call *pk* - Song of 3 or 4
syllables - Also *pirr* or *pirr..rruí* - Very
much like 732), 734) & 735) - Concealed crown - Greyish malar - Breast
lacks olivaceous - Lower belly rather
whitish ... S. America except Chile -
URUGUAY ... Forests, savannas &
plantations   IV

734) OLIVACEOUS ELAENIA
(Fiofío Oliváceo) *Elaenia mesoleuca*
14 cm - Difficult to tell apart from
sympatrics 733) & 735) - Typical call
prrrt..prrprrírrr - High, fast, loud *woú*
call & repeated *peerr* - Lacks concealed crown - Bill wider than in 732) &
735) -Somewhat dark underparts, due
to olivaceous breast & flanks - Olive
malar ... Brazil & Paraguay ... Forests
in NE   III

735) LESSER ELAENIA
(Fiofío Belicoso) *Elaenia chiriquensis*
13 cm - Nests in plantations, not in
humid forests - Characteristic *wip* - Bill
like in 732), thinner than sympatrics
730), 733) & 734) - Concealed crown-
Brownish grey back, with slight or **no
olivaceous** - Conspicuous bars on
inner remiges - Smaller & with less
crest than 730) ... From Costa Rica,
except Chile ... Capueras & rural
areas in **Misiones**   III

736) GREENISH ELAENIA
(Fiofío Corona Dorada)
Myiopagis viridicata
12 cm - Resembles 737.) - Both look like *Elaenia* - Conspicuous & continuous *peeue..* - Semi concealed **golden band on crown** - Olivaceous back - **Lacks bars on coverts** - Conspicuous **whitish eyelid** - Breast olivaceous grey turned yellow on rest of underparts - Short & thin bill with orange mandible ... S. America, except Chile ... Medium & high strata in edges of forests in N   III

737) GRAY ELAENIA
(Fiofío Ceniciento)*Myiopagis caniceps*
11 cm - Shrill *weep* or *weep weep* - Brown wings with conspicuous **yellowish bars on coverts** & inner remiges, not in sympatric 736) - Also pale eyelid - Grey - Semi-concealed **white band on** plumbeous **crown** - Rest of upperparts plumbeous turned olivaceous - Greyish breast turned whitish on lower belly - **●: Yellow band on crown - Olive** back - With intermediate plumages ... From Panama, except Chile ... Humid forests in NW & NE   II

738) PATAGONIAN TYRANT
(Peutrén)   *Colorhamphus parvirostris*
12 cm - Tame - Passive - Moves about branches - Long & sharp *peeuuuu* - **Short bill - Chestnut upperparts - Two conspicuous rufous wing bars - Face & underparts grey** turned ochraceous on lower belly ... Chile ... Low & medium strata in clearings of Araucano Forest   III

739) MOUSE - COLORED TYRANNULET
(Piojito Pardo)   *Phaeomyias murina*
10 cm - Hunts on wing - Call *psh.. pee reereep* - Brown back - Blackish brown wings with two **whitish bars on coverts** reaching those of inner remiges-Greyish underparts - Yellowish lower belly - Orange mandible ... From Panama except Chile ... Low & medium strata in yungas & humid forests   III

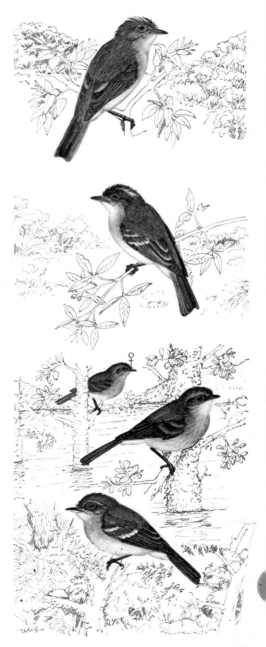

740) SEPIA-CAPPED FLYCATCHER
(Mosqueta Corona Parda)
Leptopogon amaurocephalus
12 cm - Tame - Lifts one wing
vertically- Prolonged trill similar to that of
Furnariidae - Other calls - **Crown,
wings & tail brown, contrasted
with olive back** - Ochraceous wing
bars - **Black auricular half moon
patch** ... From C. America, except
Chile ... Medium strata in forests of
NW & NE   III

**741) SOUTHERN BEARDLESS
   TYRANNULET**   (Piojito
Silbón) *Camptostoma obsoletum -2R*
9 cm - Looks like White-crested
Tyrannulet 721) - Moves less about
vegetation - Lacks concealed crown -
Whistle *fee..fwee..* - Also a series of
short notes like sharp laughter - Erect
posture - Conspicuous **erectile small
crest** - Brownish back - Ochraceous
or **cinnamon bars on coverts**
& inner remiges - **Whitish
underparts**, greyish on breast -
Cinnamon mandible ... From Costa Rica
except Chile - URUGUAY ... In foliage of
low trees in forests & savannas   . IV

**742) ROUGH-LEGGED
   TYRANNULET**   (Mosqueta
Pico Curvo) *Acrochordopus burmeisteri*
11 cm - Active - Monotonous
repetitions of sharp *sit..* - **Rather curved
maxilla** - Cinnamon mandible -
Olivaceous upperparts more uniform
than 743) - Green or cinnamon bars on
wing coverts - Forehead, eyebrow &
eyelid whitish ... From Costa Rica,
except Guianas & Chile ... Medium
strata in yungas & humid forests of
NW & NE   II

743) PLANALTO TYRANNULET
(Mosqueta Olivácea)
Phyllomyias fasciatus
10 cm - Resembles 741) & 742) -
Trisyllabic whistle - **Short bill** -
Olivaceous back - Crown browner &
darker-Bars on coverts & inner remiges
- Lores, eyelid & throat whitish -
Underparts yellow, more olivaceous on
breast ... Brazil & Paraguay ... High
strata in humid forests of **Misiones**   I

238

744) GREENISH TYRANNULET
(Mosqueta Corona Oliva)
Xanthomyias virescens

11 cm - Tail somewhat erect - **Nervous wing movement - Short bill** - Allopatric with 745) - Dull plumage - Olivaceous upperparts - Ochraceous bars on coverts & inner remiges - Whitish eyebrow - **Underparts** even underwing coverts **yellow, more olivaceous on breast** ... Venezuela, Brazil & Paraguay ... Medium strata in humid forests of **Misiones**   II

745) SCLATER'S TYRANNULET
(Mosqueta Corona Gris)
Xanthomyias sclateri

12 cm - Very much like 744) - **Brownish grey crown**, not like back- **Greyish breast turned yellowish** on rest of underparts ... Peru & Bolivia... Low & medium strata in yungas   II

746) GRAY-HOODED FLYCATCHER
(Ladrillito)   *Pipromorpha rufiventris*

13 cm - Tame - Passive - Moves wings nervously not extending them - **Plumbeous hood** - Olive back - **Cinnamon underparts** ... Brazil ... Low & medium dense strata in humid forests of **Misiones**   III

747) SOUTHERN ANTPIPIT
(Mosquitero)   *Corythopis delalandi (.)*

13 cm - Reclusive - Almost terrestrial - Passive - Hunts on wing - Loud & continuous whistle *tweet..twee.tweet.. twee.. fuiririri*   - Bill & long legs pale - Cinnamon olive back - Conspicuous **collar & spots** on breast **black - White underparts** ... Brazil, Paraguay & Bolivia ... Low strata in humid forests of **Misiones**   II

(.) Previously in Fam. Conopophagidae; no longer valid

Fam. Phytotomidae, see page 38

748) RUFOUS-TAILED PLANTCUTTER
(Rara) *Phytotoma rara*
18 cm - Passive - Pairs sit on bushes-
Eats buds - Rasping **song like
bleating** - Small crest- Thick bill-
**Rufous crown & underparts -
Back striated** black - Black wings
with conspicuous white bars - **Rufous
tail with central rectrices & wide
tip black** - Black face - White malar -
Red iris - ♥ : **Striated** - Tail like ♂:..
Chile ... Araucano Forest & shrubby
steppes in SW   III

749) WHITE-TIPPED PLANTCUTTER
(Cortarramas) *Phytotoma rutila-2R*
17 cm - Appearance & behavior of
748) - Bigger **crest - Wide forehead & underparts rufous -
Plumbeous back, without striations** - Black **tail with** outer tip
white- ♥:**Striations** more **conspicuous** than ♀748) - Tail like ♂...
Brazil, Paraguay & Bolivia - URU-
GUAY ... Savannas, forests, plantations, shrubby steppes & prepuna IV

Fam. Hirundinidae, see page 38

750) BARN SWALLOW
(Golondrina Tijerita) *Hirundo rustica*
15 cm - Flocks of adults & JJ - Soft
witwit - **Long deeply forked tail**
blackish, **with ventral white band -**
Blue collar & upperparts - **Rufous
throat** - Rest of underparts cinnamon
- J: Shorter tail - Forehead & throat cinnamon - Ochraceous underparts ...
URUGUAY ... Savannas, rural areas &
marshes - Migrant A, although a small
population breeds in Mar Chiquita, B.
Aires   IV

751) CLIFF SWALLOW
(Golondrina Rabadilla Canela)
        Petrochelidon pyrrhonota-2R
13 cm - Flocks flying in open areas -
Often with 750) - Soft warble -
Conspicuos **cinnamon white
forehead** & underparts - Blue crown -
Chestnut nape band & throat -
Cinnamon rump - J: Browner - White
forehead - Ochraceous rump ...
URUGUAY ... Migrant A - Savannas,
rural & marshy areas   IV

240

*PROGNE: **Large** - Rather wide wings-**Forked tails** black - (3 species)*

752) PURPLE MARTIN
(Golóndrina Purpúrea)   *Progne subis*

18 cm - Resembles 753) - Somewhat more purple - ●: Back more opaque - **Forehead, nape band,** belly & **throat whitish** - Breast ashy grey - [Irregular Migrant A] ... Cited in Cordoba   I

753) SOUTHERN MARTIN
(Golondrina Negra)   *Progne modesta*

18 cm - **Bluish black** with soft purple sheen - ♀: Underparts ashy grey with slight wave pattern ... Migrant B to Peru, Bolivia, Paraguay, Brazil & Guianas - URUGUAY ... Hills, savannas, rural areas, villages & seacoasts   V

754) GRAY-BREASTED MARTIN
(Golondrina Doméstica)
                     Progne chalybea

18 cm - Sometimes large **flocks** on trees **in towns** - Blue black back - [Throat & breast ashy grey with pale wave pattern] - Rest of **underparts white** - ♀: Browner back ... Migrant B to C. America, except Chile - URUGUAY ... Hills, savannas, rural areas, villages & seacoasts   V

755) BROWN-CHESTED MARTIN
(Golondrina Parda)
                     Phaeoprogne tapera

16 cm - Breeds **in horneros' nests** - **Glides with wings below horizontal** - Warble like an arpeggio - Resembles 754) - Tail barely forked - **Upperparts brown - Brown collar** [turned into spots along center of belly]- Rest of underparts white ... Migrant B to Panama, except Chile ... URUGUAY ... Forests, savannas & rural areas   V

*TACHYCINETA: Medium size - Tails barely forked - **Rumps** & underparts **white** - JJ: Backs browner - (3 species)*

756) WHITE-RUMPED SWALLOW
(Golondrina Ceja Blanca)
Tachycineta leucorrhoa
13 cm - Blue back with **slight green sheen** - Inconspicuous **white forehead & half eyebrow** - White **underwing coverts** ... Brazil, Paraguay, Bolivia & Peru - URUGUAY ... Savannas, forests, lakes, rural & inhabited areas   V

757) CHILEAN SWALLOW
(Golondrina Patagónica)
Tachycineta leucopyga
13 cm - Very similar to 756) - Allopatric in breeding period - Lands more on ground - **Slight violaceous dorsal sheen** - Lacks white forehead & eyebrow [except in J] - White bar on inner remiges more conspicuous & contrasted than in 756) - **Ashy grey underwing coverts** ... Chile ... Migrant C to Brazil, Paraguay & Bolivia - [URUGUAY] ... Forests & nearby areas in Patagonia   IV

758) WHITE-WINGED SWALLOW
(Golondrina Ala Blanca)
Tachycineta albiventer
13 cm - Very tame - Attractive **pattern of greenish sky blue & white** - Conspicuous **white band in folded wing** ... From Venezuela, except Chile ... Rivers & marshes in forests (Always present in Iguazu Falls)   III

759) BANK SWALLOW
(Golondrina Zapadora) *Riparia riparia*
11 cm - Looks like a small 755) - Tail barely forked - **Brown upperparts** - [Slight whitish eyebrow & lores] - **Brown collar** somewhat prolonged ventrally - Rest white ... [URUGUAY]... Savannas, wetlands & rural areas - Migrant A   III

760) BLUE-AND-WHITE SWALLOW
(Golondrina Barranquera)
Notiochelidon cyanoleuca-2R

11 cm - Around cliffs - Loose flocks - Sometimes sitting on ground - **Looks like a small 754)** - Tail barely forked **Back** & undertail coverts **bluish black - Lacks white rump** - Underparts white -J: Back & half collar brown, not full collar like in 759) ... From C. America - URUGUAY ... Various habitats, including villages & forests V

761) BLACK-COLLARED SWALLOW (Golondrina de Collar) *Atticora melanoleuca*

14 cm - Low flight over water - Sits on emergent rocks - **Long deeply forked tail** - Back, undertail coverts & **collar bluish black** - Underparts white - J: Brown instead of black ... Colombia, Venezuela, Guianas & Brazil ... Rivers in humid forests of **Misiones** (Iguazu Falls) III

762) ROUGH-WINGED SWALLOW
(Golondrina Ribereña)
Stelgidopteryx ruficollis

13 cm - Resembles 763) - More elegant - **Brown upperparts - Pale rump** - Cinnamon face & throat turned brown on breast - Rest of underparts ochraceous ... From N. America except Chile - URUGUAY ... Rivers, streams & marshes III

763) TAWNY-HEADED SWALLOW (Golondrina Cabeza Rojiza) *Alopochelidon fucata*

11 cm - Tail more forked than in 762) - Lacks pale rump - **Head & nape band cinnamon - Blackish crown-** Brown back - Cinnamon breast - Rest of underparts white ... Venezuela, Peru, Brazil, Paraguay & Bolivia - URUGUAY ... Savannas, rural areas & wetlands IV

243

Fam. *Corvidae, see page 38*

CYANOCORAX: Gregarious - Noisy - Varied calls, even mocking - Tame & even audacious - Arboreal & somewhat terrestrial - Large - Long tails - Strong bills - Striking colors with sheen - (3 species)

764) PURPLISH JAY
(Urraca Morada)
Cyanocorax cyanomelas

33 cm - **Purple** - Slight frontal tuft - Black hood & large bib - Tail violaceous blue ... Brazil, Paraguay, Bolivia & Peru - [URUGUAY] ... Forests in N (Guaycolec, Formosa)   III

765) AZURE JAY
(Urraca Azul) *Cyanocorax caeruleus*

35 cm - Resembles 764) - **Blue** with sky blue & violaceous sheens - Frontal tuft - Hood & large bib black ... Brazil & Paraguay ... Forests, often of *Araucaria*, in NE   II

766) PLUSH-CRESTED JAY
(Urraca Común)
Cyanocorax chrysops-2R

32 cm - Conspicuous - Striking colors- **Crown & small crest velvet black- Eyebrow & nape lilaceous sky blue** - Back & bib violaceous black - Wide tip on tail & rest of **underparts yellowish cream** - Golden iris J: Lack sky blue areas ... Brazil, Paraguay & Bolivia - URUGUAY ... Forests, including gallery forests & capueras
V

244

767) RUFOUS-THROATED DIPPER

(Mirlo de Agua)   *Cinclus schulzi*
14 cm - Aquatic - Jumps from stone to stone like *Cinclodes* - [Goes under water] - Shakes wings while **short tail** is lowered - Long fluttering flight almost skimming - Chubby - **Dark grey - White wing band** - Conspicuous **cinnamon bib** ... Bolivia ... Fast flowing mountain **streams** in forests - (Rio Los Sosa, Tucuman) - In winter in humid forests   III

Fam. Troglodytidae, see page 39

*WRENS: Small - Active - Tame - Short flight - Wings & **erect tails** barred black - Underparts ochraceous - Flanks & undertail coverts cinnamon - (3 species) (.)*

768) GRASS WREN

(Ratona Aperdizada)
            Cistothorus platensis - 3R
10 cm - Reclusive - Comes out above grass - Pleasant sharp call in pairs of strophes - **Ochraceous** - Striated black on crown - Conspicuous **black & whitish dorsal striation** - Cinnamon rump - Orange legs ... From N. America... Reed beds & grasses near water   III

769) HOUSE WREN

(Ratona Común)
            Troglodytes aedon - 5R
10 cm - Varied & pleasant song ended in long trill - Also *chrrrc* - **Near houses-** Moves about bushes & hedges - **Brown - Wings & tail chestnut** (barred) ... From N. America- URUGUAY ... Various habitats VI

770) MOUNTAIN WREN

(Ratona Ceja Blanca)
            Troglodytes solstitialis
9 cm - Looks like Tapaculo (606) - Lacks white throat - Also resembles 769) - **Climbs well** - Cricket like *yeep..yeep* - Shorter tail - Conspicuous **white eyebrow** - Barred undertail coverts ... From Venezuela along the W...Low & medium strata in yungas III

MIMUS: In open - Terrestrial & on bushes- Alike - Look like thrushes - More slender - Bills more curved - Not in humid forests - Songs varied, pleasant & conspicuous - Whistle & immitate - Long tails- White eyebrows- (4 species)

771) BROWN-BACKED MOCKINGBIRD

(Calandria Castaña) *Mimus dorsalis* 21 cm - Resembles 772) - **Chestnut back** - Rufous rump - Conspicuous **white wing patch - White tail with central rectrices black** - Underparts white ... Bolivia ... Prepuna (Humahuaca, Jujuy)   IV

772) WHITE-BANDED MOCKINGBIRD

(Calandria Real)   *Mimus triurus* 20 cm - **Brownish grey** back - Rufous rump - **Tail, like 771)**, & more conspicuous **white wing band** form **striking pattern in flight** - Ochraceous flanks - Bordering countries ... URUGUAY ... Savannas, shrubby steppes & rural areas   IV

773) CHALK-BROWED MOCKINGBIRD   (Calandria Grande)   *Mimus saturninus* **25 cm** - Slight **dorsal striation** - White wing bars less conspicuous than in 774) - **Longer tail semierect, with outer web & wide tip on rectrices white** (except central ones) - **Conspicuous eyebrow** & underparts whitish ... Brazil, Paraguay & Bolivia - URUGUAY ... Savannas, forest edges, rural & **inhabited areas**   IV

774) PATAGONIAN MOCKINGBIRD

(Calandria Mora) *Mimus patagonicus* **22 cm** - Resembles 773) - Different song - **Uniform back** - Two conspicuous **dotted white bars** on coverts - **Tail** barely shorter, **only with tip white - Underparts cinnamon ochre** ... Chile ... Andean & Patagonian, also in arid & shrubby steppes - Part of southern population migrates N   IV

775) BLACK-CAPPED MOCKINGTHRUSH
(Angú) *Donacobius atricapillus -2R*
20 cm - In marshes - Different to *Mimus* - Showy coloration - Tame - Does not imitate - Loud melodious screams, sometimes in duet - **Black head** - Chestnut back - Conspicuous **white wing patch** - Long graded **black tail bordered white** - Cinnamon underparts - **Golden iris** ... From Panama, except Chile ... Marshes & reed beds in NE   III

Fam. Turdidae, see page 39

776) SPOTTED NIGHTINGALE-THRUSH
(Zorzalito Overo)   *Catharus dryas*
16 cm - Almost terrestrial - Shy & reclusive - More heard than seen - Series of double repeated, variable & flute like notes - Conspicuous **black head** - Olivaceous brown black - Striated throat - **Underparts yellowish spotted black** - Orange bill, eyelid & legs ... From Mexico along W - Yungas - (Calilegua NP)   II

777) SWAINSON'S THRUSH
(Zorzalito Boreal) *Catharus ustulatus*
16 cm - **Small flocks** on tree tops - Sonorous cheep & weak feew - Does not look like *Turdus* - **Small** - Bill somewhat short - **Breast spotted** like pipit - Underparts whitish - Pale eyelid - Migrant A ... Yungas & forests in NW   II

778) YELLOW-LEGGED THRUSH
(Zorzal Azulado) *Platycichla flavipes*
20 cm - Sings perches in open - Sometimes imitates - Call *tsrip* - Loud, varied & melodious song - **Hood to breast, wings & tail black** - Rest grey (may look blackish or bluish) - Bill, eyelid & legs yellow - ♀ : Olivaceous brown - Striated throat - Whitish lower belly - Eyelid & legs yellow (not black as 779) ... From Caribbean along E - Humid forests & capueras in **Misiones**   I

247

TURDUS: Terrestrial & on bushes - Often reclusive - Flick tails - Alike - Sing well - Do not imitate - Often humid forest dwellers - Yellow eyelids ... From 779) to 783): Backs olivaceous brown - Throats striated- (8 species)

779) CREAMY-BELLIED THRUSH
(Zorzal Chalchalero)
Turdus amaurochalinus
21 cm - Song less melodious, similar to 781) - Call *puk* - Sharp **mewing** - On wing *psib* - Much tail flicking - Black lores - Breast ashy grey turned **whitish on lower belly** (Lacks rufous)- ♂ adult: yellow bill - J: Spotted breast... Bordering countries & Peru - URUGUAY ... Forests, plantations & villages   IV

780) PALE-BREASTED THRUSH
(Zorzal Sabiá)   *Turdus leucomelas*
21 cm - Song softer & less melodious than 781) - Call *schra* - Similar to 779) & 781) - Dull plumage - **Ashy grey head** - Inconspicuous **cinnamon remiges & underwing coverts** - Throat striation little conspicuous - Underparts uniform cinnamon grey (individual variation) - Undertail coverts whitish - Dark bill ... From Venezuela, except Chile ... Humid forests, capueras & villages in NE (Iguazu NP)   IV

781) RUFOUS-BELLIED THRUSH
(Zorzal Colorado)   *Turdus rufiventris*
23 cm - Repeated & melodious *koro..cheeere* from early morning - Loud *dru..wip* & other calls - Throat striation continued on breast - **Belly & lower belly orange rufous** more conspicuous in NP - ♂ adult: Yellow bill... Brazil, Paraguay & Bolivia - URUGUAY... Forests, plantations & **villages**   V

782) AUSTRAL THRUSH
(Zorzal Patagónico)
Turdus falcklandii-2R
24 cm - More showy coloration than previous ones - Looks somewhat like NW race 784) - Allopatric - **Head & tail blackish** - Cinnamon underparts - **Bill & legs orange yellow** - J : Lacks black on head - Spotted breast ... Chile Araucano Forest & nearby areas, plantations & villages in **Patagonia**   IV

783) WHITE-NECKED THRUSH
(Zorzal Collar Blanco)
Turdus albicollis-2R
19 cm - Reclusive - Nasal *nac* - Song reminding that of Rufous-bellied Thrush (781) - Often imitates - Scrapes more - Blackish head & tail - **Black throat** with slight white striation sharply separated from ashy grey breast by conspicuous **white collar** - White lower belly - **Cinnamon flanks** J: Breast spotted ... S. America, except Chile - URUGUAY ... Humid forests & capueras in NW (I) & NE   III

784) SLATY THRUSH
(Zorzal Plomizo) *Turdus nigriceps* 2R *(.)*
19 cm - Call *tsok* like 779) - Reclusive- Often metallic, rasping or brittle flock song *teeee..tee..teeee..tee* - **Plumbeous back** -Wings & tail blackish - (**Head black** in NW) - Black throat striation - Lower throat white turned **ashy grey on underparts** - Yellow mandible - Orange legs - ♀ : Resembles 779) - Smaller & lacks black lores - J: Spotted ochraceous breast ... Ecuador, Peru, Bolivia, Brazil & Paraguay ... Yungas, forests & ravines in NW (IV) & humid forests & villages in NE   II

785) CHIGUANCO THRUSH
(Zorzal Chiguanco) *Turdus chiguanco*
25 cm - In open - Tame - Rather terrestrial & on rocks - Sharp song lacking musical notes - **Blackish brown - Orange yellow bill & legs** - ♀ : Browner ... From Ecuador along W... Forests, plantations, grasslands & ravines in hills   V

786) GLOSSY-BLACK THRUSH
(Zorzal Negro)   *Turdus serranus*
24 cm - **Reclusive** - Flocks - Glossy **black,** not brown like 785) - **Bill & legs yellow** -♀: Dull plumage - Brown- Wings blackish - Paler underparts - Throat striated brown ... From Vene- zuela along W to Bolivia ... Yungas- (Calilegua NP)   II

(.) The NW & NE forms, *nigriceps* & *subalaris*, often considered different species

● *Fam. Motacillidae, see page 39*

*ANTHUS: Terrestrial - In open areas - Walk, do not jump - **High display flight descend gliding while singing** - Alike - Mimetic - Some seasonal color variation - Long hind toe nails Backs striated & spotted black & ochre - Dark tails with pale outer rectrices - (8 species)*

787) SHORT-BILLED PIPIT
(Cachirla Uña Corta)
Anthus furcatus - 2R
14 cm - Tame - Relatively **short nail- Back** greyer & more **opaque,** lacks conspicuous bars on wings & central rectrices - Visible malar line - Auricular uniform brown - **Ochraceous breast spotted brown, contrasting with rest of** whitish **under- parts-** Flanks much less spotted than in 788) ... Brazil, Paraguay, Bolivia & Peru - URUGUAY ... Grasslands, steppes & rural areas   IV

788) CORRENDERA PIPIT
(Cachirla Común)
Anthus correndera-5R
14 cm - More contrasted than 787) - Very long nail - **Back with two white bordered black lines** - Conspicuous bars on wings & central rectrices- **Breast spotted blackish striated on flanks** - Rest of underparts whitish... Bordering countries & Peru - URUGUAY ... Steppes, grasslands & rural areas   V

789) YELLOWISH PIPIT
(Cachirla Chica)   *Anthus chii*
12 cm - Long buzz *cheeeee* - Wings & central rectrices blackish with little edging - Outer rectrices somewhat ochraceous - **Yellowish under- parts** speckled brown on upper breast - Flanks slightly striated ... S. America - URUGUAY ... Grasslands near water & rural areas   III

790) CHACO PIPIT
(Cachirla Trinadora) *Anthus chacoensis*
12 cm - **Resembles 789)** (Has been considered conspecific) - Tail brown not blackish - **Underparts whitish** (not yellowish) **barely striated on upper breast** ... Paraguay ... Grasslands in savannas in Oriental Chaqueño District   I

250

791) HELLMAYR'S PIPIT
(Cachirla Pálida) *Anthus hellmayri-2R*

14 cm - **Back** like Correndera (788) but **lacks characteristic white lines** - **Ochraceous underparts barely striated** blackish **on upper breast** & flanks - Outer rectrices ochraceous -In Patagonia more whitish, even outer rectrices ... Bordering countries & Peru- URUGUAY ... Steppes, grass-lands & rural areas   III

792) OCHRE-BREASTED PIPIT
(Cachirla Dorada)   *Anthus nattereri*

14 cm - Almost vertical flight - Showy coloration for genus - The **yellow**est-Cinnamon rump - Ochre auricular - **Breast yellowish ochre barely striated** black - Rest of underparts ochraceous - **Yellow mandible** ... Brazil & Paraguay ... Wet grasslands in NE   I

793) SOUTH GEORGIA PIPIT
(Cachirla Grande)   *Anthus antarcticus*

16 cm - Looks like Correndera 788) - Allopatric - **Back black & ochre**, lacks white - Ochre **breast with thick black striations** - Rest of underparts ochraceous barely striated - Wide tail with only outer web white ... Steppes & grasslands in **Georgias**   III

794) PARAMO PIPIT
(Cachirla Andina)   *Anthus bogotensis*

14 cm - Resembles 791) - More **cinna-mon** - Lacks wing bars - **Ochre breast with few & soft** brown **stria-tions - Flanks lack spots** - Outer rectrices whitish ... From Venezuela along W ... Grasslands & High Andean steppes - (Aconquija)   II

251

795) MASKED GNATCATCHER
(Tacuarita Azul) *Poolioptila dumicola*
11 cm - Restless - Moves about vegetation - Delicate & varied song, even imitating - Slender - **Rather erect, narrow black tail with white outer rectrices** - **Bluish** - Paler underparts turned white on lower belly- White bars on inner remiges - **Black mask** - ♀: Somewhat paler - Lacks mask ... Brazil, Paraguay & Bolivia - URUGUAY ... In bushes in forests, savannas & plantations   V

796) CREAM-BELLIED GNATCATCHER
(Tacuarita Blanca) *Polioptila lactea*
10 cm - Resembles 795) in appearance, voice & behavior - Different habitat - Back & pectoral flanks plumbeous (less bluish) - **Black crown** - Eyebrow & face white - **Underparts creamy white** - ♀: Lacks black on crown ... Brazil & Paraguay ... Medium & high strata of humid forests & capueras in **Misiones**   III

797) RUFOUS-CROWNED GREENLET
(Chiví Coronado) *Hylophilus poicilotis*
11 cm - Tame -Restless - Repeated series of monotonous whistles - Bill short & pointed - Looks like a small greenish tyrant - **Rufous crown** - Green back - Black auricular spot - Greyish throat - Underparts yellow ... Brazil, Paraguay & Bolivia ... Medium & high strata in humid forest of **Misiones**   II

798) RED-EYE VIREO
(Chiví Común)) *Vireo olivaceus-2R*
13 cm - Tame - Acrobatic - More heard than seen - Repeated & loud *cheevee..cheeveevee* - Slender - Strong bill - **Grey crown - Long white eyebrow** heightened by black ocular line & upper eyebrow - Olive back - Whitish underparts - Brown iris, not red ... From N. America - URUGUAY ... Medium & high strata in forests & plantations   IV

(.) Some authors consider the Argentine species included in Fam. Polioptilidae & others in Muscicapidae.

799) RUFOUS-BROWED PEPPERSHRIKE

(Juan Chiviro) *Cyclarhis gujanensis- 3R (.)*
15 cm - More heard than seen - Tame - Passive - Rapid, loud & melodious whistle *cheeveecheeveeereeoh* & other audible calls - Brown crown - **Chestnut eyebrow** - Ashy grey face- Upperparts olive - Yellowish breast - **Bill** (like a parrot's) **rosy pearl** - Orange iris ... From C. America, except Chile - URUGUAY ... High strata in forests & plantations   IV

Fam. Ploceidae, see page 40

800) HOUSE SPARROW

(Gorrión)   *Passer domesticus*
13 cm - The best known bird - Near houses - Noisy - Opportunistic - Thick bill - **Crown** & rump **grey** - **Collar on nape chestnut** - Back striated chestnut & black - **Black bib** - Wing bar & rest of underparts white - ♀: Lacks black or rufous - Introduced from Europe ... Bordering countries & Peru - URUGUAY ... Villages & rural areas   VI

Fam. Parulidae, see page 40

801) BLACKPOLL WARBLER

(Arañero Estriado)   *Dendroica striata*
12 cm - Restless - In mixed flocks - Olivaceous upperparts striated - Eyebrow & malar line whitish - **Two wing bars** & undertail coverts **white** - **Striated black on flanks - Orange legs** - [♂ **in NP: Black cap with white**] Irregular Migrant A ... [URUGUAY]   I

BASILEUTERUS: Tame - Curious - Restless - Sharp bills lack hooks- Orange legs-(5 species)

802) WHITE-BROWED WARBLER

(Arañero Silbón)
Basileuterus leucoblepharus
12 cm - Hops & turns hind third of body sideways - Almost terrestrial - Loud & melodious voice with many flute-like notes - Sharp whistle - Black crown with central band, face & nape grey - Slight eyebrow & **periocular white** - Olive back - Underparts white with grey breast ... Brazil & Paraguay - URUGUAY ... Dense low strata in forests & capueras   IV

(.) Previously in Fam. Cyclarhidae no longer valid

803) RIVER WARBLER
(Arañero Ribereño)
Basileuterus rivularis
13 cm - Terrestrial - Hunts running or hopping along **stream shores** - Tame - Sharp *chee* & long series of notes end in prolonged trill - Restless- Flicks tail - Plumbeous crown turned **olivaceous on back** - Conspicuous **white eyebrow** - Underparts cinnamon whitish ... From Honduras, except Chile ... Streams in humid forests & capueras of **Misiones**   III

804) TWO-BANDED WARBLER
(Arañero Coronado Grande)
Basileuterus bivittatus
13 cm - Tame - Continuous *feet..feet..feet..feetfeetfeet* - Also a more sonorous song than Hooded Siskin (924) - Resembles sympatrics 805) & 806) - Barely bigger - Plumbeous **crown with semi concealed orange golden band** - Olive back -**Eyebrow,** lower eyelid & all **underparts yellow** ... Guyana, Venezuela, Brazil, Peru & Bolivia ... Borders of rivers & canals & bushes in yungas   IV

805) PALE-LEGGED WARBLER
(Arañero Ceja Amarilla)
Basileuterus signatus
12 cm - Similar call to 590) - Inconspicuous - Looks like ♀ 809) - Different habitat - Lacks band on crown (present in 804 & 806) - **Short yellow eyebrow** - Blackish lores ... Colombia, Peru & Bolivia ... Low & medium strata in yungas   II

806) GOLDEN-CROWNED WARBLER   (Arañero Coronado Chico)   *Basileuterus culicivorus - 2R*
12 cm - Acrobatic - Restless - Tame - Quick crescendo of sharp whistles & warbles - Call *chreek* - Olivaceous brown back - **White eyebrow** heightened by black ocular line & upper eyebrow - Semiconcealed **orange band on crown** - Yellow underparts... From Mexico, except Ecuador, Peru & Chile - URUGUAY ... Medium (even low) strata in forests & capueras   V

807) BROWN-CAPPED REDSTART (Arañero Corona Rojiza) *Myioborus brunniceps* 12 cm - Tame - Restless - Shorter trill than 808) - Conspicuous **rufous crown** - Plumbeous back & olive upper back - Black tail with **white outer rectrices** conspicuous when opened- White eyelid - **Golden yellow underparts** - J: Grey head ... Guyana, Venezuela, Brazil & Bolivia ... Forests, ravines & plantations in NW - Expanding

V

808) TROPICAL PARULA (Pitiayumí) *Parula pitiayumi* 9 cm - Tame - Restless - Moves about vegetation - Very sharp trill ascending & descending - Short tail - **Bluish back with olive upper back** - White on outer rectrices & coverts - **Underparts golden yellow, orange breast** ... From N. America, except Chile - URUGUAY ... High & medium strata in forests & plantations   IV

809) MASKED YELLOWTHROAT (Arañero Cara Negra) *Geothlypis aequinoctialis* 13 cm - Often reclusive - Varied & melodious warble - **Plumbeous crown - Black mask** - Olive back - Yellow underparts - ♀: Inconspicuous - Lacks mask & plumbeous crown - Short eyebrow & eyelid pale ... From Costa Rica, except Chile - URUGUAY... Capueras, forests & marsh vegetation   IV

Fam. Coerebidae, see page 40

810) BANANAQUIT (Mielero) *Coereba flaveola (.)* 10 cm - Tame - Acrobatic - Pierces flowers for nectar - Frequently in wild fruit trees - Chirping warble - Short tail- Curved bill - Conspicuous **white eyebrow - Grey throat sharply separated from yellow underparts** - J: Lacks eyebrow - Underparts ashy grey... From C. America, except Chile ... Medium strata in humid forests, capueras & plantations of NE   III

(.) If Fam. Coerebidae not valid, it would remain in Fam. Parulidae

811) CHESTNUT-VENTED CONEBILL (Saí Común) *Conirostrum speciosum (.)* 10 cm - Moves about vegetation - Acrobatic - Slender - Looks like 795) - Bill thin & pointed - Tail rather short - **Grey sky blue back** - White on wing visible in flight - Underparts pale grey- **Rufous undertail coverts** - ♀: Grey sky blue crown - Olive back - Ochraceous white underparts ... S. America, except Chile ... Medium & high strata in forests & capueras of N   IV

812) SLATY FLOWER-PIERCER (Payador) *Diglossa baritula (..)* 11 cm - Noisy - Often *peereebeer-eebee* - Eats flowers - Looks like 832) **Hooked bill slightly curved upwards** - Bluish upperparts - Black lores - **Cinnamon underparts** - ♀: Brown back - Ochraceous underparts barely striated breast ... From Mexico along W to Bolivia ... In low & medium strata in forests in NW   II

813) BLUE DACNIS (Saí Azul) *Dacnis cayana (..)* 11 cm - Acrobatic - Frequently on tops of wild fruit trees - Bill thin, pointed & rather curved, different from 814) - **Shiny colors - Sky blue - Black** lores, **throat & upper back** - Wings & tail black with blue bars - **Rosy legs- ♀: Green - Sky blue crown & face** - Grey throat ... From Nicaragua, except Chile ... Medium & high strata in humid forests & capueras in NE III

● Fam. Tersinidae, see page 40

814) SWALLOW-TANAGER (Tersina) *Tersina viridis* **14 cm** - Tame - In open - Crisp *tseep-* Hunts on wing - ♂ & ♀ look like 813)- Thick & short bill - **Sky blue - Forehead, lores, throat,** primaries & tail **black - Flanks waved** black - **White belly - ♀: Green** without black- Forehead, periocular & throat pale - Whitish belly - Flanks waved green ... From Panama, except Chile... High strata (sometimes on ground) in forests & villages in **Misiones**   III

(.) If Fam. Coerebidae not valid, it would remain in Fam. Parulidae
(..) If Fam. Coerebidae not valid, it would remain in Fam. Thraupidae

EUPHONIA: Small groups [mixed flocks] look in epiphytes - Eat wild fruits - Restless- Small - Bills short & strong - Short tails - Colorful - ♀♀ 815), 817) & 818): Alike-Olive backs - Whitish underparts with yellowish olivaceous flanks - (5 species)

815) GREEN-THROATED EUPHONIA
(Tangará Picudo) *Euphonia chalybea* 11 cm - Very rapid series of short *cheek-* Thick & high bill - **Upperparts** shiny **bluish green** - Forehead & underparts yellow ´- **Black chin** ... Brazil & Paraguay ... Humid forests in **Misiones** II

816) BLUE-HOODED EUPHONIA
(Tangará Cabeza Celeste)
Euphonia musica
10 cm - Noisy - Looks like a small 837)- **Crown & nape sky blue - Forehead, face, throat** & upperparts violaceous **black** - Golden yellow rump - Underparts orange yellow - ♀: **Rufous forehead** - Sky blue crown & nape - Olivaceous back - J: Like ♀ lacks rufous forehead´ - Whitish center of underparts ... From Mexico, except Chile ... Forest clearings III

817) PURPLE-THROATED EUPHONIA
(Tangará Común) *Euphonia chlorotica* 9 cm - Audible call (both sexes) *bee..bee* - **Wide forehead** & underparts **golden yellow** - Hood, even **throat,** & upperparts **violaceous black** - Undertail with white patches ... From Venezuela, except Chile ... Forests & **savannas** IV

818) VIOLACEOUS EUPHONIA
(Tangará Amarillo) *Euphonia violacea* 10 cm - Very pleasant warbles including imitations - Resembles 817) - Head (not hood) violaceous black - Forehead & underparts, even **throat, golden yellow** - More white on undertail - ♀: Yellowish forehead ... Venezuela, Guianas, Brazil & Paraguay ... Humid forests in **Misiones** (Iguazu NP) IV

257

819) CHESTNUT-BELLIED EUPHONIA

(Tangará Alcalde)*Euphonia pectoralis* 10 cm - Sharp & metallic *schree..schree..schree* - Shiny dark blue - Conspicuous **golden yellow on** pectoral **flanks - Dark rufous belly** & lower belly - Sky blue mandible - ●: Olive - **Underparts ashy grey,** yellowish flanks - **Rufous undertail coverts** ... Brazil & Paraguay... High & medium strata in humid forests of **Misiones**   II

820) BLUE-NAPED CHLOROPHONIA

(Tangará Bonito) *Chlorophonia cyanea* 10 cm - Restless - Descending & melodious whistle - Shiny colors - **Green hood** - Sky blue periocular & back - Yellow underparts - ●: **Sky blue nape band** - Rest of upperparts green - Underparts greenish yellow ... From Venezuela, except Chile ... High strata in humid forests of **Misiones**   III

821) GUIRA TANAGER

(Saíra Dorada)*Hemithraupis guira-2R* 12 cm - Moves about wild fruit trees - Often mixed flocks - Showy coloration with yellow predominant - Upperparts bronzed green - **Face & throat black surrounded with yellow - Cinnamon** lower back & **breast - Yellow bill** with black culmen - ♀: Olivaceous - Rump & underparts yellowish - Greyish flanks - Bill like ♂ ... From Venezuela, except Chile ... High & medium strata in forests of NW (II) & NE   IV

822) COMMON BUSH-TANAGER

(Frutero Yungueño)

Chlorospingus ophthalmicus 13 cm - Tame - Restless - Strong & pleasant call - Brownish crown - **Olive back - White postocular** - Breast golden yellow, paler on flanks - Rest of underparts whitish ... From Mexico to Venezuela, Colombia, Ecuador, Peru & Bolivia ... Medium strata in yungas IV

TANGARA: *More brightly colored &*
larger than Euphonia - Similar behavior-
Mixed groups & flocks - ♂♂ resemble ♀♀
High & medium strata - (3 species)

823) GREEN-HEADED TANAGER
(Saíra Arcoiris)　　*Tangara seledon (.)*

13 cm - Striking - Metallic shine -
Upperparts: greenish sky blue head,
greenish yellow upper back,
violaceous blue coverts, black mantle
& **orange lower back** - Underparts:
black bib, sky blue breast & green belly
- ♀: Paler-J: Lacks black & orange ...
Brazil & Paraguay ... Humid forests &
capueras in **Misiones**　　　　IV

824) CHESTNUT-BACKED TANAGER
(Saíra Castaña)　　*Tangara preciosa (..)*

14 cm - Series of various sharp *tsee* -
Crown & upper back coppery
chestnut - Coverts, rump & belly sil-
very ochraceous - Underparts greenish
sky blue - ♀: Paler - Cinnamon crown -
Greenish sky blue back ... Brazil &
Paraguay - URUGUAY ... Forests in NE
　　　　　　　　　　　　　　II

825) BURNISHED-BUFF TANAGER
(Saíra Pecho Negro)　*Tangara cayana*

13 cm - **Black on forehead & face**
end in central band on under-
parts - Rest silvery ochraceous -
Wings & tail sky blue with black bars - ♀:
Paler & more greenish - Lacks black ...
From Venezuela, except Chile ...
Humid forests in NE　　　　II

(.) *T. cyanocephala* has been cited for Misiones
(..) *T. arnaulti* is considered hybrid

826) MAGPIE TANAGER
(Frutero Overo)   *Cissopis leveriana*

27 cm - In open - Small flocks - Sharp whistles - Unmistakable - Looks like Black-billed Magpie - **White & black-Long & graded** black **tail** with white tips - Large bluish black hood, ended in fringes on breast - **Golden iris** ... S. America, except Chile ... Medium & high strata in clearings of humid forests & capueras in **Misiones**   III

827) BLACK-GOGGLED TANAGER
(Frutero Corona Amarilla)
              Trichothraupis melanops

15 cm - Restless - Noisy - Flocks - Call *cheek* - Dull plumage except when **golden crest** erect **- Mask, wings & tail black - White wing band** conspicuous on flight - Olivaceous brown back - Cinnamon underparts - ♀: Paler - Lacks mask & crest ... Brazil, Paraguay, Bolivia & Peru ... Medium strata in humid forests of NE   IV

828) RUBY-CROWNED
TANAGER   (Frutero Coronado)   *Tachyphonus coronatus*

16 cm - Call *cheek,* while quickly waggling body - Violaceous **black - White on wing** only conspicuous in flight - Rarely visible **red crown**, not present in 829) - **Whitish mandible-** ♀: Chestnut - Brownish head - Cinnamon underparts with **breast barely striated** ... Brazil & Paraguay... Low & medium strata in humid forests & capueras of NE   IV

829) WHITE-LINED TANAGER
(Frutero Negro)   *Tachyphonus rufus*

17 cm - Resembles 828) - Lacks red - **White on shoulders**, sometimes visible when perched - ♀: More **uniform** than ♀828) - Lacks striations ... From Costa Rica, except Chile ... Clearings in forests & **savannas** - (E Formosa)   IV

830) DIADEMED TANAGER
(Frutero Azul)
Stephanophorus diadematus
18 cm - Call *cheep* - Song sounds like that of Rufous-browed Peppershrike (799) - **Violaceous blue** (looks black)- Forehead, lores & chin black - **White on crown** with shiny red feathers, less conspicuous in subadult - J: Brownish grey ... Brazil & Paraguay - URUGUAY ... Medium strata in capueras & forests of E (Delta of Parana River)   III

831) SAYACA TANAGER
(Celestino Común) *Thraupis sayaca-2R*
15 cm - Tame - Series of sharp *sh..hwee* - Sky blue grey - Back greener - **Wings & tail sky blue** ... Venezuela, Colombia, Brazil, Paraguay & Bolivia - URUGUAY ... Clearings in forests, savannas, plantations & **villages**   V

832) FAWN-BREASTED TANAGER
(Saíra de Antifaz)
Pipraeidea melanonota-2R
13 cm - Somewhat passive - Moves about leaves, branches & fruit trees - Looks like Blue-and-Yellow Tanager (837) & 812) - **Crown,** rump **& shoulders sky blue** contrasted with bluish black upper back - **Black mask - Cinnamon underparts** - ♀: Paler - J: Lacks mask ... S. America, except Chile- URUGUAY ... Medium & high strata in yungas, humid forests & capueras of NW & NE   III

833) HOODED TANAGER
(Frutero Cabeza Negra)
Nemosia pileata
12 cm - Arboreal - Sharp call *see..see.sle* - Nape & **back greyish sky blue - Black head - Lores & underparts white - Iris** & legs **yellow** - ♀: Lacks black on head - Ochraceous white on throat & breast ... S. America, except Ecuador & Chile ... Open forests in N   II

834) BRAZILIAN TANAGER
(Fueguero Escarlata)
Ramphocelus bresilius

17 cm - Showy coloration - **Purplish red - Black wings & tail** - Mandible with silvery base - ♀: Brown - Rufous rump & belly - Bill lacks silver ... Brazil... High strata in clearings of humid forests & capueras in **Misiones**   I

835) RED-CROWNED ANT-TANAGER
(Fueguero Morado)   *Habia rubica*

18 cm - Reclusive - Almost terrestrial - Noisy - Small flocks even mixed - Harsh *tsak* or *tcha..tcha* - **Purplish brown - Shiny red small crest** rarely visible - Rump & breast more reddish - Wings & tail with purple bars- ♀: Brown, more ochraceous than ♀ 828) - Barely cinnamon forehead - Rosy legs ... From C. America, except Chile ... Low & dense strata in humid forests of **Misiones**   III

836) HEPATIC TANAGER
(Fueguero Común)   *Piranga flava*

17 cm - Tame - Perched high in open or flying: continuous *cheep* - **Orange red** - Rufous back - ●: Very different - **Yellow** - Back olive - Intermediate plumages ... From N. America, except Chile - URUGUAY ... Capueras, forests & savannas   III

837) BLUE-AND-YELLOW TANAGER
(Naranjero) *Thraupis bonariensis-2R*

17 cm - Arboreal - Showy coloration - **Violaceous sky blue hood** - Black lores & back - Wings & tail with sky blue bars - **Orange rump & breast-** Yellow underparts ♀: Dull plumage - Olivaceous back - Ochraceous under- parts - Intermediate plumages ... Bor- dering countries, Ecuador & Peru - URUGUAY ... Forests, savannas, ru- ral areas & villages   V

262

838) CHESTNUT-HEADED TANAGER
(Pioró)　　　*Pyrrhocoma ruficeps*

12 cm - Restless - Flicks tail - Two series of 3 similar sharp & musical notes - **Plumbeous - Chestnut hood** - Black forehead & lores - ♀: Olivaceous back - **Cinnamon hood** without black ... Brazil & Paraguay ... Dense low & medium strata in clearings in humid forests of **Misiones**　　　III

839) RUST-AND-YELLOW TANAGER
(Tangará Alisero)　　*Thlypopsis ruficeps*

12 cm - Tame - Restless - Acrobatic - Series of sharp *shee sheeeah* - Resembles 840) & ♀ 838) - Smaller than 853) - **Cinnamon head** - Lacks yellow lores & moustaches - **Back** more **olive** than 840) - **Underparts golden yellow** - J: Greenish yellow hood ... Peru & Bolivia ... Montane forests in NW　　　III

840) ORANGE-HEADED TANAGER
(Tangará Gris)　　*Thlypopsis sordida*

13 cm - Tame - Restless - Looks & sounds like Saffron Finch 884) - **Golden yellow hood with wide rufous crown** - Olivaceous **grey back** - Ochraceous grey breast - Rest of **underparts whitish** - J: Olivaceous crown & back - Yellow face, throat & breast - Whitish belly ... S. America, except Peru & Chile ... Forests　　　III

● *Fam. Catamblyrhynchidae, see page 41*

841) PLUSH-CAPPED FINCH
(Diadema)
　　　Catamblyrhynchus diadema

13 cm - Little known - Graded tail - Short flat bill - Wide **golden small frontal crest** of stiff feathers - **Black nape** - Plumbeous upperparts - **Rufous underparts** - J: Olive grey back - Underparts paler ... From Venezuela along W to Bolivia ... Montane forests in **Jujuy** (Cerro Santa Barbara)　　　!

263

*SALTATOR: More heard than seen - Melodious song - Large - Somewhat long tails - Thick bills - **Conspicuous eyebrows** - (5 species)*

842) GOLDEN-BILLED SALTATOR
(Pepitero de Collar)   *Saltator aurantiirostris - 3R*

18 cm - Repeated whistle *wit..bich..bichío* - Plumbeous upperparts - **Black face, sides of neck & collar** - Long postocular eyebrow & throat white or cinnamon - Underparts cinnamon brown - **Orange bill** [black maxilla] - J: Dark bill ... Brazil, Paraguay, Bolivia & Peru - URUGUAY ... Forests & savannas   IV

843) RUFOUS-BELLIED SALTATOR
(Pepitero Colorado)   *Saltator rufiventris*

20 cm - Resembles 846) - **Olivaceous grey breast** - Rest of **underparts rufous** - Bill somewhat short with ivory mandible ... Bolivia ... Montane forests in **Jujuy**   II

844) GREEN-WINGED SALTATOR
(Pepitero Verdoso)   *Saltator similis*

19 cm - Looks & sounds like 846) - Song *few..chew.. cheechee* - **Back & bars on remiges olive** - Long white eyebrow - Black lines on sides of white throat - Underparts greyish - Blackish bill ... Brazil, Paraguay & Bolivia - URUGUAY ... Forests & capueras in E   III

845) THICK-BILLED SALTATOR
(Pepitero Picudo)   *Saltator maxillosus*

19 cm - Loud call of 4 chirps - Resembles 846) - Conspicuous **bill stronger** & more **curved - Maxilla yellow** with black culmen - Possible intermediates with 842) - ♀: Olive back- J: Black bill ... Brazil & Paraguay... Humid forests in NE   II

846) GRAYISH SALTATOR
(Pepitero Gris) *Saltator coerulescens*

20 cm - Pleasant & varied whistles *cheew..cheew..chew.. weew* - Back plumbeous not olive as in 844) - Face grey not black as in 842) - **Short & conspicuous white eyebrow** - Black lines on sides of whitish throat - **Cinnamon underparts** barely ashy grey on breast - Black bill ... From Mexico, except Chile - URUGUAY ... Capueras & forests   IV

847) BLACK-THROATED GROSBEAK
(Pepitero Negro)   *Pitylus fuliginosus*

21 cm - Tame - Short loud call - Loud bisyllabic song - Bill & appearance of *Saltator* - **Bluish black** - Black face, throat, wings & tail - **Large red bill** - White underwing coverts - ♀: Grey throat ... Brazil & Paraguay ... Humid forests of **Misiones**   II

848) RED-CRESTED CARDINAL
(Cardenal Común) *Paroaria coronata*

17 cm - Tame - Pairs or flocks sometimes on roads - Often on bushes - Various songs, some warbles - Often in captivity - **Erect red crest & hood red down to breast** - Plumbeous back - **White underparts** - Whitish bill - J: Paler hood ... Brazil, Paraguay & Bolivia - URUGUAY ... Forests & savannas   IV

849) YELLOW-BILLED CARDINAL
(Cardenilla)   *Paroaria capitata*

15 cm - Tame - Often in marshes - Terrestrial & on bushes - **Red carmine hood** (lacks crest) - **Black triangle on throat** - Blackish upperparts - **White underparts** - Orange bill - J: Paler hood ... Brazil, Paraguay & Bolivia ... Forests, even gallery forests, & savannas   IV

265

850) BLACK-BACKED GROSBEAK (Rey del Bosque) *Pheucticus aureoventris*

19 cm - Loud & melodious song - **Black** - **Shoulders** & **underparts from breast golden yellow** - Conspicuous **wing patches** & tip of outer rectrices **white** - **Very thick** greyish **bill** - ♀: Browner - Spotted breast ... S. America mainly along W except Chile... Yungas, Chaqueño foothills & humid ravines - Decreasing   III

851) SAFFRON-BILLED SPARROW (Cerquero de Collar)
                    Arremon flavirostris - 2R

15 cm - Very tame - Curious - Terrestrial & in low strata - Loud & continuous *gep* - **Black head & collar** - Conspicuous **white eyebrow & underparts** - Center of crown grey (absent in E) - Olivaceous back (grey in E) - **Orange bill** with black culmen ... Brazil, Paraguay & Bolivia ... Forests in NW (V) & NE   II

852) STRIPE-HEADED BRUSH-FINCH (Cerquero Vientre Blanco) *Atlapetes torquatus*

15 cm - Sharp *feet* .. - Non musical warbles - **Resembles** NW race of **851),** even behavior - **Lacks collar**-**Black bill** ... From Venezuela along W, except Chile ... Yungas   IV

853) FULVOUS-HEADED BRUSH-FINCH (Cerquero Cabeza Castaña) *Atlapetes fulviceps*

15 cm - Terrestrial & in bushes - Tame-Resembles 839) - **Rufous head** - **Spot on lores, moustache & underparts yellow** - Olivaceous back & flanks ... Bolivia ... Montane forests in NW   III

854) YELLOW-STRIPED BRUSH-FINCH (Cerquero Amarillo) *Atlapetes citrinellus*

15 cm -ξ - Behavior & habitat like 851)- Allopatric with 855), 856) & 857) - **Black crown, mask & moustache** with **yellow eyebrow & malar** in between - Olivaceous upperparts & breast - Rest of underparts yellow ... Paraguay ... Yungas   IV

855) YELLOW CARDINAL (Cardenal Amarillo)
Gubernatrix cristata
18 cm - In bushes - **Greenish yellow-** Conspicuous **crest & throat black -** **Upper back striated** olive & black - Golden yellow eyebrow & malar - **Golden yellow tail with central rectrices black -** ♀: Grey cheeks & breast ... Brazil - URUGUAY ... Savannas & shrubby steppes (S B. Aires) - Decreasing   III

856) YELLOW-BRIDLED FINCH (Yal Andino)
Melanodera xanthogramma-2R

15 cm - Tame - Terrestrial - Flocks - Looks like 855) - Allopatric - Plumbeous- **Long yellow eyebrow -** **Yellow edge** (not white) **around black bib** - Underparts greenish yellow - Whitish lower belly - Yellowish outer rectrices (or: olive back - Underparts & outer rectrices yellow) - ♀: Resembles ♀898) Brownish grey striated black - Underparts whitish striated... Chile ... Arid or snow covered peaks, steppes, seacoasts or near streams in Southern Andes   II

857) BLACK-THROATED FINCH (Yal Austral)
Melanodera melanodera-2R

14 cm - Resembles 856) even in behavior - **White eyebrow & edge of bib -** Conspicuous coverts & bars on remiges yellow - Plumbeous head - Olivaceous grey back - Olive rump - ♀: Whitish striated - **Primaries & outer rectrices yellow** ... Chile ...Wet grasslands in S (II) & in **Malvinas**   IV

858) ULTRAMARINE GROSBEAK (Reinamora Grande) *Cyanocompsa brissonii-2R* **16 cm** - Continuous & melodious call- **Very thick black bill** - **Blue** - Sky blue gloss on wide forehead & shoulders - Periocular sky blue - ♀ & J: Chestnut back - Cinnamon underparts- Periocular as ♂'s - Also intermediate plumages ... Venezuela, Colombia, Brazil, Paraguay & Bolivia - [URUGUAY] ... Forests & savannas
IV

859) INDIGO GROSBEAK (Reinamora Chica) *Cyanoloxia glaucocaerulea* **14 cm** - Call *psit* & soft song similar to 809)'s - Resembles 858) - Much more **sky blue** - Shorter thick bill - **Whitish** base of **mandible** - ♀ & J: Like 858) ... Brazil & Paraguay - URUGUAY ... Forests in E
III

860) BLACKISH-BLUE SEEDEATER (Reinamora Enana) *Amaurospiza moesta* **11 cm** - Similar to small & dark 858) - Similar song - Smaller bill - Looks like a seedeater - **Opaque bluish black**- Barely conspicuous white wing coverts - ♀: Chestnut back - Brown wings & tail - Cinnamon underparts ... Brazil ... Low & medium strata in humid forests & capueras of **Misiones**
II

861) BLUE-BLACK GRASSQUIT (Volatinero) *Volatinia jacarina* **9 cm** - Restless - Continuous & short **vertical jumps** from perch, flashing **white** axillaries & **underwing coverts** while emitting metallic chirp - Looks like 860) - Bill more pointed - **Shiny bluish black** - ♀: Passive - Does not jump - Brown back - Ochraceous underparts - **Striated breast** - Often intermediate plumages ... From C. America - URUGUAY... Savannas, grasslands & rural areas
III

Memorize the Topography of a Bird

862) DULL-COLORED GRASSQUIT
(Espiguero Pardo)   *Tiaris obscura*

10 cm - Tame -Almost terrestrial - **Dull plumage** - Like ♀ *Sporophila* - Closed nest - Bill thinner, with **orange mandible** - Lacks white on wing - Brown upperparts - Olivaceous grey underparts turned whitish on lower belly - Rosy legs ... From Venezuela along W to Bolivia ... Savannas & clearings in humid forests of NW (Oran, Salta)   II

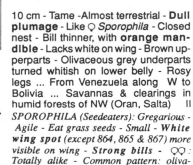

SPOROPHILA (Seedeaters): Gregarious - Agile - Eat grass seeds - Small - White wing spot (except 864, 865 & 867) more visible on wing - Strong bills - ♀♀: Totally alike - Common pattern: olivaceous brown backs & ochraceous underparts - White wing spot only in 866), 868) & 876) - Migrants B - (14 species)

863) PLUMBEOUS SEEDEATER
(Corbatita Plomizo) *Sporophila plumbea*
9 cm - Soft & melodious song - Sky bluish **grey** - Wings & tail black with grey bars - Chin & **moustache**, [subocular] & belly **white** - [Yellowish bill] - ♀: Common pattern ... S. America except Ecuador, Peru & Chile ... Grasslands in **Misiones**   II

864) DOUBLE-COLLARED SEEDEATER   (Corbatita Común)   *Sporophila caerulescens*
10 cm - Often in cages - Plumbeous back - **Black chin** surrounded with white, **black collar** & rest of **underparts white** - Yellowish bill - ♀: Common pattern ... From Brazil & Ecuador, except Chile - URUGUAY ... Savannas, shrubby steppes, rural & inhabited areas   V

865) BUFFY-FRONTED SEEDEATER   (Corbatita Oliváceo)   *Sporophila frontalis*
12 cm - Loud *pitz* & *pichochó* - **Olivaceous** brown - [Plumbeous head] - [Forehead &] **postocular white** - Wingbars & underparts whitish (except breast & flanks) - ♀: More olive - Lacks eyebrow - Ochraceous bars ... Brazil & Paraguay ... In bamboo thickets near water, abundant when seeding - Humid forests in **Misiones**   II

269

866) RUSTY-COLLARED SEEDEATER (Corbatita Dominó) *Sporophila collaris*

11 cm - Unmistakable - Often in marshes - **Black & cinnamon - Crown,** tail, cheeks **& collar black** - Forehead & subocular dots & throat white - **●: White throat** - Cinnamon rump, wing & rest of underparts ... Brazil, Paraguay & Bolivia - URUGUAY ... Grasslands, savannas & marsh vegetation III

867) YELLOW-BELLIED SEEDEATER (Corbatita Amarillo) *Sporophila nigricollis*

11 cm - Metallic *tzi* shorter than that of 864) - **Hood black** to breast - Olivaceous back - Rest of **underparts yellowish** - Bluish grey bill - ♀: Common pattern ... From Costa Rica, except Chile ... Rural areas & savannas in **Misiones** I

868) WHITE-BELLIED SEEDEATER (Corbatita Blanco) *Sporophila leucoptera*

11 cm - Slow & repeated whistle *fweet*- **Plumbeous upperparts - Underparts &** conspicuous **wing band white** - Dark orange bill - ♀: Common pattern - Cinnamon underparts ... Brazil, Paraguay & Bolivia ... Grasslands & wetlands in Eastern Chaqueño District (E Formosa) III

869) LINED SEEDEATER (Corbatita Overo) *Sporophila lineola*

10 cm - **Black & white - Crown band, malar,** rump **& underparts white** - ♀: Common pattern ... S. America, except Chile ... Savannas & forests in N III

270

870) MARSH SEEDEATER
(Capuchino Pecho Blanco)
Sporophila palustris

9 cm - **Plumbeous back - Wide white bib** - Rufous rump & under-parts- ♀: Common pattern ... Brazil & Paraguay - URUGUAY ... Marsh vege-tation in E   II

871) WHITE-COLLARED
SEEDEATER   (Capuchino de Collar)   *Sporophila zelichi*

9 cm - **Rufous back** unlike 870) - Plumbeous crown & rump - **Wide complete collar & bib white** - Rufous underparts - ♀: Common pat-tern - Winter distribution unknown ... [Brazil] ... Grasslands & marsh vegeta-tion in **Entre Rios**   II

872) CHESTNUT SEEDEATER
(Capuchino Corona Gris)
Sporophila cinnamomea

9 cm - Conspicuous & wide **plum-beous crown - Back & underparts rufous** like 871), lacks white collar - ♀: Common pattern ... Brazil & Para-guay... Grasslands & marsh vegetation in E (El Palmar NP)   III

873) RUFOUS-RUMPED
SEEDEATER   (Capuchino Castaño)   *Sporophila hypochroma*
9 cm - Resembles 875) - Much **dark**er-Wide crown & back plumbeous - **Rump & underparts rufous** not cin-namon - ♀: Common pattern ... Bo-livia... Grasslands in **Corrientes**   I

271

874) DARK-THROATED SEEDEATER
(Capuchino Garganta Café)
Sporophila ruficollis

9 cm - Plumbeous crown & back - **Wide black bib - Rest of underparts & rump rufous** - ♀: Common pattern ... Brazil, Paraguay & Bolivia -[URUGUAY] ... Savannas, grasslands, thistle beds & rural areas IV

875) RUDDY-BREASTED SEEDEATER (Capuchino Canela) *Sporophila minuta*

9 cm - Plumbeous crown & back - **Rump & underparts cinnamon** not rufous - ♀: Common pattern ... From C. America, except Peru & Chile... Savannas, grasslands & marsh vegetation IV

876) CAPPED SEEDEATER
(Capuchino Boina Negra)
Sporophila bouvreuil

9 cm - **Black cap** - Brownish back - **Ochraceous white underparts** - Opens & shuts black tail rapidly - ♀: Common pattern ... Surinam, Brazil & Paraguay ... Grasslands in NE III

877) LESSER SEED-FINCH
(Curió) *Oryzoborus angolensis*

11 cm - Looks like *Sporophila* - In open- Good singer - Melodious loud voice descending - **Black - Underparts rufous from breast - Wing spot & underwing coverts white** - ♀: Brown back - Underparts cinnamon brown ... From C. America, except Chile ... Edges of humid forests & capueras in NE III

878) BAND-TAILED SEEDEATER (Piquitodeoro Común) *Catamenia analis*

11 cm - Looks like *Sporophila* - Often in cages - Plumbeous - Forehead & lores black - **Wing band, tail band & belly white** - Rufous undertail coverts - **Thick golden yellow bill** - Dark legs - ♀: Brown back & ochraceous underparts striated - Wing & tail bands less conspicuous ... From Colombia, along W, to Chile ... High Andean steppes, Chaqueño foot hills, & high altitude grasslands - On plains in Winter   III

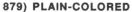

879) PLAIN-COLORED SEEDEATER (Piquitodeoro Grande) *Catamenia inornata-2R*

13 cm - Similar to & sympatric with 891), 892), 893) & 878), lacks conspicuous characters of the latter - **Undertail coverts** also **rufous** - Plumbeous **back** somewhat **striated**- Underparts dark ashy grey - **Orange bill & legs** - ♀: Browner ... From Venezuela, along W, to Bolivia ... High Andean & high elevation steppes   IV

880) COMMON DIUCA-FINCH (Diuca Común) *Diuca diuca-3R*

14 cm - Terrestrial & in bushes - Tame-Slow, continuous, melodious & loud song of 4 or 5 notes - **Ashy grey back & waistcoat - Tip of outer rectrices & rest of underparts white-**Cinnamon abdominal spot - ♀ & J: Browner ... Chile & Brazil - [URUGUAY]... Prepuna, rural areas, high Andean, Patagonian & shrubby steppes ... Southern population Migrant C   IV

881) WHITE-WINGED DIUCA-FINCH (Diuca Ala Blanca) *Diuca speculifera*

15 cm - Terrestrial - Showier than 880)- Lacks cinnamon spot - **Subocular patch**, only outer web & **conspicuous wing patch white** ... Peru, Bolivia & Chile ... High Andean meadows in **Jujuy**   I

273

Memorize the symbols

SICALIS: Gregarious - Tame - Sing on wing - Yellow - Striated backs - Andean species differ only in details (Make good field description) - (8 species)

882) STRIPE-TAILED YELLOW-FINCH

(Jilguero Cola Blanca)   *Sicalis citrina*
12 cm - Not gregarious - Almost terrestrial - Sing on wing like 883)`- Loud whistle *few*- **Olivaceous head with wide yellow forehead** - Rump & underparts yellow - Olivaceous flanks- **Black tail with white ventral patch** - ♀: Brown striated - Yellow belly- Less white on tail ... Guyana, Venezuela, Colombia, Peru & Brazil ... Alder trees & fields in **Tucuman**   II

883) GRASSLAND YELLOW-FINCH

(Misto)   *Sicalis luteola*
12 cm - Sometimes enormous flocks like bee swarms - Often in cages - Display flight slowly gliding down - More terrestrial than 884) - Nests on ground - Bisyllabic *zi..ziss* - Ochraceous **upperparts,** heavily **striated brown** - Olive rump - Eyelid & underparts yellow - **♀**: **Similar** - Paler - Ochraceous breast & flanks ... From C. America - URUGUAY ... Savannas, grasslands & **rural areas**

884) SAFFRON FINCH   V

(Jilguero Dorado) *Sicalis flaveola-2R*
12 cm - More often in pairs - Often in cages - Golden yellow - **Back olive striated black - Forehead** slightly orange - Wings & tail black with yellow edges - **♀ & J:** Different from ♂- **Lacks yellow** - Back brownish grey striated black - Underparts whitish- **Breast & flanks striated** ... From Panama - URUGUAY ... Forests, **rural & inhabited areas**   V

885) BRIGHT-RUMPED YELLOW-FINCH

(Jilguero Cara Gris) *Sicalis uropygialis*
12 cm - Greyish color distinguishes it from other Andean yellow finches - Crown & underparts yellow contrasted with almost uniform **grey back** - Wings & tail with grey edges - Olive rump - Conspicuous **grey face** - ♀: Striated crown - Browner back ... Peru, Bolivia & Chile ... High Andean steppes & prepuna in NW (Abra Pampa, Jujuy)   II

886) GREATER YELLOW-FINCH
(Jilguero Grande) *Sicalis auriventris*

14 cm - Quite golden - **Golden yellow forehead & underparts - Head yellowish not olivaceous** - Back & flanks olivaceous grey - Ashy grey coverts - Olivaceous yellow rump - **Blackish tail with yellow outer web** - ♀: Paler & more striated - Little yellow ... Chile ... High Andean steppes
III

887) PUNA YELLOW-FINCH
(Jilguero Puneño) *Sicalis lutea*
13 cm - Looks a little like ♀ siskin - Melancholic & loud *treewee* - **Yellowish olive back & golden rump** contrasted with yellow edged **blackish wings & tail** - Uniform golden yellow underparts - ♀: Paler - Olivaceous crown - Back, wings & tail brownish grey - Rump & underparts yellow, greyish on breast ... Peru & Bolivia ... High Andean steppes & prepuna in NW
III

888) GREENISH YELLOW-FINCH
(Jilguero Oliváceo) *Sicalis olivascens-2R*
13 cm - Musical, rapid & repeated chatter *teereereeree* - **Olivaceous on crown & nape**, on brown back & yellow rump & underparts - Blackish wings & tail with yellow bar - Pale eyelid- Pale orange legs - ♀: Upperparts brown somewhat striated - Olivaceous rump - Yellowish underparts ... Peru, Bolivia & Chile ... High Andean steppes & prepuna
IV

889) PATAGONIAN YELLOW-FINCH
(Jilguero Austral) *Sicalis lebruni*
13 cm - Display flight as Grassland Yellow-Finch (883) although lower - **Olivaceous grey** crown & **back - Forehead yellow**er - Olivaceous rump - Blackish wings & tail with grey bars - Olivaceous yellow coverts - Underparts yellowish grey turned yellow on lower belly - **Reddish** or rosy **legs** - ♀: More brownish grey ... Chile... Patagonian steppes & high grasslands in Sierra de la Ventana, B. Aires
III

275

890) SHORT-TAILED FINCH
(Yal Grande) *Idiopsar brachyurus*
16 cm - Terrestrial - **Long** (2 cm) **&
thick bill** - Greyish - **Plumbeous
back** - Wings & somewhat short tail
blackish - Pale bars on remiges -
Subocular dotted white - Whitish
throat & undertail coverts - Long legs
& iris yellowish ... Peru & Bolivia...
High Andean steppes & ravines in NW
II

*PRYGILUS: Terrestrial - Flocks even
mixed - Andean & Patagonian - Bills not
very thick - (9 species)*

891) BAND-TAILED SIERRA-FINCH
(Yal Platero) *Phrygilus alaudinus*
14 cm - On wing two chirping notes -
Call *peewk* - Plumbeous - **Tail with
white band** only **conspicuous** on
wing - Cheeks & dorsal striations
black- White belly - **Orange yellow
bill & legs** - ♀: Plumage pattern of
pipit- - Back & breast ochraceous,
striated black - Bill, legs & tail like ♂ ...
Ecuador, Peru, Bolivia & Chile ... High
Andean steppes & **grasslands on
high elevations** III

892) PLUMBEOUS SIERRA-FINCH
(Yal Plomizo) *Phrygilus unicolor-3R*
13 cm - Prolonged trill - **Back uniform plumbeous,** not striated as
891) & 893) with whom it coexists-
Lacks eyebrow - Grey underparts -
Dark bill - Rosy legs - ♀: Similar to ♀
891) - Less contrasted - Underparts
more striated - Lacks white on tail &
yellow on bill ... From Venezuela along
the Andes to Chile ... High Andean
steppes & high altitude grasslands -
(Pampa de Achala, Cordoba) IV

893) ASH-BREASTED SIERRA-FINCH
(Yal Chico) *Phrygilus plebejus-2R*
12 cm - Sharp & musical *tzi..* - ·Smaller
than 891) & 892) - **Upperparts
brownish** grey striated black - Wide
plumbeous rump - **Whitish eyebrow
& underparts** - Pale bars on remiges &
coverts - Dark bill & legs - ♀: Underparts
less striated than ♀ 892) - Slight pale
eyebrow ... From Ecuador along the
Andes to Chile ... High Andean steppes &
high altitude grasslands V

894) GRAY-HOODED SIERRA-FINCH
(Comesebo Andino)*Phrygilus gayi-2R*
15 cm - Terrestrial - **Paler than 895)**-
Hood & wings bluish grey - **Olivaceous back** - Yellowish underparts -
Lower belly & undertail coverts white -
♀: **Striated hood** - Olivaceous ochre
back - **Whitish throat with brown
on sides** - Cinnamon breast turned
ochre on belly & undertail coverts ...
Chile ... Andean & Patagonian dry
lands   IV

**895) PATAGONIAN
SIERRA-FINCH** (Comesebo
Patagónico) *Phrygilus patagonicus*
14 cm - Arboreal - Repeated & musical
tweet..teeoh.. - Resembles 894) - Colors more contrasted - Like an intermediate between 894) & 896) - Olivaceous
**cinnamon back - Golden yellow
rump** & underparts -Blackish wings &
tail - ♀ : Paler - **Hood like ♂**- [Two
lines on throat] - Olive back-Greenish
yellow underparts ... Chile ... Araucano
Forest   IV

**896) BLACK-HOODED
SIERRA-FINCH** (Comesebo
Cabeza Negra) *Phrygilus atriceps*
15 cm - In bushes - Delicate, repeated
& musical *trili* - **Large black hood -
Cinnamon back** turned yellow on
rump - **Wings & tail** blackish **with
grey bars - Cinnamon under-
parts-** White undertail coverts - ♀ :
Paler - Hood somewhat striated - Olivaceous brown back - Yellowish underparts ... Peru, Bolivia & Chile ... Prepuna & High Andean steppes in NW
(Humahuaca, Jujuy)   IV

897) RED-BACKED SIERRA-FINCH
(Comesebo Puneño) *Phrygilus dorsalis*
15 cm - Duller plumage - Looks like
Diuca-Finch 880) - Grey head,
hindneck & rump - **Rosy cinnamon
upperback** - Blackish coverts - **White
throat** - Grey underparts turned white
on lower belly - ♀: Barely paler ... Bolivia
& Chile ... High Andean steppes in
NW   II

277

898) MOURNING SIERRA-FINCH
(Yal Negro)   *Phrygilus fruticeti*
15 cm - Nasal *peeree..peeree.. peeee..peereepee* when perched or in display gliding with wings below horizontal - Blackish - Dorsal striation, **breast**, wings & tail **black- White wing bars - Rest of underparts whitish - Orange bill & legs - ♀:** Brownish grey striated black -**Cinnamon brown auricular - White moustache** ... Peru, Bolivia & Chile ... Andean & Patagonian   IV

899) CARBONATED SIERRA-FINCH
(Yal Carbonero) *Phrygilus carbonarius*
13 cm - ♂ - More reclusive than 898) - Display flight with wings upwards - Striated **back** (or uniform), tail & **underparts black** - Orange yellow bill & legs- ♀: Tame & passive - Resembles ♀ - Saffron Finch (884) - Upperparts striated brown & ochraceous - Pale periocular - Underparts whitish, breast striated brown - **Bill yellow**, culmen black- **Yellowish legs** - Migrant C ... Shrubby & Patagonian steppes & salt pans   III

900) UNIFORM FINCH
(Afrechero Plomizo) *Haplospiza unicolor*
11 cm - Bisyllabic & rapid cricket-like chirp - Resembles allopatric 892)- Small pointed bill - **Uniform plumbeous** - Lilaceous legs - ♀: Brownish olivaceous -Underparts striated - Pale mandible ... Brazil & Paraguay ... Bamboo thickets along edges of humid forests & capueras in **Misiones**   II

901) TUCUMAN MOUNTAIN-FINCH
(Monterita Serrana)
                    Compsospiza baeri
16 cm - ♂ - Terrestrial & in bushes - Tame- Restless - Olivaceous plumbeous - **Wide forehead & bib orange rufous** - Cinnamon undertail coverts - Humid ravines in high altitude grasslands & edges of montane forests in Aconquija (El Infiernillo, Tucuman) III

902) GRAY-CRESTED FINCH
(Soldadito Gris)
Lophospingus griseocristatus

13 cm - **Ashy grey** - Resembles 903) - Brownish crest barely smaller - **Lacks eyebrow & black marks on head-Outer rectrices with white tip** - Underparts grey turned white on lower belly - ♀: Paler ... Bolivia ... Prepuna II

903) BLACK-CRESTED FINCH
(Soldadito Común)
Lophospingus pusillus

12 cm - Terrestrial & arboreal - Mixed flocks - Looks like 902) - **Crest, mask & throat black** with conspicuous **eyebrow & malar white** in between - Rest ashy grey - ♀: Browner - Lacks black - White throat ... Paraguay & Bolivia ... Forests & savannas of Chaqueño type IV

904) COAL-CRESTED FINCH
(Afrechero Canela) *Charitospiza eucosma*

10 cm - Unmistakable - **Crest, bib & pectoral splash black - White cheeks** & dots on wing - Grey back - **Cinnamon underparts** -♀: Paler & browner ... Brazil ... Fields in **Misiones** I

905) RED-CRESTED FINCH
(Brasita de Fuego)
Coryphospingus cucullatus - 2R

12 cm - Terrestrial & in bushes - Call *cheep..* - Dark reddish - **Glossy red** erectile **small crest - Carmine rump & underparts** - White periocular & mandible - ♀: Paler - Lacks glossy red ... Guianas, Brazil, Paraguay, Bolivia & Peru - URUGUAY ... Forests, capueras & savannas IV

Reread the Glossary

SPARRROWS (906 to 909): Back striated black - Underparts whitish - (4 species)

906) STRIPE-CAPPED SPARROW
(Cachilo Corona Castaña)
Aimophila strigiceps-2R
15 cm - Small flocks - Continuous, short & metallic *tich*.. - Looks like House-Sparrow - Resembles 907) - Somewhat long tail - **Dark rufous crown with grey center** - Rufous shoulders - Grey eyebrow, malar, breast & flanks - Black moustache ... Paraguay & Bolivia ... Forests & savannas - In NW high altitude grasslands   IV

907) RUFOUS-COLLARED SPARROW
(Chingolo)
Zonotrichia capensis-7R
12 cm - Tame - Three warbled whistles [followed by a trill] - Coloration of head variable according to race - **Crest & cheeks grey** [with sides black] - **Cinnamon hindneck** - Slight black & cinnamon half collar - **J:** Lacks grey & cinnamon - Underparts **striated black** ... From Mexico - URUGUAY ... Almost all habitats including villages   VI

908) GRASSLAND SPARROW
(Cachilo Ceja Amarilla)
Ammodramus humeralis
11 cm - Tame - Terrestrial - Perched in open but more heard than seen - Soft warble followed by nasal note [& trill] - Duller plumage than 907) - Lacks crest & cinnamon - **Yellow eyebrow** ending whitish - **Golden yellow shoulders** ... S. America except Ecuador & Chile - URUGUAY ... Savannas, grasslands & rural areas   III

909) BLACK-MASKED FINCH
(Cachilo de Antifaz)
Coryphaspiza melanotis
12 cm - Terrestrial - Looks like Saffron-billed Sparrow (851) - **Black head** - Conspicuous **long eyebrow & underparts white** - **Yellow coverts** - Upperparts olive striated - Graded tail with white tip - Yellow mandible - ♀: Browner - Striated head - Resembles Saffron Finch (884) - Yellow coverts like ♂ ... Brazil, Paraguay, Peru & Bolivia ... Grasslands in NE   II

280

910) LONG-TAILED REED-FINCH
(Cachilo Canela)*Donacospiza albifrons*

14 cm - Tame - Vertical posture - Looks like *Poospiza* - **Long tail** (8 cm) ending in points - Small bill - Plumbeous head - **Whitish eyebrow** - Brown **back striated** black - Cinnamon underparts - J: Pale - Short tail ... Brazil & Paraguay - URUGUAY ... Grasslands & marsh vegetation   III

*POOSPIZA: Agile - Flocks in Winter, sometimes mixed - Dark **tails** with **white tip on outer rectrices** - Bills not thick for Emberizidae - (7 species)*

911) CINNAMON WARBLING-FINCH
(Monterita Canela)   *Poospiza ornata*

12 cm - ♂ - Plumbeous head, lower back & rump - **Rufous upper back, flanks & breast - Wide eyebrow & rest of underparts cinnamon** - Blackish wings with two wide ochre bars on coverts - ♀: Brownish back - Ochraceous eyebrow & underparts ... Winters in central provinces ... Shrubby steppes & forests   IV

912) RUSTY-BROWED WARBLING-FINCH   (Monterita
Ceja Rojiza)   *Poospiza erythrophrys*

13 cm - Resembles 911) - Sympatric in Winter - Brown upperparts - Conspicuous **rufous eyebrow** not cinnamon - Rufous subocular - **Rufous breast turned cinnamon on rest of underparts** ... Bolivia ... Yungas   III

913) RUFOUS-SIDED WARBLING-FINCH   (Monterita
Pecho Gris)   *Poospiza hypochondria*

14 cm - Brownish grey upperparts - **White eyebrow** - Black upper eyebrow- White malar & throat separated by **black moustache** - Grey breast - **Rufous flanks** - Rest of underparts ochraceous ... Bolivia... Bushes in prepuna, High Andean steppes & high altitude grasslands in W   III

914) RED-RUMPED WARBLING-FINCH

(Monterita Litoral)   *Poospiza lateralis*
13 cm - Groups - Tame - Often reclusive-
Loud, continuous & sharp: *gep..* & other
calls - Cinnamon - Plumbeous
upperparts - **Rufous rump**, undertail
coverts **& flanks** - Conspicuous & **long
eyebrow** & malar **white** - Greyish
underparts with white center .. Brazil &
Paraguay - URUGUAY ... Low strata in
forests, specially in gallery forests in E
(Delta of Parana River)   III

915) BLACK-AND-RUFOUS WARBLING-FINCH

(Sietevestidos) *Poospiza nigrorufa-2R*
13 cm - Low flight - More heard than
seen - Continuous & sharp *juít..juít..tiú* -
Mountain race: very different melodious
song - Blackish - **White eyebrow &
malar** surrounding black mask -
**Rufous underparts - White on
lower belly** V-shaped toward breast -
J: Lacks rufous - **Underparts spotted
black** - Tail lacks white ... Brazil, Paraguay & Bolivia - URUGUAY ... Forests,
savannas & marsh vegetation   IV

916) RINGED WARBLING-FINCH

(Monterita de Collar)*Poospiza torquata*
12 cm - Moves about vegetation - Plumbeous upperparts - Conspicuous **white
eyebrow & throat** - Upper eyebrow,
mask & wide collar black - Bar on
coverts & rest of underparts white -
Rufous undertail coverts - ♀:
Paler... Paraguay & Bolivia ... Savannas
& shrubby steppes & in rural areas in
Winter   IV

917) BLACK-CAPPED WARBLING-FINCH   (Monterita

Cabeza Negra) *Poospiza melanoleuca*
12 cm - Tame - Moves about vegetation-
Repeated & loud *tsp* - Looks like
Masked Gnatcatcher (795) - **Black
head** - Plumbeous back - **White underparts** - ♀:Browner - Lacks black
head ... Brazil, Paraguay & Bolivia -
URUGUAY ... Savannas & near forests
                                      IV

282

918) MANY-COLORED CHACO-FINCH

(Pepitero Chico) *Saltatricula multicolor*
15 cm - Looks like a small & colorful 842)-
Repeated *víreo..* - **Black tail with
white outer tip** - White postocular
eyebrow - **Black on face continued
along sides of white throat** [sur-
rounding it] - Grey collar - **Underparts
cinnamon with white center -
Orange yellow bill with black culmen** ... Paraguay & Bolivia - [URU-
GUAY] ... Forests & savannas of
Chaqueño type   IV

919) LESSER GRASS-FINCH

(Coludo Chico)
                Emberizoides ypiranganus
16 cm - In marshes - Reclusive - Quite
terrestrial - Call *gek..* - Long, graded tail
ending in points - Very similar to 920) -
More contrasted - **Olivaceous back
striated black** - Greenish yellow coverts - Pale eyebrow - **Plumbeous face-**
Whitish underparts - Orange yellow bill
with black culmen ... Brazil ... Grasslands & marsh vegetation in NE   II

920) WEDGE-TAILED GRASS-FINCH

(Coludo Grande)   *Emberizoides herbicola*
18 cm - Looks like 921) - Behavior &
appearance of 919) - Less in marshes -
Different call - Soft *sbit* & *pic* -
Ochraceous brown back striated
blackish - Lacks eyebrow - Pale lores &
periocular - **Face** & underparts
ochraceous - Cinnamon rump - J: Eyebrow & underparts yellowish ... From
Costa Rica, except Ecuador & Chile ...
Wet grasslands in NE (Ibera, Corrientes)
                                   III

921) GREAT PAMPA-FINCH

(Verdón)   *Embernagra platensis-3R*
20 cm - Tame - In pairs - [Along roads]-
From bush tops: pleasant notes, pene-
trating & short - Also *cheep* - Grey head-
Olivaceous back (striated in E) - **Wings
& tail greenish yellow** - Conspicuous
orange bill (black culmen in E) - J:
Heavily striated - Yellow eyebrow - Cinnamon rump & lower belly - Blackish
bill... Brazil, Paraguay & Bolivia - URU-
GUAY ... Savannas, high altitude & plain
grasslands & marsh vegetation   IV

283

CARDUELIS (922 to 927): Looks like Sicalis - Gregarious - Varied song; sometimes whole group sings - Conspicuous wing band, visible even with folded wings & base of forked tails golden yellow -(7 species)

922) BLACK SISKIN
(Negrillo) *Carduelis atrata*

12 cm - Tame - **Black** - Yellow lower belly & undertail coverts - ♀: Barely paler... Peru, Bolivia & Chile ... High Andean steppes & prepuna III

923) YELLOW-RUMPED SISKIN
(Cabecitanegra Andino)
Carduelis uropygialis

12 cm - Looks like intermediate between 922) & 924) - **Hood, including bib,** & upper back **black** - **Rump** & rest of underparts **yellow** - ♀: Paler - Striated back - Blackish hood ... Peru, Bolivia & Chile ... High Andean steppes II

924) HOODED SISKIN
(Cabecitanegra Común)
Carduelis magellanica-4R

12 cm - Often in cages - Pleasant trilling song - **Black hood** including small bib-Olivaceous back slightly striated - Yellow rump & underparts - ♀: More olivaceous - Lacks hood ... S. America - URUGUAY ... Various habitats, rural areas, plantations & **villages** IV

284

925) THICK-BILLED SISKIN
(Cabecitanegra Picudo)
Carduelis crassirostris

12 cm - Resembles 924) - Sympatric -
Bill barely larger - Back browner - **Sides
of neck yellow** - ♠: Different to ♀924)
Brownish grey back slightly striated -
Yellow rump - **Sides of neck & under-
parts ashy grey** ... Peru, Bolivia &
Chile ... High Andean steppes & prepuna
III

926) BLACK-CHINNED SISKIN
(Cabecitanegra Austral)
Carduelis barbata

12 cm - Resembles 924) - Allopatric -
Cap & throat spot black - Olivaceous
yellow rump - **Tail almost black** - ♀:
Lacks black cap & throat - Olivaceous
breast turned ashy grey on rest of underparts ... Chile ... Araucano Forest,
nearby areas & villages III

927) EUROPEAN GREENFINCH
(Verderón) *Carduelis chloris*

14 cm - Short, rapid & loud trill *shshsh* -
Looks like ♀ 924) - **Larger bill** more
whitish - Yellow on remiges less con-
spicuous on wing but **longer & more
conspicuous when wing folded** -
Rosy legs - ♀: Greyer - J: Back striated -
Introduced from Eurasia ... URUGUAY...
Pine woods & villages in **B. Aires** (Villa
Gesell) - Expanding III

928) EUROPEAN GOLDFINCH
(Cardelino) *Carduelis carduelis (.)*

12 cm - Showy coloration - Wingband &
forked tail as other *Carduelis* - **Head
red, white & black** - Brown back -
Whitish bill & rump - J: Ochraceous
grey striated - Introduced from Eurasia
... Forests, rural areas & villages in **URU-
GUAY**

28

Fam. Icteridae, see page 41

*CACIQUES & OROPENDOLA (929 to 932): Glossy **black** - Straight & sharp bills- Long tails - Hanging nests, as if woven - (4 species)*

929) CRESTED OROPENDOLA
(Yapú)   *Psarocolius decumanus*

♂: **40 cm** - ♀: 30 - In colonies - Acrobatic-Loud *uaj,* like a bark, & other calls- Unmistakable - On wing looks like a bird of prey - Long & thin crest - Rufous rump & undertail coverts - Conspicuous **yellow tail** with black center - Large **Ivory bill** - Blue iris ... From Panama, except Chile ... Forests in NW (Aguas Blancas, Salta) (II) & in NE   I

930) GOLDEN-WINGED CACIQUE   (Boyero Ala Amarilla)   *Cacicus chrysopterus*

21 cm - Short hoarse mewing - Other calls including pleasant song - **Coverts & wide rump golden yellow** - Rosy iris - Sky blue mandible ...Brazil, Paraguay & Bolivia - URUGUAY ... Forests
                                           III

931) RED-RUMPED CACIQUE
(Boyero Cacique) *Cacicus haemorrhous*

24 cm - Flocks - Nests in groups, often in palm trees & near man - Noisy - Loud & rasping *rak..* & other calls, some musical - Looks like 932) - **Lower back & rump red - Ivory bill** - Sky blue iris - J: Brown iris ... S. America, except Chile... Medium & high strata in forests & capueras in NE (Iguazu NP)   IV

932) SOLITARY BLACK CACIQUE
(Boyero Negro) *Cacicus solitarius*
24 cm - Acrobatic - Bisyllabic song &
short hoarse *uegg* - Also other calls - Imitates - **All black**, lacks red & yellow -
Ivory bill ... S. America, except Chile -
URUGUAY ... Medium & high strata in
forests & savannas IV

BLACKBIRDS *(933 to 938, except 936)*
*Glossy **black** - Bills shorter than caciques'*
slightly curved - Nests not woven - 934),
937) & 938) are nest parasites - (5 species)

933) CHOPI BLACKBIRD
(Chopí) *Gnorimopsar chopi-2R*
22 cm - Small flocks - Tame - Terrestrial
& arboreal - Strong & melodious
whistles, other calls & repeated *chopi*
sometimes by whole group - Silky gloss-
Frill sometimes curled - Dark iris -
Curved bill grooved on mandible -
Decreasing alarmingly due to uncon-
trolled hunting ... Brazil, Paraguay &
Bolivia - URUGUAY ... Savannas, palm
groves & forests in NE III

934) GIANT COWBIRD
(Tordo Gigante) *Scaphidura oryzivora*
35 cm - With caciques 929) & 931)
which parasitizes - Arboreal & terrestrial-
One or two sharp whistles - Much **larger**
than 938) - Because of frill appears
humpbacked & small headed - **Bill** black
& **curved - Orange iris** - Long legs - ♀:
28 cm - Duller - Smaller hump on back -
Brown iris ... From C. America, except
Chile ... Humid forests & capueras in NW
& NE - (Iguazu NP) III

935) AUSTRAL BLACKBIRD
(Tordo Patagónico)
Curaeus curaeus-2R
26 cm -Terrestrial & arboreal - Complex
group song like 933) - Also chirping like
Brown & Yellow Marshbird (947) - Sympatric only with 938) - Larger & more
slender - Lacks purple gloss - **Bill
long**er **& straight**er - Long legs ...
Chile... Patagonian forests, nearby areas & plantations IV

287

936) EPAULET ORIOLE
(Boyerito)   *Icterus cayanensis*
19 cm - Arboreal - Restless -
Acrobatic- Various calls including
imitations - Pleasant song - **Slender -
Black** - Lacks purple gloss of 938) -
Thin bill - Long tail - **Rufous
shoulders** barely visible - **Underwing
looks whitish** ... S. America , except
Venezuela, Ecuador & Chile -
URUGUAY ... Edges of forests,
savannas & inhabited areas   IV

937) SCREAMING COWBIRD
(Tordo Pico Corto)
                Molothrus rufoaxillaris
18 cm - ♂ & ♀ identical - Flocks with
939) which parasitizes - Often on cattle-
Harsh & sudden *juish* & other calls -
Black - Very much like 938) - Shorter
bill - Less conspicuous gloss, **not
purple** - Inconspicuous rufous axillars-
J: Similar to 939) - Subadult spotted
black ... Brazil, Paraguay & Bolivia -
URUGUAY ... Savannas, forests & rural
areas   V

938) SHINY COWBIRD
(Tordo Renegrido)
                Molothrus bonariensis
19 cm - Large flocks mainly ♂♂ - Stands
on cattle - More elegant than 937) -
Parasitizes many species - Gurgle
followed by sharp whistle or hiss -
Pleasant song on wing - **Black -
Purple gloss** - ♀: Brownish grey (black
in Misiones) ... From Panama -
URUGUAY ... Diverse habitats,
marshes & villages   VI

939) BAY-WINGED COWBIRD
(Tordo Músico)   *Molothrus badius*
18 cm - Small flocks often with 937) &
938) - **Group song** with different
voices, like orchestra rehearsal -
Brownish grey back - **Black lores &
tail** - **Rufous remiges** more
conspicuous on wing - Ashy grey
underparts ... Brazil, Paraguay &
Bolivia- URUGUAY ... Savannas,
forests, rural areas & villages   V

J 937

288

*AGELAIUS: Marsh blackbirds - Rather thin bill - **Black** - ♀♀: Striated - (3 species)*

940) UNICOLORED BLACKBIRD

(Varillero Negro)   *Agelaius cyanopus*
18 cm - Whistle *chiu..chiu..chiu* & long warble - **Long** & pointed **bill** - Glossy - **♀: Dorsal striation & bars on remiges chestnut** - Black tail - **Underparts yellow with flanks striated black** - Lacks eyebrow - ♂ J : Blackish back - Striated underparts ... Brazil, Paraguay & Bolivia ... Marsh vegetation   III

941) CHESTNUT-CAPPED BLACKBIRD   (Varillero

Congo)   *Agelaius ruficapillus*
17 cm - Flocks - Noisy - Musical whistles & nasal notes - Bill somewhat short - Inconspicuous **rufous crown & bib** - **♀:** Blackish back barely striated olivaceous- Lacks eyebrow - **Ochraceous throat** ... Brazil, Paraguay & Bolivia - URUGUAY ... Marsh vegetation & nearby areas   V

942) YELLOW-WINGED BLACKBIRD   (Varillero

Ala Amarilla)   *Agelaius thilius-[2R]*
17 cm - Small flocks - Soft & varied warble - More pointed bill than 941) - **Golden yellow shoulders & underwing coverts** conspicuous on wing - **♀:** Long **whitish eyebrow** - Shoulders & underwing coverts like ♂ - Breast striated black - Bordering countries & Peru-URUGUAY ... Marsh vegetation & nearby areas   IV

943) BOBOLINK

(Charlatán)   *Dolichonyx oryzivorus*
15 cm - Flocks - Musical *pink* - Dull plumage - **Upperparts & flanks striated** black - **Line on black crown, long eyebrow & underparts ochraceous** - Orange bill - [**♂** in NP: Black - **Golden yellow on hindneck**] Wetlands & grasslands ... Migrant A ... Decreasing   II

944) TROUPIAL
(Matico)   *Icterus icterus*

21 cm - Loud & melodious whistle - Showy coloration - **Orange color - Black** forehead, **face, breast,** mantle, **tail & wings** - White on remiges - Yellow iris ... S. America, except Chile ... Savannas in **Formosa**   II

945) SAFFRON-COWLED BLACKBIRD
(Tordo Amarillo)   *Xanthopsar flavus*

19 cm - Gregarious - **Golden yellow head,** shoulders, **rump & all underparts - Black** lores & **upperparts - ●:** Looks like ♀940) - Striated brown back-Conspicuous **eyebrow**, shoulders, all underparts & **rump yellow** ... Brazil, Paraguay & Bolivia - URUGUAY ... Wetlands with vegetation, grasslands & rural areas - Decreasing   II

946) YELLOW-RUMPED MARSHBIRD   (Pecho Amarillo
Grande)   *Pseudoleistes guirahuro*

22 cm - Gregarious - Quite terrestrial - Resembles 947) - Sometimes together-Song more pleasant & trilled usually on wing - More contrasted - **Blackish brown upperparts & breast** - More yellow on coverts - **Golden yellow rump**, underwing coverts & rest of underparts ... Brazil & Paraguay - URUGUAY ... Grasslands & marshes in NE   III

947) BROWN-AND-YELLOW MARSHBIRD   (Pecho Amarillo
Común)   *Pseudoleistes virescens*

21 cm - Appearance & behavior of 946)-Less showy - Feeds in fields & roosts in marshes - Chirps & repeated group call *chrrruí* - Olivaceous **brown upperparts (including rump) breast & lower belly** - Yellow shoulders, underwing coverts & rest of underparts ... Brazil - URUGUAY ... Wetlands with vegetation & rural areas in E   IV

948) SCARLET-HEADED BLACKBIRD
(Federal) *Amblyramphus holosericeus*

22 cm - Loud *wit* - Melancholic trisyllabic whistle - Unmistakable - Long & pointed bill - Black - **Hood to breast & thighs orange red** - J: Black - Intermediate plumages ... Brazil, Paraguay & Bolivia - URUGUAY ... Wetlands with vegetation- Decreasing   III

STURNELLA: Terrestrial - Quail-like plumage - Shoulders & breasts red -♀♀: Paler - (3 species)

949) LONG-TAILED MEADOWLARK
(Loica Común)   *Sturnella loyca-4R*

22 cm - Screaming song with warbles, whistles & nasal notes - **White eye-brow started red - Underwing coverts white** - ♀: White throat with black on sides ... Chile ... Andean & Patagonian grasslands & steppes & other high elevations   IV

950) LESSER RED-BREASTED MEADOWLARK
(Loica Pampeana)   *Sturnella defilippi*

19 cm - Song on wing while gliding down- Bill & tail smaller than 949) - Darker back - **Underwing coverts black** - More intense red - ♀: Bill rather shorter & lower belly blacker than ♀ 949)... Brazil - URUGUAY ... Grass-lands- Decreasing   I

951) WHITE-BROWED BLACKBIRD
(Pecho Colorado) *Sturnella superciliaris*

17 cm - The most gregarious - In view on shrubs or posts - Song on wing like 950)- Metallic *pinng* - **Back almost black** - Long white eyebrow .- **Red throat, breast & shoulders** - ♀: Inconspicu-ous - Ochraceous eyebrow & throat - Underparts barely striated - Rosy breast & shoulders ... Brazil, Paraguay, Bolivia & Peru - URUGUAY ... Grasslands & rural areas   IV

291

· Diomedea cauta

· Pterodroma externa

· Pterodroma macroptera

· Pachyptila forsteri

· Larus modestus

· Sterna albifrons

· Vanellus cayanus

· Pitangus lictor

· Tangara cyanocephala

· Muscisaxicola fluviatilis

· Asthenes humicola

· Crotophaga sulcirostris

· Campylorhynchus turdinus

♂ ♀
• Hylocharis cyanus

♀ ♂
• Heliomaster longirostris

• Galbula ruficauda

PN PI
• Calidris minutilla

• Numenius borealis

• Gallinago undulata

• Ara caninde

• Streptoprocne biscutata

♀ ♂
• Columbina minuta

• Anodorhynchus glaucus

• Aburria cumanensis

Spheniscus humboldti
Eudyptes sclateri (M)
Taoniscus nanus
Pelecanus occidentalis
Sula variegata
Butorides virescens
Eudocimus ruber
Anas platyrhynchus
Buteogallus aequinoctialis
Penelope montagnii (pag. 99)
Charadrius occidentalis
Calidris ferruginea
Tringa nebularia
Limnodromus griseus (pag. 118)
Larus fuscus
Sterna fuscata
Columba plumbea
Ara ararauna
Amazona mercenaria
Trichlaria malachitacea (...)
Otus watsoni
Heliomaster squamosus
Thamnophilus schistaceus (pag. 197)
Contopus virens
Hylocichla mustelina (M)
Eucometis penicillata
Tangara arnaulti (pág. 259)

(.) Species included in this list are not included in the index

(...) One individual seen recently in Misiones

(M) Accidental in Malvinas

ORNITHOGEOGRAPHIC REGIONS OF ARGENTINA

There exist several works which have tried to characterize areas in Argentina that determine or influence birds' distributions. Some have been specifically ornithological (Dabbene, 1910; Pereyra, 1943; Olrog, 1959, 1963, 1984), while others have been more general given that they follow a zoogeographic criteria (Cabrera and Yepes, 1940; Gollan, 1958; Ringuelet, 1960). In spite of the data provided by these authors, specially by Olrog (1959, 1963), the ornithogeographic overview of Argentina does not seem to be at all clear, reason by which this new classification is presented here. It tries to identify areas more coherent with the distribution of birds and characterized by the presence of endemisms.

Materials and Methods

To localize ornithogeographic regions, nesting areas for species and subspecies of restricted or semirestricted range have been used, and situations which reflect climatic changes in the past (specially in the Quaternary Period) have been analyzed. Cabrera's (1976) phytogeographic divisions have been taken as a base, given that birds' distributions respond markedly to those of vegetation, and the results of the analysis mentioned have been taken into account. Although the ornithogeographic divisions are based on the distribution of birds, the limits of these have been fixed, in many cases, based on vegetation distribution, on the analysis of satellite images (Landsat) and altitude, given that -due to their mobility- birds are not good indicators of limits. For vegetation distribution the data used has been obtained personally in different parts of the country and through maps published in Báez (1937), Digilio y Legname (1966), Morello y Adamoli (1968), Hueck (1972), Cabrera (1976), Luti et. al. (1979), Vervoorst (1982), Jozami y Muñoz (1983), Carnevali (1985), del Castillo (1985). The use of the terms "dominion", "province", and "district", is based on Cabrera (1976) and it has followed this criteria:
Dominion: with endemic bird genera and sometimes families;
Province: with endemic bird species and sometimes genera;
District: with endemic bird subspecies and sometimes species.
For a Dominion to be divided into Provinces or a Province into Districts, it is an indispensable condition that each one of the resulting divisions should have endemisms, and not just a decrease of the diversity following some type of gradient.
In many cases the bird species that have been considered to characterize a Region are not exclusive to it, but they also frequent neighboring areas of other regions, although generally it is in a sporadic way or in small quantities.
Commonly, the Districts within a Province share a good part of species and subspecies, but each one -at the same time- has its own forms. Generally, only characteristic forms have been used to characterize a Region, but in some cases also common forms have been used and attributed to the most important district for it.

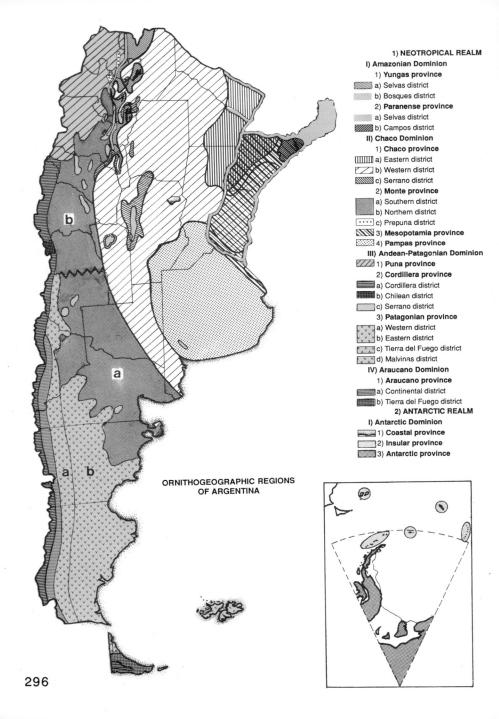

1) NEOTROPICAL REALM
I) Amazonian Dominion
1) Yungas province
- a) Selvas district
- b) Bosques district
2) Paranense province
- a) Selvas district
- b) Campos district
II) Chaco Dominion
1) Chaco province
- a) Eastern district
- b) Western district
- c) Serrano district
2) Monte province
- a) Southern district
- b) Northern district
- c) Prepuna district
3) Mesopotamia province
4) Pampas province
III) Andean-Patagonian Dominion
1) Puna province
2) Cordillera province
- a) Cordillera district
- b) Chilean district
- c) Serrano district
3) Patagonian province
- a) Western district
- b) Eastern district
- c) Tierra del Fuego district
- d) Malvinas district
IV) Araucano Dominion
1) Araucano province
- a) Continental district
- b) Tierra del Fuego district
2) ANTARCTIC REALM
I) Antarctic Dominion
1) Coastal province
2) Insular province
3) Antarctic province

ORNITHOGEOGRAPHIC REGIONS
OF ARGENTINA

296

ORNITHOGEOGRAPHIC REGIONS

1) Neotropical Realm

I) Amazonian Dominion

1) Yungas Province: It extends through the mountains of the Argentine NW, forming a strip in the middle of the provinces of Salta, Jujuy, Tucuman and Catamarca. Also in S and central Bolivia (southern sector).
Vegetation types: Transition humid forests, rain forests, forests, prairies, etc.
a) Selvas District: It extends through the above mentioned provinces, between 400 and 1,600 m approximately.
Characteristic birds: *Micrastur ruficollis olrogi, Geotrygon frenata margaritae, Ara militaris boliviana, Pyrrhura molinae australis, Pionus maximiliani lacerus, Piaya cayana mogenseni, Pulsatrix perspicillata boliviana, Caprimulgus saltarius, Picumnus dorbignyanus, Picumnus cirratus thamnophiloides, Piculus rubiginosus tucumanus, Veniliornis frontalis, Campephilus leucopogon major, Lepidocolaptes angustirostris certhiolus, Synallaxis scutatus whitii, Xenops rutilans connectens, Thamnophilus caerulescens connectens, Batara cinerea argentina, Todirostrum plumbeiceps viridiceps, Phylloscartes ventralis tucumanus, Elaenia obscura obscura, Xanthomyias sclateri sclateri, Turdus albicollis contemptus, Cyclarhis gujanensis tarijae, Basileuterus bivittatus argentinae, Hemithraupis guira boliviana,* etc.
b) Bosques District: It extends above the Selvas District, between 1,200 and 2,500 m approximately. Three types of forests are characteristic: of *Alnus acuminata,* of *Podocarpus parlatorei,* and of *Polylepis australis.*
Characteristic birds: *Penelope dabbenei, Amazona pretrei tucumana, Aegolius harrisi dabbenei, Uropsalis lyra argentina, Microstilbon burmeisteri, Mecocerculus hellmayri subsp, Cinclus schulzi, Turdus serranus unicolor, Basileuterus signatus flavovirens, Diglossa baritula sittoides, Thlypopsis ruficeps, Saltator rufiventris, Sicalis citrina, Atlapetes fulviceps, Atlapetes citrinellus.*
2) Paranense Province: It extends through Misiones and NE Corrientes provinces, and along the Parana, Uruguay, de la Plata, Paraguay, Bermejo, and Pilcomayo rivers and their tributaries. Also in E Paraguay and SE Brazil.
Vegetation types: Subtropical rain forests, *Araucaria angustifolia* forests, grasslands, etc.
a) Selvas District: It occupies the greater part of the province of Misiones and margins of the large rivers and their tributaries.
Characteristic birds: Some 170 species and subspecies partially shared with the Brazilian rain forest.
Examples: *Tinamus solitarius solitarius, Crypturellus obsoletus obsoletus, Mergus octosetaceus, Penelope obscura obscura, Penelope superciliaris major, Aburria jacutinga, Amazona pretrei pretrei, Piaya cayana macroura, Otus atricapillus sanctaecatarinae, Ciccaba virgata borelliana, Caprimulgus sericocaudatus sericocaudatus, Stephanoxis*

lalandi loddigesii, Dryocopus galeatus, Melanerpes flavifrons rubrirostris, Leptasthenura setaria, Syndactila rufosuperciliata acrita, Hypoedaleus guttatus guttatus, Chamaeza campanisona tshororo, Psilorhamphus guttatus, Pachyramphus castaneus castaneus. Turdus albicollis paraguayensis, Basileuterus rivularis rivularis, etc.

b) Campos District: It extends through S Misiones and NE Corrientes provinces.
Characteristic birds: *Athene cunicularia grallaria, Colaptes campestris campestris, Xolmis cinerea cinerea, Xolmis dominicana, Donacobius atricapillus atricapillus, Anthus nattereri, Sporophila bouvreuil pileata, Emberizoides ypiranganus, Xanthopsar flavus, Carduelis magellanica icterica.*

II) Chaco Dominion

1) **Chaco Province:** It extends through the provinces of Salta, Jujuy, Tucuman, Catamarca, La Rioja, Formosa, Chaco, Santiago del Estero, Santa Fe, Corrientes, Entre Rios, Cordoba, San Luis, La Pampa, and Buenos Aires. The sector corresponding to the phytogeographic Province of the Espinal, which is included in this Province, is so modified that in some sectors presents pampas features. Nevertheless, the presence of remnant forests as well as trees and isolated bushes show that originally it was Espinal. Also in W Paraguay and SE Bolivia.
Vegetation types: Xerophyte forests, palm groves, cacti fields, savannas, grasslands, etc.

a) Eastern District: It occupies E sectors of Formosa and Chaco provinces, NW Corrientes and N Santa Fe provinces. Characteristic vegetation is "quebracho" forests of *Schinopsis balansae.*
Characteristic birds: *Nothura maculosa paludivaga, Nothura maculosa chacoensis, Nandayus nenday, Myopsitta monacha cotorra, Celeus lugubris kerri, Lepidocolaptes angustirostris angustirostris, Thamnophilus doliatus radiatus, Donacobius atricapillus albovittatus, Anthus chacoensis, Sporophila leucoptera leucoptera, Icterus icterus strictifrons.*

b) Western District: It occupies W sectors of Formosa and Chaco provinces, NE and central Santa Fe province, S Corrientes province, and the provinces mentioned under 1) Chaco Province. It includes the phytogeographic Province of the Espinal. Typical vegetation is forests of *Schinopsis quebrachocolorado.*
Characteristic birds: *Nothura maculosa pallida, Eudromia elegans magnistriata, Eudromia formosa formosa, Chunga burmeisteri, Stix rufipes chacoensis, Dryocopus schulzi, Furnarius cristatus, Furnarius rufus paraguayae, Pseudoseisura lophotes argentina, Knipolegus striaticeps, Lophospingus pusillus, Coryphospingus cucullatus fargoi, Aimophila strigiceps strigiceps, Embernagra platensis olivascens, Poospiza torquata pectoralis, Saltatricula multicolor.*

c) Serrano District: It extends through the mountains of Salta, Jujuy, Catamarca, Tucuman, La Rioja, Cordoba, and San Luis. It behaves partly as a transition zone between the Chaco and Selvas sectors, but it has some bird species of its own or that at least mostly frequent the area. The characteristic species is *Schinopsis haenqueana.*
Characteristic birds: *Nothoprocta pentlandii doeringi, Melanopareia maximiliani argentina, Hirundinea ferruginea pallidior, Aimophila strigiceps dabbenei, Poospiza nigrorufa whitii.*

2) Monte Province: It extends through the provinces of Chubut, Rio Negro, Buenos Aires, La Pampa, Neuquen, Mendoza, San Juan, La Rioja, Catamarca, Tucuman, Salta, and Jujuy. Also Bolivia.

Vegetation types: bushy steppes, xerophyte forests, cacti fields, bromeliad beds, etc.

a) Southern District: It extend from E Chubut province up to approximately the center of Mendoza province.

Characteristic birds: *Nothura darwinii darwinii, Eudromia elegans devia, Pseudoseisura gutturalis gutturalis, Asthenes patagonica, Agriornis murina, Xolmis coronata, Neoxolmis rubetra rubetra, Anairetes parulus patagonicus, Anairetes flavirostris flavirostris, Stigmatura budytoides flavocinerea.*

b) Northern District: It extends from the center of Mendoza province to S Salta province.

Characteristic birds: *Eudromia elegans albida, Eudromia elegans riojana, Eudromia elegans intermedia, Cyanoliseus patagonus andinus, Asthenes steinbachi, Pseudoseisura gutturalis ochroleuca, Teledromas fuscus, Saltator aurantiirostris nasica, Poospiza ornata.*

c) Prepuna District: It extends through the Andean zone of Jujuy province (Quebrada de Humahuaca) and S Salta (Calchaqui River), between 2,000 and 3,400 m and partly also in Catamarca, Tucuman and La Rioja provinces.

Characteristic birds: *Metriopelia morenoi, Bolborhynchus aurifrons margaritae, Phytotoma rutila angustirostris, Mimus dorsalis, Lophospingus griseocristatus.*

3) Mesopotamia Province: It extends through S Misiones province, East of the Parana River, until Northeastern Buenos Aires province. It is superimposed with the Chaqueño Western and Eastern Districts, and with the Campos District of the Paranense Province. Also, Uruguay and SE Brazil.

Vegetation types: Humid grasslands, aquatic vegetation, reed beds, palm groves, forests, etc. Lagoons and marshes with floating vegetation are frequent.

Characteristic birds: *Leptotila verreauxi chloroauchenia, Myiopsitta monacha monacha, Chlorostilbon aureoventris lucidus, Colaptes melanochloros perplexus, Picoides mixtus mixtus, Lepidocolaptes angustirostris praedatus, Furnarius rufus rufus, Limnornis curvirostris, Limnoctites rectirostris, Troglodytes aedon bonariae, Cyclarhis gujanensis ochrocephala, Thraupis sayaca sayaca, Thraupis bonariensis bonariensis, Sporophila palustris, Sporophila zelichi, Sporophila cinnamomea.*

4) Pampas Province: It extends throughout most of Buenos Aires, E La Pampa, SE Cordoba, and S Santa Fe provinces. Also Uruguay.

Vegetation types: Prairies, grasslands, etc.; it is very rich in lagoons and marshes with aquatic vegetation (reeds, rushes, etc.).

Characteristic birds: *Nothura maculosa annectens, Eudromia elegans multiguttata, Cranioleuca sulphurifera, Spartonoica maluroides, Asthenes hudsoni, Carduelis magellanica magellanica, Sturnella defilippi.*

Although it has few bird species of its own, the Pampas Province is very important for nesting of aquatic birds which, although generally shared with Patagonia, are found in larger concentrations.

Examples: *Podiceps major major, Coscoroba coscoroba, Cygnus melancoryphus, Anas flavirostris flavirostris, Anas silbilatrix, Anas georgica spinicauda, Anas platalea, Netta peposaca, Fulica armillata, Fulica rufifrons, Fulica leucoptera, Nycticryphes semicollaris, Himantopus melanurus, Larus maculipennis.*

III) Andean-Patagonian Dominion

1) **Puna Province:** It extends through the Andean zone of Jujuy, Salta, Catamarca, La Rioja, and Tucuman, between 3,000-3,500 m. Also Chile, Bolivia, and Peru.
Vegetation types: Bushy steppes ("tolar"), gramineous steppes, etc. Lagoons with aquatic vegetation and salt beds are abundant.
Characteristic birds: Some 50 species and subspecies.
Examples: *Nothoprocta ornata, Tinamotis pentlandii, Plegadis ridgwayi, Phoenicoparrus jamesi, Anas puna, Buteo poecilochrous, Fulica cornuta, Charadrius alticola, Attagis gayi simonsi, Athene cunicularia juninensis, Oreotrochilus estella, Geositta punensis, Upucerthia andaecola, Phleocryptes melanops schoenobaenus, Asthenes modesta modesta, Astenes sclateri lilloi, Agriornis montana montana, Muscisaxicola rufivertex pallidiceps, Muscisaxicola juninensis, Lessonia rufa oreas, Tachuris rubrigastra alticola, Anthus furcatus brevirostris, Anthus correndera catamarcae, Sicalis lutea, etc.*

2) **Cordillera Province:** It extends through the mountains of W Argentine, in the Andean area as well as in other mountainous systems. It occupies a more or less continuous strip from La Rioja to Santa Cruz provinces, and in an isolated way in other mountain ranges. Also Chile.
Vegetation types: Bushy steppes, rupestrine grasslands, etc.

a) Cordillera District: It extends from La Rioja to Santa Cruz provinces, and in some way also to Tierra del Fuego.
Characteristic birds: *Nothoprocta pentlandii mendozae, Merganetta armata armata, Geositta cunicularia hellmayri, Agriornis montana leucura, Muscisaxicola albilora, Muscisaxicola frontalis, Muscisaxicola macloviana mentalis, Sicalis olivascens mendozae, Phrygilus unicolor unicolor, Melanodera xanthogramma barrosi.*

b) Chilean District: It extends through the NW of Mendoza province and neighboring areas in San Juan province. Typical of Chile.
Characteristic birds: *Laterallus jamaicensis, Geositta isabellina, Cinclodes oustaleti oustaleti, Scytalopus magellanicus fuscus, Muscisaxicola rufivertex rufivertex, Muscisaxicola cinerea cinerea, Zonotrichia capensis sanborni, Phrygilus gayi gayi.*

c) Serrano District: It occupies in a patchy way the hills of Salta, Tucuman, Catamarca, La Rioja, San Juan, Mendoza, Cordoba, San Luis, Buenos Aires, and Rio Negro provinces.
Characteristic birds: *Nothoprocta pentlandii doeringi, Geositta rufipennis ottowi, Geositta cunicularia contrerasi, Cinclodes olrogi, Cinclodes comechingonus, Cinclodes atacamensis schocolatinus, Asthenes modesta cordobae, Asthenes modesta hilereti, Asthenes sclateri sclateri, Asthenes sclateri brunnescens, Agriornis montana fumosus, Muscisaxicola rufivertex achalensis, Anthus bogotensis shiptoni, Catamenia inornata cordobensis, Phrygilus unicolor cyaneus, Phrygilus plebejus naroskyi, Compsospiza baeri, Sturnella loyca obscura.*

3) **Patagonian Province:** It extends through Mendoza, Neuquen, Rio Negro, Chubut, and Santa Cruz provinces and also Tierra del Fuego and Malvinas Islands. Also Southern Chile.

a) Western District: It extends from the province of Mendoza, south along the W to the province of Santa Cruz and Tierra del Fuego. In some way it is a transition zone between Patagonian steppe and Araucaria Forests.

Vegetation types: Bushy steppes, herbaceous steppes, etc.

Characteristic birds: *Nothura maculosa submontana, Rallus sanguinolentus landbecki, Asthenes pyrrholeuca sordida, Asthenes anthoides, Agriornis livida fortis, Anairetes parulus parulus, Phytotoma rara, Tachycineta leucopyga, Diuca diuca diuca.*

b) Eastern District: It extends through the provinces of Rio Negro, Chubut, and Santa Cruz, east of the Western District.

Characteristic birds: *Pterocnemia pennata pennata, Tinamotis ingoufi, Eudromia elegans patagonica, Thinocorus rumicivorus rumicivorus, Geositta antarctica, Eremobius phoenicurus, Neoxolmis rufiventris, Anthus correndera chilensis, Sicalis lebruni.*

c) Tierra del Fuego District: It extends mainly through Northern Tierra del Fuego; also the Beagle Channel zone and Staten Island.

Characteristic birds: *Rallus sanguinolentus luridus, Gallinago stricklandii, Cinclodes antarcticus maculirostris, Cinclodes patagonicus patagonicus, Cinclodes oustaleti hornensis, Muscisaxicola flavinucha brevirostris, Muscisaxicola capistrata, Melanodera xanthogramma xanthogramma, Phrygilus unicolor ultimus.*

d) Malvinas District: It occupies the Malvinas Islands.

Characteristic birds: *Podiceps rolland rolland, Nycticorax nycticorax falkandicus, Chloephaga picta leucoptera, Chloephaga hybrida malvinarum, Asio flammeus sanfordi, Cinclodes antarcticus antarcticus, Muscisaxicola macloviana macloviana, Cistothorus platensis falklandicus, Troglodytes aedon cobbi, Turdus falcklandii falcklandii, Anthus correndera grayi, Melanodera melanodera melanodera, Sturnella loyca falklandica.*

IV) Araucano Dominion

1) **Araucano Province:** It extends through the Andes, from Neuquen to Santa Cruz provinces, Tierra del Fuego, and Staten Island. Also Chile.

Vegetation types: Evergreen forests, deciduous forests, shrubs. Lakes, meadows, and peat bogs with aquatic vegetation are very abundant.

a) Continental District: It extends from Neuquen to Santa Cruz provinces.

Characteristic birds: *Accipiter bicolor chilensis, Buteo ventralis, Milvago chimango temucoensis, Columba araucana, Enicognathus ferrugineus minor, Strix rufipes rufipes, Sephanoides galeritus, Ceryle torquata stellata, Picoides lignarius, Colaptes pitius cachinnans, Sylviorthorhynchus desmursii, Pteroptochos tarnii, Scelorchilus rubecula rubecula, Xolmis pyrope, Colorhamphus parvirostris, Curaeus curaeus curaeus.*

b) Tierra del Fuego District: It extends through the southern half of Tierra del Fuego and Staten Island.

Characteristic birds: *Milvago chimango fuegiensis, Enicognathus ferrugineus ferrugineus, Curaeus curaeus reynoldsi.*

I) Antarctic Dominion

1) Coastal Province: It extends through the Atlantic coast from Buenos Aires province to Tierra del Fuego, Staten Island, and Malvinas Islands. Also in Laguna Mar Chiquita, Cordoba. Also Chile and Peru.

Vegetation types: Bushy steppes, grass steppes, halophytic steppes, giant algae "forests", etc.

Characteristic birds: *Spheniscus magellanicus, Eudyptes chrysocome chrysocome, Pelecanoides magellani, Phalacrocorax magellanicus, Phalacrocorax bougainvilli, Phalacrocorax albiventer, Phalacrocorax gaimardi, Tachyeres pteneres, Tachyeres brachypterus, Tachyeres leucocephalus, Haematopus ostralegus durnfordi, Haemotopus ater, Haematopus leucopodus, Charadrius falklandicus, Stercorarius skua chilensis, Leucophaeus scoresbii, Larus belcheri atlanticus, Sterna hirundinacea.*

It is an important wintering area for Charadriiformes from the Northern Hemisphere.

2) Insular province: It extends through the Malvinas, South Georgias, South Sandwich, South Orkneys and South Shetlands Islands. Also in other subantarctic islands.

Vegetation types: Bushy steppes, grass steppes, tundra, giant algae "forests", etc.

Characteristic birds: *Aptenodytes patagonica patagonica, Pygoscelis papua papua, Diomedea exulans chionoptera, Phoebetria palpebrata palpebrata, Halobaena caerulea, Pachyptila belcheri, Pachyptila turtur, Procellaria aequinoctialis aequinoctialis, Puffinus gravis, Puffinus griseus, Oceanites oceanicus oceanicus, Garrodia nereis, Fregetta tropica tropica, Pelecanoides georgicus, Pelecanoides urinator exsul, Pelecanoides urinator berard, Sterna vittata gaini.*

South Georgias have four endemic bird species: *Phalacrocorax atriceps georgianus, Sterna vittata georgiae, Anas georgica georgica, Anthus antarctica.*

3) Antarctic Province: It extends through Antarctica and neighboring islands.

Vegetation types: Lichens, moss, giant algae "forests", etc.

Characteristic birds: *Aptenodytes forsteri, Thalassoica antarctica, Stercorarius maccormicki.*

In addition 14 species and subspecies in common with Insular Province.

Manuel Nores
Investigador del Conicet
Centro de Zoologia Aplicada

The data used to carry-out this work
has been obtained in part with subsidies
from the International Council for Bird Preservation,
the Conicor, and the Secretaria de Ciencia y Tecnica.

ORNITHOGEOGRAPHIC BIBLIOGRAPHY

BAEZ, J.
1937   Mapa fitogeográfico de la provincia de Entre Ríos. Pág. 17, en Burkart, A.
            1969. Flora ilustrada de Entre Ríos (Argentina), pt. 2, Gramíneas . INTA.

CABRERA, A. L.
1976   Regiones fitogeográficas argentinas. Enciclopedia argentina de agricultura y
            jardinería. Tomo 2.

CABRERA, A. y J. YEPES
1940   Mamíferos sudamericanos. Cía. Argentina de Editores, Bs. As.

CARNEVALI, R.
1985   Esquema fitogeográfico de Corrientes. Presentado en las 20 Jornadas Ar-
            gentinas de Botánica. Salta.

DABBENE, R.
1910   Ornitología argentina. An. Mus. Nac. Bs. As. Tomo 18.

DIGILIO, A.P. y P.R. LEGNAME.
1966   Los árboles indígenas de la provincia de Tucumán. Opera Lilloana 15.

DEL CASTILLO, M.Z. de.
1985   Esquema fitogeográfico de la provincia de Salta. Secr. Est. Asuntos Agrarios,
            Salta.

GOLLAN, J.S.
1958   Zoogeografía. Págs. 211-359, en La Argentina suma de geografía. Tomo 3.

HUECK, K.
1972   As florestas da America do Sul, Sao Paulo.

JOZAMIN, J. M. y J.D. MUÑOZ.
1983   Arboles y arbustos indígenas de la provincia de Entre Ríos. IPNAYS. Santa
            Fe.

LUTI, R., M. SOLIS, F. GALERA, N. FERREYRA, M. BERZAL, M. NORES, M. HE-
RRERA y J. BARRERA.
1979   Vegetación. Págs. 297-368, en Geografía física de la provincia de Córdoba.
            J. Vázquez, R. Miatelló y M. Roqué (Eds.). Ed. Boldt.

MORELLO, J. y J. ADAMOLI
1968   Las grandes unidades de vegetación y ambiente del chaco argentino. Primera
            parte: objetivos y metodología. INTA, Serie Fitogeográfica, N° 13.

OLROG, C.C.
1959   Las aves argentinas, una guía de campo. Inst. M. Lillo. Tucumán.

1963   Lista y Distribución de las Aves Argentinas. Op. Lilloana IX. Tucumán.

1984   Las aves argentinas. Adm. de Parques Nacionales.

PEREYRA, J. A.
1943   Nuestras aves. Tratado de ornitología. Min. Obr. Públ. Bs. As.

RINGUELET, R. A.
1960   Rasgos fundamentales de la zoogeografía de la Argentina. Physis 22: 151-170.

VERVOORST, F.
1982   Noroeste. Págs. 9-24, en Simposio Conservación de la vegetación natural en la República Argentina. 18 Jornadas Argentinas de Botánica. Tucumán.

GENERAL BIBLIOGRAPHY

Alejandro Di Giacomo

ALEXANDER, W.B.
1963   Birds of the Océan. G. P. Putnam's Sons. New York.

ARAYA M., B. y G. MILLIE H.
1986   Guía de Campo de las Aves de Chile. Ed. Universitaria. Sgo. de Chile.

BARATTINI, L. y R. ESCALANTE
1958   Catálogo de las Aves Uruguayas. 1° parte. Falconiformes. Cons. Deptal.
            Montevideo. Montevideo.

1971   Catálogo de las Aves Uruguayas. 2° parte. Anseriformes. Intendencia Munici-
            pal de Montevideo. Montevideo.

BELTON, W.
1984   Birds of Rio Grande do Sul, Brazil. Part. I. Rheidae through Furnariidae.
            Bull. Am. Mus. Nat. Hist. Vol 178, art. 4. New York.

1985   Birds of Rio Grande do Sul, Brazil. Part. II. Formicariidae through Corvidae.
            Bull. Am. Mus. Nat. Hist. Vol. 180, art. 1. New York.

BLAKE, E. R.
1977   Manual of Neotropical Birds. Vol. I. Spheniscidae to Laridae. University of
            Chicago Press. Chicago.

BROWN, L. y D. AMADON
1968   Eagles, Hawks and Falcons of the World. Mc. Graw. Hill. Co. New York.

BURTON, J.A.
1984   Owls of the World. W. Collins. Glasgow.

CADE, T. J.
1982   The Falcons of the World. Cornell University Press. Ithaca. New York.

CLARK, R.
1986   Aves de Tierra del Fuego y Cabo de Hornos. Ed. L.O.L.A. Buenos Aires.

CONTINO, F.
1980   Aves del Noroeste Argentino. Universidad Nacional de Salta. Salta.

CORY, C., C. HELLMAYR y B. CONOVER
1918-1951   Catalogue of Birds of the Americas and Adjacent Islands. Fiel. Mus. Nat.
            Hist. XI. Vol. Chicago.

CUELLO, J. y E. GERZENSTEIN
1962   Las Aves del Uruguay. Lista sistemática, distribución y notas. Com. Zool. Mus. Hist. Nat, Montevideo. Vol. 6, N° 93. Montevideo.

CUELLO, J.
1985   Lista de referencia y bibliografía de las Aves Uruguayas. Mus. D. A. Larrañaga, Int. Mun. de Montevideo. Montevideo.

DABBENE, R.
1910   Ornitología Argentina. An. Mus. Nac. Bs. As. Tomo XVIII, 1. Buenos Aires.

1972   Aves de Caza. Editorial Albatros. Buenos Aires.

DE LA PEÑA, M.
1976-1977 Aves de la Provincia de Santa Fe. Fasc. I-X. Santa Fe.

1978-1979 Enciclopedia de las Aves Argentinas. Fasc. I-VIII. Editorial Colmegna. Santa Fe.

DE SCHAUENSEE, R. M., 1970. A guide to the Birds of South America. The Academy of Natural Sciences of Philadelphia. Pennsylvania.

DUNNING, J. S.
1982   South American Land Birds. Harrowood Books. Pennsylvania.

ESCALANTE, R.
1970   Aves marinas del Río de la Plata y aguas vecinas del Océano Atlántico. Barreiro y Ramos S. A. Montevideo.

1983   Catálogo de las Aves Uruguayas. 3° parte. Galliformes y Gruiformes. Intendencia Municipal de Montevideo. Montevideo.

FFRENCH, R.
1976   A guide to the Birds of Trinidad and Tobago. Harrowood Books. Pennsylvania.

FORSHAW, J.M.
1973   Parrots of the World. Lansdowne Press. Melbourne. Australia.

FRAGA, R. y S. NAROSKY
1985   Nidificación de las Aves Argentinas (Formicariidae a Cinclidae). Asoc. Orn. del Plata. Buenos Aires.

GIAI, A.
1952   Diccionario Ilustrado de las Aves Argentinas. Parte I. Mundo Agrario. Ed. Haynes. Buenos Aires.

GOODALL, J., W. JOHNSON y R. PHILIPPI
1948-1951   Las Aves de Chile, su conocimiento y sus costumbres. Tomos I y II. Platt. Establ. Graf. Buenos Aires.

GOODWIN, D.
1970   Pigeons and doves of the world. Brit. Mus. Nat. Hist. Ithaca, New York.

GORE, M. E. y A. R. GEPP
1978   Las Aves del Uruguay. Mosca Hnos. Montevideo.

HANCOCK, J. y J. KUSHLAM
1984   The Herons Handbook. Croom Helm. London and Sydney.

HARRISON, P.
1983   Seabirds an identification guide. Croom Helm. Ltd. A. H. & A. W. Redd. Beckenham.

HAVERSCHMIDT, F.
1968   Birds of Surinam. Oliver & Boyd. Edimburgo.

HUDSON, G.E.
1974   Aves del Plata. Libros de Hispanoamérica. Buenos Aires.

HUMPHREY, P.S., D. BRIDGE, P. W. REYNOLDS y R. T. PETERSON
1970   Birds of Isla Grande (Tierra del Fuego). Prelim. Smiths. Manual. University of Kansas. Mus. of Nat. Hist.

JOHNSGARD, P. A.
1981   The Plovers, Sandpipers and Snipes of the World. University of Nebraska Press. Lincoln and London.

JOHNSON, A. W.
1972   Supplement to The Birds of Chile. Platt Establ. Graf. Buenos Aires.

KOEPCKE, M.
1964   Las Aves del Departamento de Lima. Lima.

LANYON, W.E.
1978   Revision of the Myiarchus Flycatchers of South America. Bull. Am. Mus. Nat. Hist. Vol. 161, art. 4. New York.

MURPHY, R. C.
1936   Oceanic Birds of South America. Vols. 1 y 2. Amer. Mus. Nat. Hist. New York.

NAROSKY, T.
1978   Aves Argentinas. Guía para el reconocimiento de la avifauna bonaerense. Asoc. Orn. del Plata. Buenos Aires.

NAROSKY,S. ,R.FRAGA y M. DE LA PEÑA
1983   Nidificación de las Aves Argentinas (Dendrocolaptidae y Furnariidae).
            Asoc. Orn. del Plata. Buenos Aires.

NAVAS; J.
1977   Aves, Anseriformes. Fauna de Agua Dulce de la República Argentina.
            Vol. XLIII. Fasc. 2. FECIC. Buenos Aires.

            y N. A. Bo
1977   Ensayo de tipificación de nombres comunes de las aves argentinas
            Rev. Mus. Arg. Cs. Nat. Tomu XII, N° 7

NORES, M. y D. YZURIETA
1980   Aves de ambientes acuáticos de Córdoba y centro de Argentina. Sec. de
            Estado de Agric. y Ganad. Córdoba.

            D. YZURIETA y R. MIATELLO
1983   Lista y Distribución de las Aves de Córdoba, Argentina. Acad. Nac. Cienc.
            Córdoba. N° 56. Córdoba.

OLROG, C. C.
1959   Las Aves Argentinas. Una guía de campo. Inst. M. Lillo. Tucumán.

1963   Lista y Distribución de las Aves Argentinas. Op. Lilloana IX. Tucumán.

1968   Las Aves Sudamericanas. Una guía de campo. Tomo 1. Inst. M. Lillo. Tucu-
            mán.

1979   Nueva lista de la avifauna argentina. Op. Lilloana XXVII. Tucumán.

1984   Las Aves Argentinas. Adm. de Parques Nacionales. Buenos Aires.

PAYNTER, R. A. (Jr)
1985   Ornithological Gazetteer of Argentina. Harvard University. Cambridge.

PEREYRA, J.
1937   Aves de La Pampa. Mem. Jard. Zool. Tomo VII. La Plata.

1937-1938   Aves de la Zona Ribereña Nordeste de la Provincia de Buenos Aires. Mem.
            Jard. Zool. Tomo IX. La Plata.

1942   Avifauna Argentina. Mem. Jard. Zool. Tomo X. La Plata.

1943   Nuestras Aves. Min. Obr. Publ. Pcia. Bs. As. Buenos Aires.

PERGOLANI DE COSTA, M.J.I.
1970   Los nombres vulgares de las Aves Argentinas. IDIA. Buenos Aires.

PETERS, J. L.
1931-1979   Checklist of Birds of the World. 15 Vols. Harvard. Univ. Press. Cambridge.

PHELPS, W. H. y DE SCHAUENSEE, R. M.
1979   Una Guía de las Aves de Venezuela. Gráficas Armitaño, C. A. Caracas.

PRATER, A. J., J.H. MARCHANT y J. VOURINEN
1977   Guide to the identification and ageing of Holarctic Waders. British Trust for
             Ornithology. Beech Grove, Tring, Herts.*

RIPLEY, S. D.
1977   Rails of the World. M. F. Feheley Publishers Limited. Toronto.

ROBBINS, C., B. BRUUN y H. ZIM
1966   A guide to field identification Birds of North America. Golden Press. New
             York.*

SALVADOR, S.
1983   La avifauna de Villa María y alrededores. Esc. V. Mercante. Villa María.
             Córdoba.

SCOTT, D. A. y M. CARBONELL
1986   Inventario de Humedales de la Región Neotropical. IWRB y UICN. Slim-
             bridge y Cambridge.

SHORT, L.
1975   A zoogeographic Analysis of South American Chaco Avifauna. Bull. Am.
             Mus. Nat. Hist. Vol. 154, art. 3. New York.

1982   Woodpeckers of the World. Delaware Museum of Natural History. USA.

SICK, H.
1985   Ornitología Brasileira, uma introducao. Vols. I y II. Editora Universidade
             de Brasília. Brasília.

STEULLET, A. B. y E. A. DEAUTIER
1935-1946   Catálogo Sistemático de las Aves de la República Argentina. Univer. Nac. de
             La Plata. La Plata.

TUCK, G. y H. HEINZEL
1980   Guía de campo de las Aves Marinas de España y del Mundo. Ediciones
             Omega, S.A. Barcelona.

VAURIE, C.
1980   Taxonomy and geographical distribution of the Furnariidae (Aves, Passeri-
             formes) Bull. Am. Mus. Nat. Hist. Vol. 166, art. 1. New York.

VENEGAS, C. y J. JORY
1979   Guía de campo para las aves de Magallanes. Publicaciones del Instituto de la
            Patagonia. Punta Arenas. Chile.

WETMORE, A.
1960   A classification for the birds of the world. Smith. Misc. Coll. 139 (11).

WOODS, R. W.
1975   The Birds of the Falkland Islands. Anthony Nelson. Shropshire.

_____

* Useful for Northern Hemisphere migratory species.

Journals

Acta Zoológica Lilloana. Universidad Nacional de Tucumán. Instituto Miguel Lillo. Tu-
    cumán.

Comunicaciones Zoológicas del Museo de Historia Natural de Montevideo. Museo de His-
    toria Natural. Montevideo.

Historia Natural. Revista de Ciencias Naturales de aparición mensual. Corrientes.

El Hornero. Revista de la Asociación Ornitológica del Plata. Buenos Aires.

Neotropica. Notas Zoológicas Americanas. La Plata.

Nuestras Aves. Boletín de la Asociación Ornitológica del Plata. Buenos Aires.

Physis. Revista de la Sociedad Argentina de Ciencias Naturales.

The Auk. A Quarterly Journal of Ornithology. Published by The American Ornithologists
    Union. Washington, D. C.

The Condor. Journal of the Cooper Ornithological Society.

The Ibis. Journal of the British Ornithologists' Union. Published for The British Ornitho-
    logists' Union by Academic Press.

The Wilson Bulletin. Published by The Wilson Ornithological Society.

INDEX

A

320

Y

Z

RECENTLY RECORDED SPECIES

Since the first Spanish eddition of this guide (1987), several new species have been included in Argentina's avifauna, which we compile in the following, tentative list:

Spheniscus demersus - **Jackass Penguin**

Procellaria westlandica - **Westland Petrel**

Cathartes melambrotus (*) - **Greater Yellow-headed Vulture**

Xenus cinereus - **Terek Sandpiper**

Aratinga solstitialis (*) - **Sun Parakeet**

Otus guatemalae - **Variable Screech-Owl**

Glaucidium jardinii - **Andean Pygmy-Owl**

Hydropsalis climacocerca - **Ladder-tailed Nightjar**

Nyctibius aethereus - **Long-tailed Potoo**

Aeronautes montivagus - **White-tipped Swift**

Taphrospilus hypostictus (*) - **Many-spotted Humingbird**

Chloroceryle aenea - **American Pygmy Kingfisher**

Chamaeza ruficauda - **Brazilian Antthrush**

Hemitriccus obsoletum (*) - **Brown-breasted Bamboo-Tyrant**

Myiotheretes rufipennis - **Rufous-webbed Tyrant**

Myiodynastes chrysocephalus - **Golden-crowned Flycatcher**

Oxyruncus cristatus - **Sharpbill**

Sturnus vulgaris - **Common Starling**

Acridotheres critatellus - **Crested Myna**

Seiurus noveboracensis - **Nothern Waterthrush**

Thraupis palmarum - **Palm Tanager**

Sporophila falcirostris - **Temminck's Seedeater**

Sicalis luteocephala - **Citron-headed Yellow Finch**

Diglossa carbonaria - **Gray-billed Flower-piercer**

FIELD NOTES

The Asociación Ornitológica del Plata wishes to thank the following members for the help given to this book:

Carlos M. Vigil

Miguel Woites

Alfredo M. Ducos

César A. Ciocatto

Edmundo R. Guerra

José Leiberman

Rosendo M. Fraga

Elsa M. de Stein

Sigrun Schmidt

Clotaire Coulon

Carlos Martinese

Laura Rosenberg

Jorge Ricci

Colin Sharp

Adelino Narosky

César A. Valdivieso

Horacio Rodríguez Moulin